REREADING

FREUD

*Psychoanalysis
through Philosophy*

EDITED BY

JON MILLS

STATE UNIVERSITY OF NEW YORK PRESS

Published by
STATE UNIVERSITY OF NEW YORK PRESS, ALBANY

© 2004 State University of New York

All rights reserved

Printed in the United States of America

For information, address the State University of New York Press, 90 State Street, Suite 700, Albany, NY 12207

Production, Laurie Searl
Marketing, Michael Campochiaro

Library of Congress Cataloging-in-Publication Data

Rereading Freud : psychoanalysis through philosophy / [edited by] Jon Mills.
    p. cm.
Includes bibliographical references and index.
ISBN 0-7914-6047-9 (alk. paper)
    1. Freud, Sigmund, 1856–1939. 2. Psychoanalysis and philosophy. I. Mills, Jon, 1964–

BF109.F74R47 2004
150.19'52'092—dc21   2003052618

10 9 8 7 6 5 4 3 2 1

For my father, to whom I aspire

CONTENTS

PREFACE

Freud is heralded as one of the most influential yet disputed thinkers of the twentieth century, having radically affected and transformed our shifting conceptions of mind, human nature, science, religion, civilization, and gender. It has been said that no one since Jesus has been so compelling or controversial.[1] Ricoeur refers to Freud's work as a "monument of our culture,"[2] while Wollheim says he "revolutionized . . . the world."[3] Just as Kant is attributed with initiating the Copernican turn in philosophy, so is Freud credited with turning our understanding of human psychology on its head.[4] Either admired or vilified, adored or detested, we may reason with or against him, but we cannot reason without him.

Freud's ideas have become commonplace even among popular culture: nowhere can we turn without being reminded of his legacy. Currently psychoanalysis enjoys a central focus of contemporary European and North American intellectual life. We may especially observe a resurgence of interest in Freud studies among the humanities and social sciences, including philosophy, literature, sociopolitical theory, anthropology, psychobiology, ethology, cultural theory, history, religion, feminist thought, art and film studies, semiotics, neurocognitive science, and the history of ideas. Within the field of psychoanalysis, however, Freud has largely devolved into contemporary perspectives. Because the history of psychoanalysis has produced several postclassical movements from ego psychology to object relations theories, interpersonal approaches, self psychology, and relational-intersubjective viewpoints,[5] there is a culture of narcissism that informs divided group loyalties. Plagued by challenges from within its own governing institutional practices, as well as from waning public interest in analytic treatment, psychoanalysis has endured a century-long evolution from Freud's original vision. Adding to these challenges, Freud's theories have become so fundamentally distorted and misinterpreted by generations of English-speaking commentators that he is radically misunderstood even within psychoanalysis today. But whether he is renounced or subsumed, psychoanalysis is merely a footnote to Freud.

Philosophy remains largely oblivious to the psychoanalytic movement, and is equally slow to embrace the potency and ramification of Freud's ideas. But with increasing attention—both sympathetic and critical—psychoanalysis continues to generate profound philosophical consequences for the way we come to understand and live our lives. With respect to Freud, like Plato, one does not have to espouse everything he said to appreciate how certain aspects of his thought resonate within us all. Yet some of his more controversial assertions have provoked derisive attacks, including vulgar polemics, leading to modifications, extensions, critical revisions, and redirecting shifts in emphasis. This is particularly the case for certain universal pronouncements that invite reactive critique and outrage: such as his thesis of innate bisexuality, the claim that we all harbor incestuous, homicidal, and suicidal desires, the notion that dreams—no matter how disturbing, as well as jokes, slips, and symptoms—are the fulfillment of a wish; and, perhaps most provocatively, that the belief in God is merely the childhood illusion of an exalted father in the sky: it is no wonder why he generates controversy. Freud is particularly hated for his views on women, the cultural disparagement of non-Western societies, and his abhorrence of religion—perhaps in part explaining the recent unease surrounding the Freud exhibit, *Conflict & Culture*, sponsored by the Library of Congress, which was delayed for years due to political protest.

Freud remains deeply embedded in our time if not for the simple fact that he is threatening. Many people, I would say most—from the average citizen to the intellectual—are afraid of his ideas; and what we fear we must defend against in some way—from pure denial to extreme, sometimes ludicrous, attempts to justify why Freud was wrong.[6] One reason why he generates such emotive contention is that he shatters our cherished ideals—what we hold most dear; and as a result evokes anxiety, hostility, and psychic terror. But Freud ultimately threatens us with knowledge about ourselves—what we wish to know nothing about at all, knowledge that can potentially disrupt the way we experience and understand our inner worlds.

The central aim of this project is to celebrate and philosophically critique Freud's most important contribution to understanding humanity: namely, that psychic reality is governed by the unconscious mind. While philosophers from Schelling to Hegel, von Hartmann, Schopenhauer, and Nietzsche have advanced our understanding of unconscious mental processes, it was Freud who first provided a systematic framework of the psychodynamics of mind that punctured the notion of a transparency to consciousness, which had dominated scientific attitudes since the time of Descartes. The chapters in this volume attempt to shed light on the ontological commitments Freud introduces in his metapsychology and the implications they generate for engaging theoretical, clinical, and applied modes of philosophical inquiry. The contributors assembled here are eminent philosophical scholars and clinical practitioners from continental, pragmatic, feminist, and psychoanalytic paradigms. There is no collection like the present that assembles such a diverse yet concentrated group of scholars explicitly conjoined around the task of analyzing Freud's theories.

The organization of this volume is structured in terms of explicating certain key themes within Freud's masterworks, including examining points of connection to other philosophers and topics relevant in our contemporary world climate. More specifically, chapters focus on the exegesis and critique of several of Freud's most influential theories, including the nature and structure of dreams, infantile sexuality, drive and defense, ego development, symptom formation, feminine psychology, the therapeutic process, death, and the question of race.

Freud considered his work on dreams to be his most original contribution to understanding the human mind. In their chapters, John Sallis and Tom Rockmore are preoccupied with the dream-book: the former from the standpoint of understanding the logical and experiential operations of the dream, while the latter with dream interpretation as social construction. In chapter 1, John Sallis provides a meticulous explication of the process of dreaming and ultimately argues that the dream-work reconstitutes as schemata the logical categories that it disrupts. The logic of the dream-work is therefore a logic of schemata, one that yokes contradictory opposites together; and thus from the standpoint of philosophical logic based on ancient ontology, it is almost indistinguishable from illogic, indeed, the logic of the interior. In the next chapter, Tom Rockmore critiques Freud's dream theory from standard epistemological approaches to knowledge. Claiming Freud is neither a realist nor a representationalist, Rockmore argues that Freud's dream theory is constructivist, a position he argues is eminently defensible.

Freud's treatise on infantile sexuality is a bedrock of psychoanalytic thought. In chapter 3, John Russon examines Freud's essays on sexuality and defends a notion of the unconscious as the continuing presence of infantile and intersubjective embodiment in adult experience. Russon shows that the human body is a determinate, self-transcending openness, yet one radically influenced by our early familial resonances and the internalized desire of the other. Emphasizing a phenomenological approach to psychoanalytic methodology, Russon further concurs that our mature adult experience cannot outstrip the forms of childhood life whose traces it bears.

It may be argued that Freud's views on the nature and role of the ego underwent more transformations than any other construct. Chapter 4 is by Stephen David Ross who examines the role and function of the image in Freud's theory of dreams, creativity and the unconscious, and in its relation to the ego. Through Blanchot, Ross pursues the role images, imagination, and exposition play in Freud, psychoanalysis, and language, thus arguing that the self may only be formally expressed in imagistic, imaginative terms. In chapter 5, Emily Zakin examines, through close readings of Freud, three related concepts: namely, narcissism, melancholia, and femininity, and shows how identification is operative within each of these phenomena. Relying on Irigaray and Kristeva, Zakin challenges Freud's claims on melancholia and sadism, and explores the nature of the masochistic ego in its relation to the melancholic bond with femininity and loss.

In chapter 6, Wilfried Ver Eecke explicitly examines the ontological dimensions of denial in Freud's metapsychology and specifically traces its phenomenal appearances through a case study. Ver Eecke shows that recognizing the truth behind a denial is more than just an epistemological process, rather it requires laborious emotional work. Extending beyond Freud's work on negation, he argues that undoing denial in the service of truth further requires acts of separation from internalized significant others and the linguistic enlistment of metaphor. By examining the case of Anthony Moore, Ver Eecke points out the complexifications of unconscious defense and its impact on consciousness.

Among contemporary psychoanalytic paradigms, Freud is often criticized for his biologicalism and emphasis on sexuality; while his mature views on mental functioning go selectively unacknowledged. In my chapter, I provide an exegesis and critique of Freud's mature model of the psyche as represented in his pivotal work, *The Ego and the Id*. Using a process psychological approach to conceptualizing the soul, I attempt to trace the dialectical origins of psychic reality from its most primitive unconscious configurations to self-conscious ego development. Through a dialectical logic of self-differentiation and modification, I provide a naturalistic-idealist interpretation of the coming into being of unconscious agency.

Psychoanalysis is both a general psychological theory of mental health and disease as it is a psychotherapeutic form of treatment. In chapter 8, Maria Talero examines several key concepts in the practice of psychoanalysis, including the phenomenology of transference, repetition, repression, and the working-through process of effective cure. Employing Merleau-Ponty's notion of the habitual body as an intrinsically temporal phenomenon, Talero shows how the very nature of embodiment is a temporal trajectory of habitual transformation that affects the process of therapy and the meaning of lived subjective experience.

The implications of psychoanalytic thought have far-reaching sociopolitical consequences. In our current ethnopolitical climate of multiculturalism and transnational identifications, prejudice and hate continue to grip world attention. Nowhere do we observe such atrocities than in the phenomenology of genocide and racism. In chapter 9, Bruce Wilshire explores the relation between Freud's notion of the death drive and its contemporary application to the problem of genocide. Relying on a classical model of fixation, conflict, and sadistic repetition, Wilshire traces the derivatives of death and destruction from psychosexual development and collective identify formation to displaced primal masochism and projected self-hate. Using Kierkegaard to analyze the experience of guilt and dread, Wilshire poses that because antithetical cultural groups have disparate experiential worlds, each projects their own suffering onto the other as designated concrete pain that must be destroyed. In the end, Wilshire contends, genocidal aggression is deflected masochism from a group that is insecure, self-deflated, and guilt-ridden.

In our final chapter, Shannon Sullivan examines the unconscious life of prejudice and its impact on racial, ethnic, religious, and gendered identities. Through critical race theory, Sullivan specifically challenges white privilege as well as Freud's own prejudicial predilections informing his conceptions of castration and circumcision, thereby lending legitimacy to misogynistic attitudes and the deprecation of non-Europeans. Sullivan's analysis of group identity ultimately shows that prejudice and its derivatives lurk in the unconscious of all people. Given that racism in general—and white privilege in particular—operate unconsciously, Sullivan argues that we may only alter such racist tendencies by first becoming aware of them.

Taken together, the chapters in this volume offer a comprehensive account of Freud's ontology of the unconscious and its philosophical implications for advancing our understanding of human nature. One aspiration Freud harbored was that psychoanalysis, which he ultimately defined as "the science of unconscious mental processes," would inspire appreciation among the disparate fields that psychoanalysis itself attempts to explain. In the end, Freud was humble: "Something will become of . . . my life's labours . . . in the future, though I cannot myself tell whether it will be much or little. I can, however, express a hope that I have opened up a pathway for an important advance in our knowledge."[7]

NOTES

1. This was attributed to Freud by the narrator of A & E's Biography of Sigmund Freud.

2. Paul Ricoeur, Freud and Philosophy (New Haven: Yale University Press, 1970), xi.

3. Richard Wollheim, Sigmund Freud (Cambridge: Cambridge University Press, 1971/1990), x.

4. Lacan compares the significance of Freud's discoveries to that of Copernicus. See Écrits: A Selection, trans. Alan Sheridan (New York: Norton, 1977), 114, 295.

5. For an in-depth historical overview of the evolving paradigms within the psychoanalytic domain, see my article, Dialectical Psychoanalysis: Toward Process Psychology, Psychoanalysis and Contemporary Thought 23, no. 3 (2000): 417–450.

6. See Richard Webster, Why Freud Was Wrong: Sin, Science, and Psychoanalysis (New York: Basic Books, 1995), for the most recent account of Freud-bashing. In my opinion, this work is an irresponsible, untenable, and misinformed attack on the main tenets of psychoanalysis under the guise of scientific idolatry that denigrates Freud while deifying Darwin. Certainly this is not new criticism, but one here presented more for sensationalism rather than based on philosophical merit. Historically

within philosophy, psychoanalysis has been labeled "mythology" by Wittgenstein, "unintelligible" by James, "illegitimate" by MacIntyre, "unscientific" by Grünbaum, and, more recently, "pseudoscience" by Cioffi (Cf. Ludwig Wittgenstein, *The Blue and Brown Books*, Oxford: Blackwell, 1958 [First dictated in 1933–1934]; "Conversations on Freud," in *Lectures and Conversations on Aesthetics, Psychology and Religious Belief*, ed. C. Barrett (Berkeley: University of California Press), 1966;.William James, *The Principles of Psychology*, 2 Vols. (New York: Dover, 1890/1950); Alasdair MacIntyre, *The Unconscious: A Conceptual Study* (London: Routledge, 1958); Adolf Grünbaum, *The Foundations of Psychoanalysis* (Berkeley: University of California Press, 1984); and Frank Cioffi, *Freud and the Question of Pseudoscience* (Chicago: Open Court, 1998). Some have gone so far to deny the existence of the unconscious altogether (e.g., Webster; also see Sartre's existential critique in *Being and Nothingness*, trans. H. Barnes (New York: Washington Square Press, 1943/1956); and T. R. Miles, *Eliminating the Unconscious* (Oxford: Pergamon Press, 1966), to which Freud would merely reply is "absurd" (*Standard Edition*, 19, fn, p. 16.). While Freud has been championed by some philosophers such as Richard Wollheim, John Wisdom, Jonathan Lear, and others, Donald Levy recently shows how many of Freud's critics have repeatedly focused on very selective and prejudicial arguments that have misunderstood key theoretical concepts and neglected the broader domain of psychoanalytic inquiry. Scrutinizing the claims that psychoanalysis is mythology, incoherent, self-contradictory, and scientifically unverifiable, Levy exposes these selective philosophical biases and misunderstandings that have dominated Anglo-American philosophy's critique of psychoanalytic doctrine. Cf. Richard Wollheim, *op. cit.*; John Wisdom, *Philosophy and Psychoanalysis* (Berkeley: University of California Press, 1969); Jonathan Lear, *Love and Its Place in Nature: A Philosophical Interpretation of Freudian Psychoanalysis*. (New York: Noonday Press, 1990); and Donald Levy, *Freud Among the Philosophers* (New Haven: Yale University Press, 1996).

　　7. Freud, "An Autobiographical Study," *Standard Edition*, 1925, Vol. 20 (London: Hogarth Press), 70.

ACKNOWLEDGMENTS

I wish to sincerely thank Andrew MacRae and the Research Institute at Lakeridge Health for providing me with a research grant for this project. I am also appreciative of the critiques and constructive suggestions that were offered from the anonymous reviewers whom evaluated this current volume. Chapter 7 largely comprises a previously published essay: "Deciphering the 'Genesis Problem': On the Dialectical Origins of Psychic Reality." *The Psychoanalytic Review,* (2002) 89 (6), 763–809; and I wish to thank Guilford Publications for permission to reproduce it here. Most important, I am deeply grateful to Jane Bunker, Senior Acquisitions Editor, and Laurie Searl, Senior Production Editor, State University of New York Press, for their continued support, encouragement, and interest in my work.

Through the detour of being a physician . . . I most secretly nourish the hope of reaching my original goal, philosophy.

—*Freud*, Letter to Fliess, January 1, 1896

ONE

THE LOGIC AND ILLOGIC
OF THE DREAM-WORK

JOHN SALLIS

THE DREAM-WORK is a matter of translation, a work of translation. Only of translation. Nothing else. Nothing more. In and through the dream-work nothing is produced except a translation.

This at least is what Freud says of the dream-work, that its work consists solely in translating, that its work produces nothing but a translation. In the dream-work as such—though not in the constitution of what is given to it to be worked—the psyche functions solely as a translator, carries out— below the level of consciousness—the work of translating.

But what, then, gets translated? Of what does the dream-work produce a translation? Freud identifies it again and again, names it in various formulations, various translations, says—perhaps most directly—that the dream-work "accomplishes nothing else but a translation of the dream-thoughts" [eine Übersetzung der Traumgedanken].[1] This name already in effect says what is produced by translating the dream-thoughts, what they are translated into— namely, the dream itself. Or rather, the dream-thoughts are translated into what in other contexts, contexts other than that of psychoanalysis, one would commonly take as simply the dream itself. Thus, one would perhaps say—or at least wish to say—that the dream-thoughts are simply the thoughts underlying the dream. Yet if it is a matter of translation and not just of expression, the relation of the dream-thoughts to what they would thus underlie cannot be constituted by simple relocation or transposition, for translation, as nearly all will attest, invariably produces distortion and loss in what is translated, in what undergoes translation.

1

This difference is what, on the one hand, allows Freud to "work out the solution *[Lösung]* of the dream" (p. 280) in a new way while, on the other hand, endlessly complicating that solution. No longer will it be a matter of deciphering the mere surface, or, rather, what is now recognized as being mere surface; merely interpreting as such the dream's manifest content—which otherwise one would have taken as the dream itself—cannot suffice. For this content is—proves to be—only the result of a process of translation of something else, of the dream-thoughts that underlie the dream-content and yet are concealed from the dreamer both in the course of dreaming and afterward when the dream is remembered. Thus distinguishing between the manifest content of the dream and the latent content, the underlying dream-thoughts, Freud identifies a task, the "new task," one "that did not exist before" (p. 280), that could not exist as long as one adhered to the surface of the dream without recognizing it as such, as long as one took the mere surface, the manifest content, to be the dream as such. The task is to investigate the relationship between the two distinctly posited levels, to trace *(nachspüren)* the processes *(Vorgänge)* by which the manifest content has come to be from the latent content.

The way in which Freud introduces his new solution tends initially to dissolve the very difference that makes it possible. He begins: "Dream-thoughts and dream-content lie before us *[liegen vor uns]* like two representations *[Darstellungen]* of the same content in two different languages" (p. 280). But—one will ask—do they both *lie before us*? And to whom is it that the first-person plural pronoun refers? Before whom—if before anyone—do they lie, both of them—so it seems—uniformly, both to the same degree? Certainly not before the dreamer, not even when, having awakened, he remembers the dream and perhaps narrates it. The dream-content may indeed lie before him, but the dream-thoughts definitely do not. They remain concealed as long as the psychoanalyst has not carried out an interpretation of the dream sufficient to reveal them. Before whom, then, do they lie revealed? Primarily before the psychoanalyst, though the associations carried out before him by the dreamer will typically have played an indispensable role in the interpretation of the dream. Many years later Freud reinforces this structure by distinguishing between two tasks.[2] The first is the practical task carried out by means of dream interpretation *(Traumdeutung)*: it consists in transforming *(umwandeln)* the manifest dream—Freud calls it here the dream-text—into the latent dream-thoughts. The second task, the theoretical task, consists in explaining how in the dreamer—in his *Seelenleben*—the latent dream becomes the manifest dream. It would seem that the second task must indeed be second, that is, subsequent to the practical task, which would first have exposed the depth, the under-lying dream-thoughts, lying under the surface, under the manifest dream. Whatever theoretical anticipation might have been in play, the practical interpretation of dreams is what would first actually open up the space in which the theoretical task geared to the dream-work could commence. Only through the interpretation of dreams does the theoretical work presented in *The Interpretation of Dreams* become possible. The question is whether the logic of this configuration can be other than simply circular, whether the practical task of interpreting dreams can proceed without presupposing what only the theoretical task can establish: the dream-work, which sustains the difference precisely by distorting the dream-thoughts into something quite other.

Even at this very general level it is a question of a logic and a hermeneutics that would negotiate the pertinent circularity in terms laid down by that logic. At this level the logic would be determined by the way in which the function of the dream-work within the theoretical-practical configuration as a whole came to be construed. Yet it is a logic of the configuration, not the logic of the dream-work proper (assuming that *propriety* can retain a determinate sense in reference to the dream-work).

One may put aside, then, all the complications posed by the supposition that dream-thoughts and dream-content *lie before us*. In reference to this passage, which orients the entire chapter on the dream-work, what is more to the point is to observe how close Freud has already come to construing both dream-thoughts and dream-content as texts: he says that they are like representations of the same content in two different languages. Because they are like texts in different languages, one of them can be taken as a translation of the other: "or better said, the dream-content looks to us like a translation [*erscheint uns als eine Übertragung*] of the dream-thoughts into another mode of expression" (p. 280). Freud formulates the—presumably theoretical—task: "we are to get to know its [i.e., the translation's] signs and laws of grammatical construction." How are we—whoever the *we* may be—to do so, to become familiar (*kennenlernen*) with the signs and the syntactical laws of the translation? Again, it seems that both must to some degree lie before us; for Freud says explicitly that this familiarity with the signs and syntax of the translation is to be acquired "by comparing the original and the translation" [*durch die Vergleichung von Original und Übersetzung*]. In any case Freud insists that "the dream-thoughts become understandable to us without further ado, as soon as we have learned these" [*sie* is formally ambiguous here; though it could refer to *dream-thoughts*, presumably its reference is to *signs and laws of grammatical construction*]. The point is that once one recognizes the manifest content *as* a translation and—by comparison with the dream-thoughts—becomes acquainted with its manner of construction, with the laws of translation, then the dream-thoughts underlying that manifest content become understandable. In what does this becoming understandable without further ado (*ohne weiteres verständlich*) consist? Freud answers: "The dream-content is given, as it were, in a pictograph [*Bilderschrift*] whose signs are to be translated individually into the language of the dream-thoughts," as one would translate—Freud develops the example—a rebus. Once one knows how in general the translation has come about, once one knows the laws governing the translation of the dream-thoughts into the dream-content, then it will not be difficult, beginning with a dream-content, to counter-translate it back into the dream-thoughts of which it is a translation. Everything will depend, then, on discovering the laws governing the original translation, that is, governing the translation of the original. Yet one wonders whether this discovery can completely dispense with—or postpone until after its work is done—all countertranslating. Can the circularity—which already has proven not to be simple—be so simply put aside?[3]

It is in the penultimate chapter of *The Interpretation of Dreams*, entitled simply "The Dream-work," that everything preceding is finally brought together into a definitive orientation. Afterward, in the final chapter, a transition is made to another level; Freud could hardly have marked this more clearly than he did at the outset of the final chapter where he contrasts the previous paths, which "led us into the light," with those on which he is about to venture and that, he confesses in advance, "lead into the dark" (p. 490).[4] In this sense, one can say that *The Interpretation of Dreams* culminates or is centered in the chapter on the dream-work. In this respect it mirrors the operative structure that it articulates; for that structure, differentiating between manifest and latent dream-content, is itself centered in the dream-work.

The chapter "The Dream-work" is devoted to determining how the translation of the dream-thoughts into the dream-content is carried out, to formulating the laws or principles that govern the translation. In other words, Freud's task is to distinguish and to describe the various forms of work, the modes of working, that, taken together, constitute the dream-work as such. Throughout the delimitation of these moments of the dream-work, there remains continuous tacit reference to the translational character of the work carried out. Indeed, in the case of one moment, the work of displacement (*Verschiebungsarbeit*), the translational character is so emphasized that a word translatable as *translation* becomes a synonym for the proper name of the moment. According to Freud's account, the work of displacement is what brings it about that the dream is centered differently from the dream-thoughts. The value had by particular elements among the dream-thoughts is not retained in the dream-content; the most valuable elements among the dream-thoughts are stripped of their value, and their place is taken by other elements to which little value was attached at the level of the dream-thoughts. Thus, the work consists here in a displacement of the psychical intensity of the individual elements, as in Freud's own dream of the botanical monograph in which the element of the dream-thoughts concerned with "the complications and conflicts arising from obligations incurred by services between colleagues" is displaced into the element "botanical" (see pp. 183–189). To designate this work, this moment of the dream-work, Freud uses two terms: *Verschiebung* (displacement) but also *Übertragung*, translatable as *transference* but equally—especially considering the common etymology (Latin *transfero*)—as *translation*. Freud's way of expressing the consequence of such *Übertragung*

gives further warrant for translating the word as *translation*: "as a consequence the difference between the texts [*Textverschiedenheit*] of the dream-
content and the dream-thoughts appears" (p. 307). Construing them as texts,
Freud is declaring that the difference between the dream-thoughts and the
dream-content—indeed the very formation of the manifest dream in its difference from the latent content—is brought about by such translating.

Yet, as he proceeds to delimit successively the individual moments of
the dream-work (condensation, displacement, regard for representability),
Freud comes finally to the conclusion that in the dream-content there is one
element, one kind of content, that has no correlate in the dream-thoughts.
This element occurs among those that, within the dream, are expressive of
a certain criticism of the dream, of a certain resistance to its content. To be
sure, Freud insists that most of the stirrings of criticism in which the dreamer
is, for instance, astonished or annoyed by the dream or even recoils from its
content derive from the dream-thoughts no less than does the dream-
content to which these are reactions. Yet he grants that some critical responses within the dream cannot be so derived, have no correlate in the
dream-thoughts. Freud cites a criticism that he says is quite often met with
in dreams, a criticism that is no longer merely a mute, affective striving but
that is expressed in the declaration "After all, it's only a dream." To explain
such a case, Freud has recourse to the concept of the censor, to the supposition that a psychic censorship is decisively operative in dreams. In *The
Interpretation of Dreams* this supposition is axiomatic; the operation is neither
put into question nor analyzed in a thorough and rigorous manner. It is not
insignificant that Freud introduces the notion of a censor behind dream-
distortion by elaborating an analogy between such censorship and that operative in political situations, the censorship in face of which political writers
can avoid having their words completely suppressed only if they speak allu-
sively or conceal their objectionable views behind some disguise. Freud says:
"The correspondence, traceable down to the last detail, between the phenomena of censorship and those of dream-distortion justifies us in assuming
similar preconditions for both" (p. 160).

One could say indeed that the notion of the censor is one of the
primary axioms of Freud's text, for even in those modes—the principal modes:
condensation, displacement, regard for representability—in which the dream-
work consists in translating the dream-thoughts into dream-content, what
prompts the translation, what makes the dream-work necessary, is the operation of censorship. Because the dream-thoughts come under censor, they can
enter consciousness as dream-content only if, like the views of political writers
in a situation of censorship, they are sufficiently disguised. They come to be
disguised by being translated into something different, as into another language. It is as if political writers were to publish their texts only in translation into a language illegible to those in power—or at least, as such writers
have always done, into a tale whose genuine intent remains illegible.

In the case of the criticism expressed within the dream yet against the dream, the criticism expressed in the words "After all, it's only a dream," the role of the censor is not to prompt or require a translation of the content but rather to intervene directly. Freud would have these words be the words of the censor, words uttered when, caught unaware, it is too late to suppress an objectionable content, to disguise it by the usual means, by translation. In such cases, something enters the dream that does not derive from the dream-thoughts. Thus, the dream-content proves not to consist solely of elements translated from the dream-thoughts. In such cases there will also be elements that derive from the direct intervention of the censor, something interjected to compensate for a lack of vigilance or, in any event, for some lack or other that otherwise would throw the economy of psychic censorship off balance: "There is no doubt that the censoring agency, whose influence we have so far recognized only in restrictions and omissions in the dream-content, is also responsible for interpolations and additions" (p. 471). These products of what Freud calls secondary revison or reworking (die sekundäre Bearbeitung) display certain features, which he marks: they are not particularly vivid, are less easily retained by the memory, and are always to be found at points in the dream-content where they can function to link two pieces of dream-content. Most significantly, the purpose served by secondary revision is to fill the gaps in the structure of the dream: "The result of its labor is that the dream loses its appearance of absurdity and incoherence and approaches the pattern of an intelligible experience" [dem Vorbilde eines verständlichen Erlebnisses] (pp. 471–472).

Thus, in secondary revision the dream undergoes a very deep and thorough reworking by, as Freud describes it, "a psychic function that resembles waking thought" (p. 472), by a function that in any case introduces into the dream the form and coherence demanded by waking thought. Or rather, more precisely, this function imposes form and coherence on what has been produced by the other three moments of the dream-work, the translational moments of condensation, displacement, and regard for representability. Though in The Interpretation of Dreams he refers explicitly to secondary revision as a part of the dream-work (dieses Stück der Traumarbeit [p. 471]), Freud will later qualify this assignment, remarking that, strictly speaking, secondary revision is not a part of the dream-work.[5] One could say of secondary revision: it belongs to the dream-work inasmuch as it contributes to the formation of the dream-content, but it is set apart from the other moments inasmuch as it does not translate dream-thoughts, does not deform them into dream-content, but rather imposes form on the deformed content. With its form, its coherence, restored, the dream seems to make sense, to have a meaning (einen Sinn zu haben [p. 472]). But this sense is not the sense—not even a sense—belonging properly to the content of the dream; it is an imposed sense and is even, says Freud, "furthest removed from the actual sense of the dream" (p. 472).

There is reason to say that secondary revision institutes the logic of the dream-work. But then one would be obliged to add that this logic is not properly the logic of the dream-work—whatever that logic might be, if there is such a logic—but only a logic that serves to conceal the absurdity and incoherence of the translation produced by the dream-work, by its (other) three moments. It would be the logic of the dream-work only as the logic of a single moment of the dream-work, of a moment that later will be said not to be, strictly speaking, a part of the dream-work. It is a logic of the dream-work that serves precisely to conceal the illogic of the dream-work.

In this regard the question of the logic of the dream-work is insepa-rable from the question of sense or meaning (*Sinn*). Here the word *logic* does not designate a discipline that would determine the ideal laws governing thought in various regards but rather those laws themselves, not in the form of laws but rather as they must be exemplified by whatever becomes an object of thought. In other words, *logic* designates here the forms of connec-tion that must be had by something, by some content, in order for it to be thought in some regard or other. In the case of the logic instituted in the dream-work through secondary revision, this regard has to do with meaning. Whereas the translational moments of the dream-work give it the appear-ance of absurdity and incoherence, the logic instituted through secondary revision renders it intelligible or understandable (*verständlich*). But whatever is understandable is so precisely because it has a meaning, because it offers a meaning to understanding. Whereas the product of the translational mo-ments has the appearance of absurdity and incoherence, of non-sense, whereas it displays an apparent illogic, the dream-content acquires, through second-ary revision, forms of connection such that the dream comes to make sense, to have a meaning. And yet, it is a meaning that does not belong to this content, an alien meaning that must be forced to adhere to it by the very force of censorship but that nonetheless remains "furthest removed from the actual sense of the dream" (p. 472). This logic of the dream-work is a false imposition, a false sense, a sham logic.

But can there be a false meaning otherwise than in contrast to a true meaning? Freud is confident that dreams have a meaning, one that properly belongs to them, that is true to them. After the critical survey with which *The Interpretation of Dreams* begins, Freud's very first move is to posit such meaning. As the title of his text indicates, the task he undertakes is "to show that dreams are capable of an interpretation" [*Deutung*]; and, as he continues, " 'to interpret a dream' is to determine its 'meaning' " [*heisst, seinen 'Sinn' angeben*] (p. 117). Freud's very undertaking is linked to the supposition that beneath the dream there is meaning, that dreams are not ultimately non-sense. He gives every appearance of being confident that, as he says of cer-tain absurd dreams that he discusses, "the absurdity of the dream-content is only apparent [*ein Anschein*] and disappears as we go deeper into the meaning of the dream" (p. 413). And yet even to refer to the process of going deeper into the meaning of the dream is to grant that the meaning may not be revealed all at once, that it can be extended, articulated in depth, and that its various moments—the various dream-thoughts—may be such as can be revealed only gradually. Indeed Freud grants that one always remains less than certain of having revealed all the dream-thoughts underlying a dream: "actually one is never certain of having completely interpreted a dream; even when the solution seems satisfying and without gaps, it remains always possible for a further meaning to announce itself through the same dream" (p. 282). Thus, the meaning of a dream is open-ended; even if nothing whatsoever has indicated that it is outstanding, a further meaning can always come to light. No interpretation could ever be declared finished and in itself complete.

There are passages in which Freud goes beyond even this open-endedness of meaning. The most remote and yet severe and enigmatic limit to the interpretation of dreams is broached in two passages, both of which, though they are far apart in Freud's text, refer to what he calls the navel of the dream. The first passage is a note that Freud appends to his analysis of the dream of Irma's injection. In this connection he writes of concealed meaning, of not having gone far enough in his interpretation of the dream to follow all the hidden meaning ("um allem verborgenen Sinn zu folgen" [p. 130]). Then he adds, generalizing: "Every dream has at least one place where it is unfathomable [unergründlich], the navel, as it were, by which it is connected to the unknown" [durch den er mit dem Unerkannten zusammenhängt]. One will want to ask: What is this navel of the dream? Yet one would first have to determine—even to make the question a possible question—that the navel is a what, an essence, a meaning, whereas this is precisely what remains questionable at this place where the dream is unfathomable and connected to the unknown. It is little wonder that Freud makes no attempt to say what this place is but instead has recourse to the metaphorics of the navel.

The second of the two passages comes much later in Freud's text, in the final chapter where, as he acknowledges, "all paths lead into the dark" (p. 490). This passage extends the metaphors of the first, compounding it with the figures of light and darkness: "The best-interpreted dreams often have a place that has to be left in the dark, because one notices in the course of interpretation that at this place a knot [ball, tangle: Knäue] arises, which refuses to be unraveled but which also offers no further contribution to the dream-content. This is, then, the navel of the dream and the place beneath which lies the unknown" (p. 503). No matter how thoroughly interpreted, a dream may have a place of utter resistance, a tangle that cannot be unraveled, the threshold of the unknown and presumably unknowable. One wonders in what sense—whether still in the order of sense—this tangle "offers no further contributions to the dream-content." Is it only that, since the tangle cannot be unraveled, the meanings that it harbors cannot be revealed and thus shown to contribute, by way of the dream-work, to the dream-content? Or is it that the tangle has nothing to offer to the dream-content, that it harbors no dream-thoughts that could be translated into dream-contents, that it is the place where meaning ceases so that what lies beneath it is unknowable by virtue of being anterior to the very order of meaning and understanding. Derrida puts the question succinctly: "one may wonder whether the in-soluble knot, the umbilicus, is of the stuff of sense [sens] or whether it remains radically heterogeneous, in its very secret, to signifiable sense, as well as to the signifier, and one may also wonder whether what discourages the analyst, provisionally or definitively, is homogeneous or not with the space of analytic work, the work of interpretation (Deutungsarbeit)."[6]

This question of the limit of meaning, of the character of this limit, will return in another guise, from a direction that still has to be laid out. Yet, regardless of how it might be decided, even if it should prove quite undecidable, the question of the logic of the dream-work would remain unanswered, would remain in a sense—by its reduction to a question of sense—untouched. For just as the logic, the meaning, imposed by secondary revision is a logic apart from the dream-work and is in this respect a false meaning, a sham logic, so the meaning that would be revealed through the interpretation of dreams is situated at the limit of the dream-work, at a point where the dream-work has not yet commenced. For the meaning of a dream is nothing other than the underlying dream-thoughts, which in and through the dream-work come to be translated into the dream-content. In other words, the meaning of the dream is what gets taken up by and into the dream-work and under the surveillance of censorship gets reworked—that is, distorted—into the dream-content. It is not the meaning—or, more precisely, the logic—of the dream-work as such. Anterior to the dream-work in the order of translation, the meaning of the dream is what gets translated, in distinction from the forms of connection that are produced in and through the dream-work and that would constitute its logic proper.

But if the logic of a content or process lies in the forms of connection that must be had by it in order for it to be thought in some regard or other, can one even suppose that there is a logic of the dream-work, since the work of the dream-work consists, not in instituting form and connection, but in deforming and disconnecting? In different terms, the question is whether there is some regard in which this deforming and disconnecting can be thought and, if so, what it is; for certainly these accomplishments of the dream-work cannot be thought as a coherent congeries of meaning.

One might attempt to determine the logic of the dream-work by following the directives that logic as a discipline traditionally followed. These directives prescribe attending to speech and to judgment; for it is in speech and in judgment that those forms that logic as a discipline would thematize occur concretely. Even if logic is, in the end, to determine the ideal laws governing speech and judgment, this priority would be reversed in the order of discovery. What about the speech and judgment carried out in the dream-work? Do these offer access to the logic of the dream-work?

Freud considers the case of dreams that contain speech, dreams in which the speech is distinct from thought. In these cases, he insists, "the rule holds without exception that the dream-speech derives from the remembered speech of the dream-material" (p. 304). The words spoken may be retained intact or they may be slightly altered, and in either instance their sense is likely to be changed. Thus, the dream-work itself issues in no speech at all but at most deforms the meanings of words taken over from the dream-material. As Freud writes: "The dream-work is also incapable of newly creating speech" (p. 406). In this sense there is no speech *of* the dream-work but only its deforming of the speech taken over from the dream-material. Freud insists that analysis in this regard always shows the same thing: that the dream-work takes up mere fragments of speech and deals with them quite arbitrarily (*willkürlich*), at least in ways that, measured against the speech as it was, appear quite arbitrary.

The dream-work is no more capable of judgment than it is of speech. In this connection Freud is even more emphatic: "*A moment in the dream that appears to be an activity of the function of judgment is not to be taken as an act of thinking [Denkleistung] on the part of the dream-work [der Traumarbeit]; rather, it belongs to the material of the dream-thoughts and has passed from there as a ready-made structure into the manifest dream-content*" (p. 430). Thus, within the translational dream-work itself—as distinct from what, in very different ways, is given to it by the underlying dream-thoughts and by secondary revision—there is indigenously neither speech nor judgment. The traditional directives that the logical forms are to be sought in speech and judgment provide no aid in gaining access to the logic of the dream-work.

Indeed, if one considers what Freud says directly about the relation of the dream-work to logic, one may well wonder whether there is in any sense—or even beyond sense—a logic of the dream-work. For Freud depicts the dream-work primarily as undoing the logic that, anterior to the dream-work, lies in the connections between the dream-thoughts. It would seem that in the dream-work itself, prior to the onset of secondary revision, there is no logic but only the illogic that secondary revision then covers up with its facade of form and coherence.

For this depiction Freud sets the stage by declaring that between the individual parts of the complicated structure of the dream-thoughts there are the most various logical relations. Next comes the scene of the dream-work: "Then, when the entire mass of these dream-thoughts is submitted to the pressure of the dream-work, and the pieces are turned about, broken up, and pushed up against one another, rather like surging ice-floes, the question arises: what has become of the bonds of logic that had previously given the structure its form . . . [and] without which we can understand neither propositions nor speech?" (p. 310). Freud offers an initial answer, one that is still provisional: "one must initially [*zunächst*] answer that the dream has no means at its disposal for representing these logical relations among the dream-thoughts. For the most part it disregards all these prepositions and takes over only the factual content [den sachlichen Inhalt] of the dream-thoughts to work upon. It is left to the interpretation of the dream to reestablish the connections that the dream-work has destroyed" (pp. 310–311). The dream-work—so this initial answer goes—dismantles the logical structure of the dream-thoughts; it leaves the dream-material largely "divested of its [logical] relations" (p. 335).

Yet this is only an initial, provisional answer. While continuing to maintain that the dream-work undoes the logical relations of the dream-material, Freud grants, on the other hand, that the dream-work can take a certain account of particular logical relations by means of certain modes of representation. Freud compares the process to that of painters, who, unable to make use of speech in painting and unwilling to have recourse to scrolls issuing from the mouths of painted figures, found distinctively painterly means for expressing—for instance, through gestures—the intention of the words spoken by the figures. Thus, the dream-work renders *logical connection* as such by means of *simultaneity*, concentrating all the pieces of the dream-thoughts in a representation of a single situation or event. Freud compares such representation to that of the painter (Raffaelo) who assembles all the philosophers and poets in a single painting (*The School of Athens*). Spatial proximity, in dreams as in painting, can serve to represent significant relations of another order, whether the order of logical relations or that of an intellectual and artistic legacy.

The dream-work also carries out such representation with respect to specific logical connections. For instance, causal relations between things thought in the dream-thoughts can be represented in the dream-work by presenting the cause or condition as an introductory dream and then the effect or conditioned as the main dream. Another method of representing causal relations is by actually transforming one image (the cause) into another (the effect). Freud concludes: "in both cases *causation* is represented by *succession* [Nacheinander], in the first case by one dream following another, in the second by the immediate transformation of one image into another" (p. 314).

The dream-work is less effective in representing alternation ("either . . . or"). The alternatives are represented either as options having equal rights or by the division of the dream into two halves. But what Freud finds most striking—and what indeed has the most far-reaching consequences—is the way in which the dream-work represents the category of opposition and contradiction (*die Kategorie von* Gegensatz *und* Widerspruch): "This is simply disregarded. To the dream 'No' seems not to exist. In particular, it prefers to draw opposites together into a unity or to represent them as one" (p. 316). A similar means is used—more effectively, in Freud's judgment—to represent similarity, congruence, having features in common; this is represented by concentration, by drawing together into a unity whatever is thus related.

In the last chapter of *The Interpretation of Dreams*, Freud returns to the question of how the dream-work takes up the logical relations that connect the dream-thoughts. In raising this question again, his primary intention is to explain what happens to these logical relations, to explain this happening in terms of the theoretical representation of the psyche that he introduces at this final, very different stage of his investigation. His explanation is based on the concept of regression: regression occurs in psychic activity when, instead of moving toward the motor end of the system, an excitation moves toward the sensory end and finally reaches the system of perceptions. Instead of a motor response to the excitation, the response is hallucinatory, as in the case of dreams, which, Freud insists, "have a *regressive* character" (p. 518). It is because of this regressive character that logical relations get lost, because such relations lie beyond the circuit of regression. But what in this discussion is most important for the question of the logic of the dream-work is the forcefulness with which—despite all that he has said about how the dream manages certain sorts of representations of logical relations—Freud reaffirms the loss of these relations and the difficulty with which they are represented. Here is Freud's statement: "If we regard the process of dreaming as a regression within our hypothetical psychical apparatus, this explains without further ado the empirically established fact that all the logical relations between the dream-thoughts are lost in the course of the dream-work or are expressed only with difficulty. . . . *In the course of regression the structure* [Gefüge] *of the dream-thoughts is dissolved into its raw material*" (p. 519).

And yet, a trace of that structure remains in the guise of the representations that the dream-work forms of the logical categories, that it forms precisely in deforming these categories.[7] What exactly is involved in this deforming–forming through which the categories are lost but a kind of representation of them remains in place of them? In virtually every case that Freud describes, the representation that comes to replace a category is a representation of a spatial or temporal relation. Thus, logical connections in general, says Freud, come to be represented by simultaneity or spatial proximity. It is likewise with the representations of specific logical relations. Causal relations are represented by separating cause from effect in the form of the temporal sequence of an introductory dream followed by a main dream; or such a relation can be represented by transforming one image (cause) into the other (effect), that is, as temporal succession and spatial coincidence. Two equal portions in temporal succession can represent alternation. And both similarity and opposition/contradiction are represented by spatiotemporal concentration. Hence, in each case something corresponding to the category comes, by way of the dream-work, to take the place of the category and, as it were, to function in its stead. This representative of the category is not just an image that would somehow exemplify it but rather is a schema by which in each case the image, the dream-material, is given a spatiotemporal ordering that corresponds to the pertinent category. Here it would not be inappropriate to speak of categorial or transcendental determinations of space/time, that is, of determinations that are of the same order as Kant's transcendental schemata.[8] Thus, what the dream-work accomplishes with respect to the logical categories is precisely a schematizing; for each logical connection in the dream-thoughts, the dream-work substitutes a corresponding schema. If, in reference to the history of philosophy, one considers the enormity of the difference between concept and schema,[9] then it is not surprising that Freud—without regarding that history, indeed on quite different grounds—declares that logical connections can be thus represented "only with difficulty."

Thus, the logic of the dream-work is a schematized logic, a logic of schemata, of spatiotemporal determinations corresponding to the various logical categories. Yet if measured by traditional philosophical logic or by what Freud often calls waking thought, this logic of schemata cannot but appear to be contaminated by illogic. To mark its divergence, one could call it an exorbitant logic, a logic outside the orbit of the philosophical logic rooted in ancient ontology. It is exorbitant in that it is a logic that tolerates and even institutes the effacement of difference, as in the schema of causality, which can produce the transformation of one image into another different from it, a transformation of one into the other as if they were not different but mutually substitutable. This logic is perhaps even more exorbitant—or rather, exorbitant in a way that is paradigmatic of this exorbitancy as such—in the case of the schema provided for opposition and contradiction (Gegensatz und Widerspruch). Freud says that this logical connection "is simply disregarded" by the dream-work, for which " 'No' seems not to exist." In the stronger case, that of contradiction, Freud's point is that the necessity—prescribed by philosophical logic—of rejecting one or the other of two contradictory terms is simply disregarded, that the "No" that philosophical logic would require be said to one or the other term seems not to exist for the dream-work. Rather, the schematizing of contradiction consists in carrying out what philosophical logic could never—absolutely never—tolerate: it draws the contradictory terms together into a unity, lets them be together, holds them together, in their very contradictoriness. If measured by the logic of philosophy or of waking thought, with this schema, whose effects will spread throughout, the logic of the dream-work becomes virtually indistinguishable from illogic.[10]

If contradictory opposites are retained side by side, yoked together in a unity in which they remain nonetheless contradictorily opposed, then, by the usual standards, the very possibility of truth is undermined, the fundamental law of thought and discourse, the so-called law of non-contradiction, is violated. One could say that the dream-work is attached by its logic—most notably by its schema of contradiction—to a point where, by the standards of philosophical logic and waking thought, truth ceases, breaks off no less decisively than meaning breaks off at that place in the dream-thoughts that Freud calls the navel of the dream. The dream-work, too, so it seems, has its navel.

The peculiarities of the logic of the dream-work can be seen taking shape almost from the beginning of *The Interpretation of Dreams*. Following his analysis of the dream—his own dream—of Irma's injection, which is the first dream treated in Freud's text, he notes that there are intrinsic inconsistencies operative. He says that the "explanations of Irma's illness"—that is, the various moments of the explanation as a whole as it emerges from the analysis—"which concur in exonerating me [of blame for her illness] are not consistent with one another but on the contrary are mutually exclusive" [*schliessen einander aus*] (p. 138). Freud draws a comparison with "the defense offered by the man accused by his neighbor of returning a kettle to him in a damaged condition: in the first place the kettle was not damaged at all, in the second it already had a hole in it when he borrowed it, and in the third he had never borrowed a kettle from his neighbor" (pp. 138–139). This "kettle logic," as Derrida calls it,[11] exemplifies the logic of the dream-work. It is likewise with that found in what Freud calls the embarrassment-dream of being naked. In such dreams one thing that is essential is "the embarrassing sensation of shame, of wanting to hide one's nakedness, usually by mobility, and of being unable to do so." One the other hand, "the people in whose presence one feels ashamed are almost always strangers, their faces left indefinite"; most significantly, "these people are indifferent." Hence the contradiction: "Between them the shame and embarrassment of the dreamer and the indifference of the other people produce a contradiction of the kind that often occurs in dreams. After all, the only thing appropriate to the dreamer's feeling would be for the strangers to gaze at him with astonishment and laugh at him, or be indignant at the sight" (p. 248). Here, then, there is a logic that yokes contradictory opposites together in the dream. Here, again, the exorbitant logic of the dream-work is operative.

Almost at the end of *The Interpretation of Dreams*, Freud returns to this theme: "Thoughts contradicting each other do not aim to cancel each other out, but persist side by side, often combining *as if there were no contradiction* into products of condensation, or they form compromises which we would never forgive our logical thinking for committing" (p. 566). Again, an exorbitant logic, a logic that borders on being indistinguishable from illogic: such is the logic of the dream-work.

With the dream-thoughts, however, it is quite otherwise. Freud insists that, prior to their being submitted to the dream-work, the dream-thoughts have a rational form (Freud's phrase is: "*die vorher rationell gebildeten Traumgedanken*" [p. 566]). More often he characterizes the dream-thoughts as *korrekt*. Here is the most explicit passage, which occurs near the end of Freud's text: "Thus we cannot deny the insight that two essentially different psychical processes play a part in forming dreams; the one creates perfectly correct [*korrekt*] dream-thoughts, just as valid [*gleichwertig*] as normal thinking; the other treats these in a highly disconcerting, incorrect way" (p. 567). The latter Freud then identifies as the genuine or proper dream-work (*die eigentliche Traumarbeit*), which he declares has been separated off or isolated (*abgesondert*).

What is most remarkable in this regard is the relation that Freud proposes between the dream-thoughts and phantasy (*Phantasie*). Referring to Scherner's view, which he had discussed in the initial chapter of *The Interpretation of Dreams*, Freud writes: "It is not that the dream forms phantasy, but that the unconscious activity of phantasy has the greatest share in the formation of the dream-thoughts" (p. 562). Most remarkably indeed, Freud is declaring that the dream-thoughts, which are rationally formed, correct, and as valid as normal thinking, are for the most part the product of phantasy. But *Phantasie* is just one of the names given to what more generally is called *imagination*. The dream-thoughts are for the most part formed by imagination, by an unconscious activity of imagination.

The question is whether imagination, thus operative in forming the dream-thoughts, can be kept out of the dream-work. A passage in which Freud is discussing the various modes of representation that the dream-work has at its disposal suggests otherwise. In this passage he considers the creation of the composite formations that often give dreams their fantastic character (*ein phantastisches Gepräge*). He writes: "The psychical process of forming composites [*Mischbildung*] in a dream is clearly the same as when, while awake, we represent or depict before us [*uns vorstellen oder nachbilden*] a centaur or a dragon" (p. 321). But this process, admitted into the dream-work, is just the process of phantasy, of imagination. It would seem, then, that the dream-work is perhaps less thoroughly separated off than Freud would like, that the limit that would separate the dream-thoughts from the dream-work is more fragile, more unstable, than one would have supposed.

Yet if imagination is engaged in the dream-work in the mode that Freud virtually acknowledges, will there be any limit to its engagement? To what extent does the logic of the dream-work prove to be a logic of imagination? For what other than imagination could produce a logic of schemata—granted, as Kant says, that "the schema is in itself always a product of imagination" and that such schematism is "an art concealed in the depths of the human soul."[12]

NOTES

1. Sigmund Freud, *Die Traumdeutung*, vol. 2 of *Studienausgabe* (Frankfurt a.M.: S. Fischer, 2000), 429. Translations are my own, though I have often consulted the translations by Joyce Crick (*The Interpretation of Dreams* [Oxford: Oxford University Press, 1999]) and by James Strachey (*The Interpretation of Dreams* [New York: Avon Books, 1965]). Subsequent references to this work are given in the text according to the pagination of vol. 2 of the *Studienausgabe*.

2. In 1932 in his *Neue Folge der Vorlesungen zur Einführung in die Psychoanalyse*, in vol. 1 of *Studienausgabe*, 453.

3. This question of circularity, already posed by the difficulties arising from Freud's supposition that both the dream-thoughts and the dream-content "lie before us," formulates in a hermeneutical mode the same question that Derrida raises about the limit of the "metaphorical concept of translation." In "Freud and the Scene of Writing," Derrida writes: "Here again, the metaphorical concept of translation (*Übersetzung*) or transcription (*Umschrift*) is dangerous, not because it refers to writing, but because it presupposes a text that would be already there, immobile, the serene presence of a statue, of a written stone or archive whose signified content might be harmlessly transported into the element of another language, that of the preconscious or the conscious" (Jacques Derrida, *L'Écriture et la différence* [Paris: Éditions du Seuil, 1967], 312–313).

4. Freud has especially in mind the schematic representation of the psyche as a whole that he is about to introduce and that governs much of the discourse of the final chapter. Following his reference to paths that "lead into the dark," he writes: "we will be obliged to put forth a set of new assumptions touching speculatively [mit Vermutungen streifen] on the structure of the psychic apparatus and the play of forces active in it, though we must take care not to spin them out too far beyond their first logical links, since otherwise their worth will vanish into uncertainty" (490).

5. This is noted by James Strachey in his translation of *The Interpretation of Dreams*, 528 n. 1.

6. Jacques Derrida, *Résistances de la psychanalyse* (Paris: Galilée, 1996), 29.

7. As noted earlier, Freud uses the word *Kategorie* in reference to the logical relations of opposition and contradiction.

8. I. Kant, *Kritik der reinen Vernunft*, A137/B176–A147/B187.

9. The relation between concept and schema goes back, by a very complicated route, to the difference that comes briefly into view at the center of Plato's *Timaeus*, the difference between the intelligible εδη and the χώρα. See my discussion in *Chorology: On Beginning in Plato's "Timaeus"* (Bloomington: Indiana University Press, 1999), esp. 154–155.

10. Freud writes: "Everything we have called the 'dream-work' appears to be so remote from the psychical processes we know to be correct, that the harshest judgment passed by our authors on the low psychical performance of dreaming cannot fail to seem perfectly right and proper" (563).

11. The expression "*la logique du chaudron* (*Résistances de la psychanalyse*, 19) is rendered as "kettle logic" in the English translation: *Resistances of Psychoanalysis*, trans. Peggy Kamuf, Pascale-Anne Brault, and Michael Naas (Stanford: Stanford University Press, 1998), 6.

12. Kant, *Kritik der reinen Vernunft*, A140/B179–A141/B180.

TWO

FREUD'S DREAM THEORY AND SOCIAL CONSTRUCTIVISM

TOM ROCKMORE

A VERY FEW IMPORTANT thinkers like Freud—Marx also comes to mind—tend to breach the boundaries of established intellectual domains, however understood. The conceptual richness of Freud's writing is suggested by the concerted attention, including the devastating critique, it has attracted from so many disparate angles of vision. An indication of the importance of his position many of his critics depict as unimportant, or on the contrary as a vast mistake, lies in the very considerable, even obsessive, lengths to which some of them are willing to go to reject it.

Freud was interested in philosophy and even attended Brentano's lectures between 1874 and 1876, but he is certainly not a philosopher in any ordinary sense. It is worth pointing out in passing that the frequent claim that his position is phenomenological in taking precisely what is given without presuppositions[1] is questionable since, like the German idealists, he always presupposes unconscious activity. But his theoretical corpus arguably has important philosophical ramifications. The suspicion that there is something philosophical about his theories, or that they are fair play for philosophical discussion, has attracted much philosophical attention. This ranges widely from sympathetic efforts to understand, say, how his approach differs from other forms of (philosophical) hermeneutics,[2] and studies on his contribution to analytic philosophy of mind,[3] to aggressive, even very dogmatic efforts to refute it, often on the grounds that it is unscientific, even a form of charlatanism.[4] Yet whatever else it is, his position is committed to knowledge—more

17

precisely, knowledge about human individuals—in order to treat various neurotic conditions.

In psychoanalysis, a main source of knowledge about the hidden nature of the mind and neurosis lies in the claimed access to the unconscious through the interpretation of dreams. This claim suggests a possible link between Freud's interpretation of dreams and the more general problem of knowledge. Accordingly, this chapter will consider Freud's dream theory as a source of psychoanalytic knowledge, including knowledge about the hidden conflicts of neurotic patients, as well as the import of this theory for the general problem of knowledge. Because I think that philosophers have routinely misunderstood Freud's position in criticizing it against traditional epistemological approaches, I will be arguing that Freudian dream theory is neither realist nor representationalist, but constructivist, and that a constructivist approach to psychoanalytic knowledge through dream interpretation is eminently defensible.[5]

A METHODOLOGICAL REMARK

Before going further, a methodological remark seems necessary. It would be relatively easy to devote a chapter or even a whole book to aspects of the many criticisms raised against Freud. But since philosophical debate, as psychoanalysis is only reputed to be, is in actual fact interminable, to do so would surely prevent us from ever reaching Freud's theories. For that reason, and since I believe that Freud has been largely misunderstood concerning philosophy, I will mainly be concentrating on Freud's writings and their interpretation. Other than as it comes into the discussion, I will for the most part avoid commenting on the large and growing philosophical critique of Freud.

Freud has often been attacked, in recent years, so sharply that at the present time it is unclear whether he will continue to have enough defenders to maintain theoretical interest in psychoanalysis or whether, like other positions that have been similarly attacked, it will recede into the history of the Western intellectual tradition.[6] Philosophical attack has been focused on the unconscious, a cornerstone of Freudian psychoanalysis, empirical verifiability, a central issue in positivist and neopositivist philosophy of science since the heyday of the Vienna Circle, and the supposed scientific status of psychoanalysis.

Such attacks, although sometimes very interesting, often constitute a refusal to engage with Freud in attacking his conceptual framework by denying one or more of its crucial elements. Typical here is the sharp struggle waged over the unconscious. The idea of the unconscious goes all the way back to Plato's conception of recollection (*anamnesis*) in the *Meno*. Even before Freud, William James was sharply opposed to a precursor of the Freudian unconscious.[7] This critique was later developed independently in the French discussion. French philosophy, which still exploits the Cartesian vein, is temperamentally opposed to any claim that consciousness is less than fully self-transparent. Examples include Jean-Paul Sartre's very Cartesian claim that the idea of an unconscious, which conflicts with his own project that man found himself in consciousness, is a contradiction in terms[8] and Michel Henry's refusal of the concept of the unconscious in favor of what he calls life.[9]

There are several reasons for not wanting to be drawn into the virtually endless morass of philosophical debate about psychoanalysis, in preferring, so to speak, to change the subject. On the one hand, it has been argued that Freud's theory can indeed resist the philosophical attack that has been launched against it. Yet that would have to be demonstrated. On the other hand, since philosophy has no mechanism to provide closure, in practice philosophical debate is open-ended. To plunge into the existing philosophical debate would, as I have already said, prevent us ever from getting to the locus of the present discussion.

Further, much of the philosophical criticism of Freud's position seems to me to be misplaced. In saying this, I am not merely claiming that in part the criticism often rests on a failure to see Freud's point but rather that it often consists in a basic refusal to enter into the psychoanalytic framework. One is reminded of Cardinal Bellarmine's celebrated refusal to look through Galileo's telescope. Like other theories, Freud's psychoanalysis represents an effort to deal with a body of evidence. Now it cannot be shown that there is only a single possible model of science. Further, no one has a right to impose a favorite conception of scientific theory as the only permissible model. It would have made no sense if, in the late seventeenth century, Newton had been told that he could not model planetary orbits on the ellipse, or that Einstein had been instructed at the beginning of the twentieth century to preserve the ordinary distinctions between space and time in working out relativity theory. Like other scientific theories, Freudian psychoanalysis represents an effort to construct a model adequate to the phenomena under discussion.[10] If that is accepted, then the crucial point at issue is whether this approach allows us to discover anything like knowledge or truth, not with what concerns the unobservable—precisely what cannot be known—but rather with respect to the unconscious, here allowed as an explanatory category, which through analytic means, including free association and dream interpretation, can be brought to consciousness.

Freud's claim that dream interpretation provides us with access to the unconscious can be interpreted in different ways. It might be argued that there is no unconscious. Or it might be argued that there is an unconscious but we cannot know it. Or it might even be argued that we can at best know the unconscious in imperfect, but never in perfect fashion—for instance, through some kind of filtering medium. I will be arguing that Freud's dream interpretation commits him to knowledge of human psychic reality as it really is behind its false appearance, but which can only be reached through appropriate techniques. According to this interpretation, Freud is not claiming, like

Kant, that like a thing in itself the unconscious is unknowable. Nor is he claiming, like Kant's schematism, that it cannot be known other than as it appears. On the contrary, he is claiming that, under the appropriate conditions, it can indeed be known as it is. But unlike standard philosophical theories of knowledge, in a Freudian model what counts as psychic reality is not mind-independent reality that can be known as it is either through direct intuition or through the relation of appearance to what appears, but rather a construct that can be known through another construct due to the joint work of the patient and the analyst. I believe that Freud's position illustrates the important idea that interpretation cannot yield knowledge of the real on an other than contingent basis and that there is no reason to believe one can ever know more than a "construction" of the real, which is already a "construction," as distinguished from the so-called mind-independent real, in a word a "construction" of a "construction." At stake, then, is Freud's notion of psychoanalytic objectivity, of what it means to have truth and knowledge in the domain of the mind.

FREUD'S DREAM THEORY AND INTERPRETATION

Freud is, of course, not the first person to be interested in dreams. At least in a desultory way, the philosophical interest in dreams, even in the Western tradition, is very old. In the *Republic*, Plato talks about divinatory dreams,[11] describes his sketch of the ideal city as a dream,[12] and depicts dreaming as taking appearance for reality.[13] In *On Dreams*, so far as I know the first monograph on the topic, Aristotle suggests that a dream is the movement of imaginary sense perception, not thought, during sleep.[14] Freud's claim that for Aristotle dreams continue thinking in sleep is certainly a tendentious reading of the view, although nothing in his own position turns on this. Perhaps the most famous philosophical reference to dreams occurs in Descartes's appeal to them in his extension of Pyrrhonian skepticism. In Descartes's wake, analytic philosophers interested in dreams tend to be concerned with knowing whether they are dreaming or awake,[15] which Malcolm, for instance, bases on waking testimony,[16] and which has given rise to extensive discussion.[17] For the anti-Cartesian Freud, on the contrary, dreams are not a source of renewed skepticism but rather of a new, different kind of knowledge about the repressed unconscious mind leading in the best situation to a psychoanalytic cure.

In simplifying greatly, we can say that Freud was not concerned with philosophical skepticism, and was also not interested in distinguishing in an appropriately Cartesian apodictic manner between sleeping and waking; he was rather concerned with achieving cure that in part depends on the analysis of dreams on the basis of his theory of mind. Freud's mature theory was not in place at the time he composed *The Interpretation of Dreams*. Despite this, he considered his dream-book to be his greatest contribution to psychology. One aspect of this work argues how the manifest content of dreams may be interpreted to reveal a latent or hidden content provided in coded form within the dream, but of which the patient or dreamer is supposedly unaware. In considering Freud's position, I will be concerned with his early texts, not as it later developed in response to the important debate between Freud's defenders and detractors.

An important insight into the latter theory is sketched in his earlier article on "Screen Memories." In this paper, Freud takes up memories, especially of the childhood variety, that are connected to later thoughts by symbolic means or similar links, hence they are not merely "innocent."[18] In such cases, he contends, the raw material can be used, but in disguised form, which only partially correlates with real events.[19] It is, hence, wrong to ask for historical accuracy, although one might by implication try to recover the conditions under which such memories were formed.[20]

The central insight is, of course, that there is psychic censorship, which leads to repression as a result of which material appears only in disguised form. This insight is the basis of the dream theory that Freud expounded for the first time in The Interpretation of Dreams (1900), and restated in a series of later writings, including On Dreams (1901),[21] the Introductory Lectures on Psychoanalysis (1916–1917),[22] "An Autobiographical Study" (1924), and New Introductory Lectures on Psychoanalysis (1933).[23]

The theory of dreams originally belonged to a bipartite division into conscious and unconscious that, after the First World War, was replaced by the familiar trichotomy. The dream theory, which was stated in The Interpretation of Dreams, predates the later description of the subject (id, ego, superego) along lines recalling Plato's Phaedrus. For our purposes, it will be sufficient to provide an "average" statement of the theory that simply ignores its development in subsequent writings and editions of The Interpretation of Dreams. Although this account will omit many of the details interesting to Freudians, including practicing psychologists, psychiatrists, and psychoanalysts, it will provide access to a relatively spare form of the position in which its epistemological nucleus will be clear.

In "An Autobiographical Study" (1924), we find an excellent short summary by Freud of aspects of his very complex theory of dreams. Freud here claims that, through free association and the art of interpretation, in The Interpretation of Dreams he showed that dreams have a discoverable meaning.[24] In Freud's opinion, thoughts contained in dreams are residues of the day in the form of a wishful impulse.[25] The dream represents the disguised, hence distorted, fulfillment of a repressed wish that arises through the partial relaxation of ego censorship[26] and dream-work is the process that converts latent thoughts into manifest dream-material.[27] The dream is both a wish fulfillment but also the continuation of preconscious activity of the day, providing access to both the conscious and unconscious processes of the patient.[28] In The Interpretation of Dreams, Freud supplements this minimal account in pointing out that the structure of the dream closely depends on the twin mechanisms of dream-displacement, or the substitution of one idea for another, and dream-condensation, or compression after various relations are simply dropped and the intensity of various elements altered. And, although the objection has often been raised, according to Freud it is not the case that all dreams concern sexual satisfaction.[29]

INTERPRETING DREAM INTERPRETATION

Our task now is to interpret Freud's theory—in a word, to interpret his interpretation of dreams. Even in this very brief statement, it is apparent that, at least by philosophical standards, Freud's dream theory is very complex. It includes at least eight related claims, which we can list as follows:

- Dreams take up the materials of the current day.

- Dreams often, but not always, have a sexual and aggressive content.

- Dreams have a cognitive content.

- In dreams there is a difference between appearance and reality.

- The cognitive content is present in disguised form.

- The cognitive problem lies in penetrating beyond the disguise to what is disguised.

- What is disguised is the hidden psychic reality.

- Through the interpretation of dreams, the hidden psychic reality is uncovered (or recovered).

We can, to begin with, safely give up the idea that dreams are, or only are, residues of the day. Freud held to this conviction in successive editions of *The Interpretation of Dreams*.[30] But, it may be argued, he elsewhere weakened this claim in suggesting that all dreams go back to the last few days.[31] I believe that, since it plays no useful role in his general cognitive theory, this idea can be safely discarded without harm to his overall position.

Freud's interest in sexual matters, which may reflect his own repressed state, has attracted much criticism. He has often been criticized unfairly enough for the view that dreams necessarily concern hidden sexual wishes that, even in the original version of this theory, he simply did not hold. His basic claim seems to be that dreams represent one way (but not the only way) to fulfill a wish.[32] Dreams can be described as a form of wish fulfilment,[33] which is mainly, but not exclusively, of an erotic character.

In his dream theory, one of Freud's hidden assumptions is that whatever derives from mental life is not merely somatic even if all drives always have a somatic source. In Freud's opinion, all individuals have a conflict between dream-wishes and censorship, leading to distortion, which is overcome through dream analysis.[34] According to Freud, a dream has a hidden, or latent text, as distinguished from the manifest text, which can, through free association, be satisfactorily interpreted. He thinks that dreams represent what can be recovered, but that representation must be pictorial, since dreams take the form of visual images, although there is no reason why this should be the case. His dream interpretation depends on the supposition that they obey a rational causality of psychological but not somatic or other origin, which can be traced backward from effect or manifest content to latent content or cause.

The claim that dreams have cognitive content is weaker than the further claim to recover it. The claim that dreams have cognitive content of any kind, which has been disputed,[35] can effectively be countered by recovering that content. To do so requires one to penetrate beyond the appearance, which is manifest in the dream, to the hidden psychic reality. Psychic reality is disguised or masked by the ego, which allows no more than a hidden form of the repressed wish to rise to the level of consciousness. According to Freud, the dream is only one form of the wish fulfillment whose systems are the manifestation of the unconscious.[36]

Standard philosophical theories of knowledge—for instance, all known forms of realism—are concerned with knowing a cognitive object either directly or indirectly as it is.[37] Freud's theory shares a version of that concern in a way dependent on his psychoanalytic visions. His aim is not, as is usually, perhaps always, the case in philosophical debate on knowledge to recover the mind-independent world, but rather to employ similar terminology to recover the mind-dependent world. The difficulty of this task is compounded by the claim for the existence of a psychic unconscious, which is the supposed source of the encoded content of dreams. His central epistemological claim is that, through dream interpretation, the process of psychic encoding is effectively decoded to uncover (or recover) the hidden psychic reality. The problem is enhanced in that, as Freud stresses, there is no single code, hence neither a single way of encoding psychic reality nor of deciphering it.

As concerns dream interpretation, the main clue is the idea that the dream contains wish fulfillment. There is no relevant difference between wish fulfillment and the general Aristotelian goal of human happiness. The former is the realization on the purely psychic plane of the end or goal toward which all human activity is directed. This points to a teleological view of mental life along broadly Aristotelian lines in which all activity of whatever kind is directed toward the attainment of happiness. Yet there are obvious differences between between Freud and Aristotle. Aristotle, who argues for the philosophical life as the best kind of life, had no conception of the unconscious, which is central to Freud's model. In his less intellectualized, less restrictive view of mental activity, all activity, including the activity of the unconscious, is directed toward real or ideal wish fulfillment of human goals, which ultimately concern happiness. Freud works this out in a complex theory of the human psyche whose triadic structure recalls the Platonic soul, but whose theory of repression is distinctly his own.

FREUDIAN DREAM THEORY AND REALISM

Freud's suggestion that, through dream interpretation, the analyst surpasses the manifest dream content in order to recover the latent content, is a clear assertion of knowledge about psychic reality. As a first step in evaluating this epistemological claim, it will be useful to determine what is being said. The problem of knowledge has been extensively discussed in philosophy over several thousand years. For our present purposes, let us call the two most obvious philosophical candidates Platonism and cognitive representationalism, although neither term really captures what Freud is up to.

It will be useful to distinguish between Plato and Platonism—that is, the theory attributed to Plato whose own view after several thousand years of discussion remains unknown. Freud's distinction between the manifest and the latent dream-content is closely parallel to the Platonic distinction of appearance and reality. Like Plato, starting from what is manifest or mere appearance, Freud is concerned with knowing the hidden reality that is its supposed cause. Freud's problem—that is, how to understand the reality of the patient—is analogous to the Platonic problem of knowing the real through an imitation of an imitation. Plato's solution, which is that reality can be directly known by bypassing appearance for reality, is not available for Freud. For Freud, reality is no more than a construct, which the analyst aims not to construct, but to reconstruct, although the reconstruction can never be a faithful reproduction of the original construction. Study of all the available materials, including the manifest content of dreams, ends in the supposed reconstruction of the original construction. But anything like a correspondence approach to truth as usually understood is excluded, since in Freud's position the reconstruction can never be compared with the original construction. To put the same point in other words, the difference between Plato and Freud is that the former is concerned with knowing mind-independent reality whereas the latter is concerned with knowing the mind-dependent psychic reality of the patient who is the cognitive object. Hence, in any evaluation of Freud's view, one has to dislocate the limited, special problem of understanding the psychic reality of the patient from the more general epistemological problem of understanding reality.

Platonism consists in the idea that to know is to know the real, to grasp what is as it is. This normative conception of epistemology echoes through the entire later Western philosophical tradition. A straight line connects Parmenides, who seems already to have been committed to this basic cognitive claim, with current realist thinkers, all of whom are committed to some version of the view that to know is to know a mysterious entity that can be neutrally designated as the mind-independent external world as it is.

All of the many forms of epistemological realism turn on the idea that to know is to know the mind-independent world. Hilary Putnam, who has been committed to realism in all the many successive phases of his position, is perhaps the most representative current champion of realist epistemology. In his most recent phase, in which he has given up so-called internal realism for what he calls natural realism, Putnam lays claim to direct knowledge, without an interface of any kind, of the world as it is.[38] But this general position is currently held by a wide selection of writers, including those like Donald Davidson, who are committed to some version of the correspondence approach to knowing reality,[39] and, on the contrary, those like Richard Rorty, an anti-realist skeptic, who thinks there is no knowledge since we cannot know reality, but who has no doubts about reality.[40]

Freud is certainly not a realist, or at least not one in any classical, ordinary sense of the term. He would not deny that the existence of the external world is anything other than a given. Indeed, he insists on the fact that the role of the ego is to adapt to the external natural and social world. But he is not suggesting that, say, through the interpretation of dreams, we in fact grasp mind-independent reality as it is. The cognitive object in an analytic situation is not the way the world is, but rather the situation of the neurotic individual, which can supposedly be recovered through the interpretation of dreams and in other ways.

If this is correct, then Freud's dream theory differs from garden variety forms of epistemological realism in two main senses. First, it does not depend on direct or intuitive knowledge—for instance, literally seeing the real as in Platonism, in which certain people—call them individuals of gold—on grounds of nature and nurture can be brought to the point where they supposedly literally see the forms. Second, and as emphasized, there is no mind-independent real to be grasped. Standard realism understands the real, or cognitive object, as what is in independence of the knower. But the psychic reality, which the analyst seeks to know, is not mind-independent, not like an independent object, but rather mind-dependent, like a dependent object that can be known precisely for the reason that it is constructed by the same person who further betrays its hidden nature through dreams that form the content of dream analysis. Through interaction with our surroundings, all people, including neurotic individuals, construct a view of themselves and the world, in effect a kind of highly localized worldview.

If this reading is correct, four points follow immediately, which introduce a decisive difference between Freud's position and epistemological realism, and in virtue of which his theory cannot be judged against cognitive realist lines. First, the cognitive object, in this case psychic reality, is not found, uncovered, or discovered (as it is), but is rather constructed. Second, in Freud's opinion, although there is an independent ontological reality, there is no ontologically independent but cognitively knowable real for which he substitutes a constructed psychic reality, which is directly dependent on the psychological subject. Third, Freudian psychic reality is not directly given at all, say, through direct intuition, but only indirectly through interpretation that is intended to recover what is as it were given in no more than hidden fashion, such as through the medium of dreams. Interpretation is tied to empirical data, but it is not claimed that the data are independent reality or allow us through interpretation to recover independent reality. Fourth, evaluative approaches that complain about Freud's inability to show how dream interpretation in fact provides access to mind-independent reality impose an external criterion that is unrelated to Freudian psychoanalytic theory.

FREUDIAN DREAM THEORY AND REPRESENTATIONALISM

The difference between knowing the mind-independent external world, which concerns philosophers, and mind-dependent psychic reality, which concerns psychoanalysts, forever separates Freud's task from philosophical epistemology. This can be illustrated through the distinction between Freud and Kant, who offers the most distinguished form of a representationalist approach to knowledge.

Kant, who is a leading representationalist epistemologist, revives a version of the Platonic distinction between appearance and reality. In Kant's opinion, phenomena are also appearances, and the problem of knowledge consists in understanding the relation of the appearance to the object. This yields a threefold view of the cognitive object, or object of knowledge, as phenomenon, appearance and the object, or thing-in-itself. As phenomenon, the object is given in experience; as appearance, it relates to something beyond itself that appears; and in itself, it is the way it is in independence of a knower as what can be thought but not given in experience, hence not known.

Representationalism of all kinds suffers from two basic problems that have never been solved (or resolved). One problem, which was already known to Plato, concerns the relation of the representation to what it represents, namely, to the represented. In the *Phaedo*, which may not represent his own position, through Socrates's response to Cebes, Plato explicitly rejects an ordinary scientific causal view in favor of the so-called theory of forms or ideas. Plato's objection seems to be that in the scientific model of causality cause and effect are not linked in univocal fashion since more than one cause can give rise to the same effect and conversely. Modern philosophers, who in the meantime have forgotten Plato's objection,[41] tend to prefer a causal theory of perception, although no one has ever given a satisfactory explanation of how the representation relates to the represented. Second, there is also no satisfactory account of the meaning of representation.

In avoiding epistemological representationalism, Freud's position avoids its difficulties. He is not claiming that the manifest dream content is the appearance of the latent dream content. He is rather claiming that the manifest content, which is initially present in consciousness only in encoded form, can be appropriately decoded in a way that reveals the latent, censored, distorted dream content, or hidden psychic reality. Since the latent message is already contained within the manifest content of the dream, the manifest content is not an appearance and the latent content is not the mind-independent real. In a word, the familiar Kantian distinction between appearance and reality simply cannot be drawn in the same way because as Hegel would say, the essence (*Wesen*), or in this case mind-dependent psychic reality, appears. The difficulty is not how, starting from a mere representation, one can plausibly claim to know reality that is absent, or, as Heidegger would say, present in the mode of absence. It is rather how, starting from the reported material of dreams, through working together the analyst and the patient can uncover what is hidden, or latent, by making it manifest. As concerns dreams, for Freud the idea of truth in interpretation lies in a deconstruction of myth and fantasy in order to construct, or rather to reconstruct, the psychic truth that the neurotic has constructed on the latent level but which is to be recovered through untangling the historical truth from the material reality. In this sense, the analyst is like an archeologist who sifts through the deposits of time to uncover or to recover what is only there in hidden form. Hence, standard difficulties besetting representational theories of knowledge, such as how the representation relates to the represented, or further what "representation" means, do not arise in Freud's position. More precisely, how the manifest content relates to the latent content, or what is meant by the representational function of the former to the latter, are not problematic in a Freudian model.

FREUD AND CONSTRUCTIVISM

As compared to ordinary philosophical discussion of knowledge of the real, it appears that Freud's theory of dream interpretation is neither realist nor representational, but rather constructivist. One must be careful in specifying what this means. "Constructivism" is used in many, sometimes disparate ways.[42] The term, which has a bad name, especially among those who know little about it, is often associated with the sociology of knowledge and French postmodernism, and criticized accordingly. In a recent op-ed article in the *New York Times*, it was superficially suggested that constructivism amounts to interpreting history without being bound by the facts, hence in denying truth in a way that might lead to denying the Holocaust.[43] This superficial criticism is problematic in that it suggests there is something called a fact that, a Bishop Butler would say, just is what it is—hence, by implication, is independent of any frame of reference. But what we mean by facts depends on the perspective, point of view, conceptual scheme, interpretive framework, and so on.[44] As I am using the term here, *constructivism* denotes the way in which what we call reality is a construct that is always dependent on, hence never independent of, one or another conceptual scheme. This claim can be illustrated by the early Kuhn, for whom, as he famously remarked, Priestley and Lavoisier lived in different worlds,[45] but not by the later Kuhn, for whom the input or content is the same for all parties, who may or may not interpret it differently.[46]

If we interpret constructivism on an interactionist model, then Freud is a constructivist, whose theory of dreams depends on the interpretive (re)construction of the latent psychic content present in manifest form. The interpretation of dreams, it has been emphasized, is not intended to grasp the mind-independent real, but only the unconscious psychic construct that is present to conscious in an appropriately censored, hence distorted, form. Dream interpretation is the analytic process of penetrating behind the ego censor's veil to describe whatever is only present in hidden form. What is hidden is not uncovered, since it is already there in full view, but only deciphered to recover hidden meaning. The latent content is not a mind-independent real, but triply constructed in a complex process containing different stages: first, through the interaction between the patient and that person's surroundings; second, through the interaction between the patient and the analyst; and, third, through the self-relation of the patient, that is, the patient's relation to himself mediating his developmental history, and so on. Clues furnished by the patient through free association indicate the meaning hidden in the manifest content in a way that, in cases of successful interpretation, breaks through to the latent content of the dreams. The patient and only the patient is uniquely positioned to effect this work. For the very person who constructs one's own psychic reality is the only one for whom it is potentially transparent, hence who can know it. In sum, it is possible to know psychic mind-dependent reality, although in knowing one does not know psychic reality as it is other than as a construction and then as a reconstruction.

FREUD'S CONSTRUCTIVIST DREAM MODEL
AND OBJECTIVE COGNITION

A supposed lack of cognitive objectivity is often raised as an objection against Freud and constructivist approaches to knowledge in general. Any hermeneutical discussion of dream theory needs to differentiate several potential issues, including whether Freud's view of the interpretation of dreams could possibly be correct; whether, even if it is not correct, it might still serve as a reliable way into the unconscious; and whether it has a future as a theory of interpretation. These problems all turn on the idea of cognitive objectivity—that is, the objectivity of claims to know under normal psychoanalytic conditions.

The concept of objectivity is extremely difficult even to state, much less to clarify. It is difficult to untangle such terms as objectivity, agreement, subjectivity, observation, certainty, truth, and so on. Suffice it to say here that for an empiricist, the basic insight is that claims to knowledge must in some way be determined empirically, say, by the so-called facts as opposed to personal predilection, subjective desires, and so on. This suggests a distinction between whatever a particular person or a group of people might think and, on the contrary, the way things are. A claim of this kind is routinely believed to function within natural science. If I say that the available data indicate the existence of a new planet, that assertion can be supported or undermined by the astronomical observation of a planetary body in the predicted place in the heavens.

This view of science can be applied to the interpretation of dreams. One could object that Freud's description of how this is to be done is unacceptable from a cognitive angle of vision since there is simply no way to verify the analytic interpretive claims by matching them against the reality of the situation as there is in science. Analytic philosophers of science often object that psychoanalysis has no acceptable way of justifying its claims to know, hence no notion of cognitive objectivity. This type of attack on Freud, which presuppposes the Vienna Circle idea of empirical verifiability, or at least a physicalist approach to science, was adumbrated by Karl Popper[47] and later developed by many others, such as Adolph Grünbaum. It presupposes that psychoanalysis lays claim to natural scientific status and that natural science is by definition empirically falsifiable.

To respond to this charge, it will be useful to differentiate between Freud's view of the scientific status of psychoanalysis and his constructivism. Freud's claim that psychoanalysis is science or scientific is often unclear, certainly inadequate to justify appealing to a particular scientific model. A typical instance is his suggestion, in a discussion of *Weltanschauung*, that psychoanalysis did not have need of one, since, as a part of science, it could accept the scientific *Weltanschauung*.[48] I think we must simply concede that Freud's dream theory is not verifiable in the ordinary, intersubjective sense of the term. Yet there is no reason to accept this view of intersubjective verification as normative for all forms of science, much less for all rigorous claims to know. Two points are relevant here. First, the claims for particular dreams are indeed verifiable through the technique of free association, which, admittedly, does not meet the standard the scientific verificationists have in mind. Second, there seems to be no reason to accept verifiability, or any other form of an empirical criterion of meaning, for use in psychoanalysis.

There is a difference between a claim for scientific status and a claim for empirical falsifiability. A theory might be scientific, depending on what "science" means, but unfalsifiable, certainly not falsifiable on empirical grounds. · Ordinarily these claims are run together as if for a theory to be scientific simply means that it is empirically testable in some way. Of course, many so-called scientific theories are not empirically testable, at least not obviously so. An example is so-called superstring theory, which, at the time of this writing, has been around for many years but for which an adequate empirical test has not been so far devised. If empirical testability were the criterion of scientificity, then superstring theory would not be a science, or at least would only become one when a way was found to subject it to an empirical test.

The view that there is an acceptable vision of cognitive objectivity that is simply flouted by Freudian psychoanalysis in general, particularly in dream interpretation, presupposes the sort of clarity about objective scientific knowledge that is simply nonexistent. Here three points are relevant. To begin with, the term *science* is a historical variable, which means different things in different times and places. It would be foolish to contend that we now use the term in the way, say, that it is used in ancient Greek texts. It is not as well known that the term is used differently in the main European languages. We would be hard put to find an equivalent in English for the German "*Wissenschaft*," which suggests the rigorous treatment of any domain at all, as in "*Theaterwissenschaft*," literally the science of theater. This term in ordinary German is scarcely meaningful in literal English translation, since the idea that theater studies could be a form of science is unlikely to occur to anyone. Second, we further need to resist the idea that there is only one science or only one form of cognitive objectivity. In the same way as the particular form of cognitive inquiry is a function of the cognitive domain, the relevant type of cognitive objectivity depends on the type of cognitive inquiry. Archeology, which does not permit experimental verification through predictions, has every claim to scientific status. Third, it is unclear that science need be falsifiable in any obvious way.[49] As part of the long analytic critique of empiricism in the twentieth century (waged by such writers as Russell, the later Wittgenstein, Quine, Sellars, Davidson, Putnam, and Rorty), in recent years anti-positivist philosophy of science has decisively undermined the very idea that a scientific theory can be refuted. If we take the analytic philosophical attack on empiricism seriously, then it becomes very unclear how objective claims to know differ from the fact that they are accepted by the relevant practitioners of a particular domain. It seems obvious that in the normal course of events physicists decide for physicists and poets for poets. In practice that means that those who work in a given area work out the rules, hence set the standards, in terms of which claims to know are accepted or rejected in a particular cognitive domain.

As concerns psychoanalysis, and in particular dream interpretation, claims to know arise out of and are tested within the interaction between the analyst and the analysand, between the interpretation and the source of relevant information. The analyst needs to bring the proposed reading of the material in line with the material already reported and with any other material that may be reported. Objectivity in this situation means nothing more than a basic agreement between the analytic reconstruction of psychic reality and psychic reality as mainly revealed in the patient's free associations. This is the case whether agreement is achieved immediately, or whether as what frequently happens, because of the patient's resistance, it is only achieved later on and as the result of working through the material. It follows that complaints that the analytic domain does not provide intersubjective verification of results that can be duplicated in a laboratory setting, which presuppose that the interscientific application of the standards of one science, in Grünbaum's positivist model modern physics, are simply irrelevant to analytic practice.

Wittgenstein puts the point well in a stray remark in *Philosophical Investigations*. In passing, he writes: "(Assuming that dreams can yield important information about the dreamer, what yielded the information would be truthful accounts of dreams. The question of whether the dreamer's memory deceives him when he reports the dream after waking cannot arise, unless indeed we introduce a completely new criterion for the report's agreeing with the dream, which gives us a concept of 'truth' as distinct from 'truthfulness' here.)"[50] Although I have no idea of why he was interested in dreams, I think Wittgenstein has put his finger on a point that can be expanded. For analytic purposes, it simply makes no more sense to ask whether the dreamer correctly reports a dream than whether the analyst correctly interprets it. In both cases there is no other access to the manifest dream content than what the patient reports it to be and says about it. There is, hence, no other way to access a putative mind-independent reality and there is no such reality that could be accessed in this way. Cognitive objectivity, which only exists within the analytic situation, cannot be corroborated outside it. More precisely, cognitive objectivity is corroborated only within the analytic situation in the interaction between analyst and patient.

CONCLUSION

In this chapter I have talked more about Freud than about his texts. It would be a mistake to consider Freud as a philosopher, or only as a philosopher, since that was not his intention. But his writings clearly have philosophical implications. In taking his theories out of their psychotherapeutic context, I have concentrated on stating and considering his interpretation of dreams in relation to currently standard philosophical views of knowledge. In the same way as his general position, Freud's dream theory has been more often criticized than understood. The burden of my argument has been to show that the dream theory exemplifies a nonstandard, but philosophically respectable constructivist approach to knowledge. Although it is not beyond philosophical criticism, it is able to resist much of the current philosophically motivated criticism that more often than not depends on a misunderstanding of the position. Once this is seen, I believe Freud's dream theory is able to stand on its own as a major contribution to our understanding of human beings.[51]

NOTES

1. See, for example, his discussion in *The Interpretation of Dreams*, in *The Basic Writings of Sigmund Freud*, ed. A. A. Brill (New York: Random House, 1938), 478.

2. As a phenomenologist, Ricoeur notes that psychoanalysis, which is sui generis, is like, but also basically unlike, Husserlian phenomenology. See Paul Ricoeur, *De l'interprétation, Essai sur Freud* (Paris: Editions du Seuil, 1965).

3. See, e.g., *The Analytic Freud: Philosophy and Psychoanalysis*, ed. Michael P. Levine (London: Routledge, 2000). Against those who think that the growth of cognitive sciences starting in the 1960s has made Freud's view seem like a relic of a bygone era, or that the view can be simply dismissed, Redding argues that Freud's theory resembles the so-called recently formulated "higher-order thought" (or HOT) theory in which mental contents depend on so-called higher-order concepts to become conscious [as developed by D. M. Rosenthal, "Two Concepts of Consciousness," in *Philosophical Studies* 49 (1986): 329–359; and R. J. Gennaro, *Consciousness and Self-Consciousness: A Defense of the Higher-Order Thought Theory of Consciousness* (Amsterdam: John Benjamins, 1995)] that is traceable back to Kant's view, mentioned by Freud [S. Freud, *The Standard Edition of the Complete Psychological Works of Sigmund Freud*, trans. and ed. James Strachey (London: Hogarth Press, 1953–1974, XIV, 171)] that perception is subjectively conditioned. See Paul Redding, "Freud's Theory of Consciousness," in *The Analytic Freud: Philosophy and Psychoanalysis*, 119–131.

4. A large portion of the recent philosophical discussion of Freud, especially in English, has focused on the scientific status of his theories. Freud himself seems to raise this claim. See Freud, *The Standard Edition of the Complete Psychological Writings of Sigmund Freud*, XVI, p. 452. Critique of psychoanalytic theory focussing on whether it is testable in accordance with accepted scientific procedure, includes Adolf Grünbaum, *The Foundations of Psychoanalysis* (Berkeley: University of California Press, 1984); Adolf Grünbaum, *Validation in the Clinical Theory of Psychoanalysis: A Study in the Philosophy of Psychoanalysis* (Madison, CT: International Universities Press, 1993); Edward Erwin, *A Final Accounting: Philosophical and Empirical Issues in Freudian Psychology* (Cambridge: MIT Press, 1996); Malcolm Macmillan, *Freud Evaluated* (Cambridge: MIT Press, 1997), Frederick Crews, *The Memory Wars: Freud's Legacy in Dispute* (New York: New York Review of Books, 1995), and others. For a typical response, centered on questions about what constitutes a scientific theory, see Jonathan Lear, *Love and Its Place in Nature: A Philosophical Interpretation of Freudian Psychoanalysis* (New York: Noonday Press, 1990), 216 ff.

5. For a recent discussion of social constructivism in a scientific context, see André Kukla, *Social Constructivism and the Philosophy of Science* (London: Routledge, 2000).

6. For defense of the Freudian concept of the unconscious against philosophical criticism available in English, see Donald Levy, *Freud Among the Philosophers: The Psychoanalytic Unconscious and Its Philosophical Critics* (New Haven: Yale University Press, 1996).

7. For discussion of James's critique, see Levy, *Freud Among the Philosophers*, 64–72.

8. In building on the view of Wilhelm Stekel, for whom psychosis always rests on a conscious fact, Sartre consistently argues, from the *Sketch of a Theory of*

Emotions (1943) to *Being and Nothingness* (1943), and again in his presentation to the Société française de philosophie in 1948 ("Conscience de soi et connaissance de soi") that the so-called unconscious is only a consciousness that chooses not to speak, since the psychic dimension is coextensive with consciousness, leading to his concept of bad faith. See "Existential Psychoanalysis," in Jean-Paul Sartre, *Being and Nothingness: A Phenomenological Essay on Ontology*, trans. Hazel E. Barnes (New York: Washington Square Press, 1973), 712–733. For discussion, see Alain Renaut, *Sartre, le dernier philosophe* (Paris: Grasset, 1993), 149–151.

9. See Michel Henry, *Généalogie de la psychanalyse* (Paris: Presses universitaires de France, 1985).

10. See Bas C. Van Fraassen, *The Scientific Image* (Oxford: Clarendon Press, 1980), 5.

11. See Plato, *Republic*, 383 A.

12. See Plato, *Republic*, 443 B.

13. See Plato, *Republic*, 467 B.

14. Aristotle, *On Dreams*, 1, 459a21–22 and op. cit. 3, 462a30–31.

15. See Harry Frankfurt, *Demons, Dreamers and Madmen: A Defense of Reason in Descartes' Meditations* (Indianapolis: Bobbs-Merrill, 1970).

16. See Norman Malcolm, *Dreaming* (London: Routledge and Kegan Paul, 1959), 81.

17. See *Philosophical Essays on Dreaming*, ed. Charles M. Dunlop (Ithaca: Cornell University Press, 1977).

18. See *Freud Reader*, ed. Peter Gay (New York: Norton, 1989), 123.

19. See *Freud Reader*, 125.

20. See *Freud Reader*, 126.

21. See Sigmund Freud, *On Dreams*, trans. James Strachey (New York: Norton, 1952).

22. See part 2: "Dreams," in Sigmund Freud, *Introductory Lectures on Psychoanalysis*, trans. James Strachey (London: Hogarth, 1963), in the *Complete Psychological Works of Sigmund Freud*, vol. 15, 15–239.

23. See "Revision of the Theory of Dreams," in Sigmund Freud, *New Introductory Lectures on Psychoanalysis*, trans. James Strachey (New York: Norton, 1965), 7–29.

24. See *The Freud Reader*, 27.

25. See *The Freud Reader*, 27.

26. See *The Freud Reader*, 28.

27. See *The Freud Reader*, 28.

28. See *The Freud Reader*, 29.

29. See *The Freud Reader*, 29; see also *The Interpretation of Dreams*, in *The Basic Writings of Sigmund Freud*, ed. A. A. Brill (New York: Modern Library, 1938), 236, 392.

30. See *The Basic Writings of Sigmund Freud*, 239, 240.

31. See "On Dreams," in *The Freud Reader*, 155.

32. See *The Basic Writings of Sigmund Freud*, 511.

33. See *The Basic Writings of Sigmund Freud*, 205.

34. See *The Basic Writings of Sigmund Freud*, 223–247.

35. Hobson claims that dreams are merely somatic in character. See J. Allan Hobson, *The Dreaming Brain* (New York: Basic Books, 1988).

36. See *The Basic Writings of Sigmund Freud*, 511.

37. See, e. g., Michael Devitt, *Realism and Truth* (Princeton: Princeton University Press, 1997).

38. See "Sense, Nonsense and the Sense: An Inquiry into the Powers of the Human Mind," in Hilary Putnam, *The Threefold Cord: Mind, Body and Mind* (New York: Columbia University Press, 1999), 1–70.

39. Davidson, who earlier argued in a favor of a coherence form of the correspondence theory of truth, seems to have recently abandoned this view. See his "Afterthoughts, 1987," appended to the reprint of "A Coherence Theory of Truth and Knowledge," in *Reading Rorty: Critical Responses to Philosophy and the Mirror of Nature (and Beyond)*, ed. Alan R. Malachowski (Oxford: Blackwell, 1990), 134–138.

40. For criticism of Rorty as inconsistently committed to reality that, however, on his own lights is unknowable, see Hilary Putnam, "Richard Rorty on Realism and Justification," in *Rorty and His Critics*, ed. Robert Brandom (Oxford: Blackwell, 2000), 81–87.

41. Hegel, who is an exception, revives the Platonic objection as the basis of his attack on the conception of law in Newtonian mechanics in the *Phenomenology*. See G. W. F. Hegel, *Hegel's Phenomenology of Spirit*, trans. A. V. Miller (New York: Oxford University Press, 1977), §150, 91–92.

42. For an account that usefully traces the uses of the term in sociology of knowledge to Scheler and Mannheim, see Peter L. Berger and Thomas Luckmann, *The Social Construction of Reality: A Treatise in the Sociology of Knowledge* (New York: Doubleday, 1966).

43. See Tody Judt, "Writing History, Facts Optional," in the *New York Times*, Thurdsay, April 13, 2000, A 27.

44. See Ludwik Fleck, *Genesis and Development of a Scientific Fact*, ed. Thaddeus J. Trenn and Robert K. Merton, trans. Fred Bradley and Thaddeus K. Trenn (Chicago: University of Chicago Press, 1979).

45. See Thomas Kuhn, *The Structure of Scientific Revolutions* (Chicago: University of Chicago Press, 1970) 118.

46. See Thomas Kuhn, *The Essential Tension: Selected Studies in Scientific Tradition and Change* (Chicago: University of Chicago Press, 1977) 309n.

47. See Karl R. Popper, *Conjectures and Refutations: The Growth of Scientific Knowledge* (New York: Harper and Row, 1965).

48. See "The Question of a *Weltanschauung*," in *Freud Reader*, 796.

49. Following Duhem, Quine invokes holism to deny empirical falsifiability. See "Two Dogmas of Empiricism," in W. V. O. Quine, *From a Logical Point of View* (New York: Harper and Row, 1963) 20–46.

50. Ludwig Wittgenstein, *Philosophical Investigations* (New York: Macmillan, 1953), 222–223.

51. I wish to thank Jon Mills for his useful comments on an earlier draft.

THREE

THE BODILY UNCONSCIOUS IN FREUD'S "THREE ESSAYS"

JOHN RUSSON

FREUD'S WORKS INTRODUCED a wide range of new concepts to the contemporary world, but surely among the most distinctive and significant are those of childhood sexuality, the Oedipus complex, and the formative stages of psychosexual development. These themes are the subject of his famous "Three Essays on the Theory of Sexuality," one of Freud's most significant and most original contributions to our understanding of human experience.[1] My goal is to interpret, defend, and partially transform Freud's notion of "the unconscious" as it is developed in this early work. Accordingly, this chapter will develop in four stages. Initially I will focus on the conceptions of childhood and the body that are at play in the "Three Essays," in order to develop an understanding of the self-transcending character of human experience. Next I will show that Freud's studies require that the human family be reconceived as an experiential reality, rather than a biological one. Then I will investigate the experience of other persons on which the child's experience of the family depends; this will lead to a criticism of Freud, and an argument that the unconscious must be understood as inherently intersubjective. Finally I will argue that it is phenomenological philosophy that properly lives up to the demands of method that are entailed by the Freudian conception of the unconscious.

THE BODY AS PROTOTYPE FOR THE REAL

We were all children once. That child that was me . . . I am still that same person. "The child is father to the man," as Wordsworth says.[2] Whatever I think now is a development of the perspective that began all those years ago. And that perspective itself began as the primitive openness—the basic responsiveness to my surroundings—that was the life of my body. We were all children once, and children are little bodies. The unconscious is the continued life of this child's perspective in us, which means it is the continued life of the body. That we were all children is the first great insight at play in Freud's philosophy.

As children, we do not (*pace* Descartes) enter the world with a fully developed conceptual arsenal or an encyclopedic store of factual knowledge. We are small, sensitive bodies with no resource beyond ourselves to deploy in our efforts to come to terms with our environment. How our environment is initially significant for us—what *counts* as our environment—is how we are impacted within the realm of our bodily sensitivities. What comes to be "the world" for us will be the result of the progressive interaction of the bodily sensitivities that are innate to us and the determinate stimulations and developments that these sensitivities undergo in the course of experience.[3]

The form in which the participants in our environment appear for us, then, is a form that answers to our childish, bodily interests. The child does not, for example, have an experience of "milk"—a designation of adult culture expressing nutritive, biological, and chemical significance—but experiences, rather, a pleasurable and satisfying flowing of tasty wetness, of a piece, in the case of breastfeeding at least, with the experience of the kinesthetic sense of the contracting of the lips and the varied texture and shape of the breast and nipple on which the mouth fixes itself. "It," for the child, is this interwoven undergoing of awareness that, from an educated adult perspective, we would describe as a blending of subjective with objective (pleasure + real thing), of different substances with each other and with their properties (breast + milk + tongue + lips + wet + firm + contracting, and so on), and, indeed, of one person with another (child + mother, self + other). In other words, for the adult all these are coherent, self-identical realities that are distinguished from each other, whereas for the child these initially are all roughly equal aspects of its own amorphous, singular, experiential reality. Being a child, as an act of experiencing, simply "is" this multifaceted assemblage.[4]

Experience at this level is governed by what Freud sometimes calls *the pleasure principle*.[5] What the world initially is to the child is that which responds to its desires, the realm in which it takes its pleasure. It is the child's interests that determine the "how" of the appearing of its environment— indeed, of its reality *tout court*. Experientially, the world, for the child, is the realization of its desires, and it is only within this original matrix of significance that the child undergoes the gradual development of its sense of the distinction between itself and its world and its gradual refinement of its sense of the nature of each of these two realities (self and world). It is thus from within the realm of significance opened up by the desires that animate our bodily sensitivities that reality itself is inaugurated for us, and the form reality itself takes is forever founded in the specifics of these bodily forms. That it is our character as experiencing bodies that shapes the nature of the real is the second great insight at play in Freud's philosophy. Though his "Three Essays on the Theory of Sexuality" is fundamentally an exploration of the nature of human sexuality, it has the force of introducing a new ontology, a new theory of the nature of reality. In these essays, Freud identifies the specific forms of the desires at play in the bodily sensitivities of the child that make possible the subsequent development of our sense of "reality" as a realm of distinct, self-identical objects encountered by a cognitive and moral subject.

Perhaps the most provocative claim in the "Three Essays" is its founding idea that sexuality—something we normally deem to be uniquely distinctive of adult life—is in fact the driving force in childhood development. Freud shows how it is that, defined by the standards of adult life, children are "polymorphous perverts," constantly in pursuit of the sexual satisfaction that comes from the stimulation of the body's "erotogenic" zones.[6] Freud's argument is that the biological processes essential to our maintenance (as individuals and as a species) are processes, whose enactment is accompanied by a great pleasure: eating, excretion, and reproduction, in particular, are simultaneously our most vital processes and the sites of our greatest pleasure.[7] The mouth, the anus, and the genitals are the most important erotogenic zones—areas of the body, whose stimulation is sexually pleasurable—and it is our developing experiences with these zones that structure our sexual and personal maturation. Most important for our purposes, he investigates the erotogenic character of the oral and anal structures of the child's bodily sensitivities.[8]

The first stage of the child's sexual development is the oral stage, that is, the stage dominated by the pleasures and forms of significance made available by the mouth. The child's mouth grabs and ingests, and it is thus that the world is initially experienced, namely, through incorporation: that is, the child takes its environment into itself, into its own body. This oral "logic" is initially set in motion through suckling at the breast, but the pleasurable experience thereby achieved is subsequently sought by the child-as-mouth elsewhere, initially in such experiences as thumb sucking, but ultimately in all manner of relations that enact this logic of the taking of one's object into oneself in modified forms. "Incorporation" is thus, we might say, our original "concept," our original way of getting a hold on reality.[9] It is this bodily logic that is at the foundation of our developed experience of the world, and in particular Freud refers to this incorporation of the object as the "prototype" for all subsequent "identifications" (i.e., roughly, adopting the identities of others as our own) and for every relation of love.[10] In other words, our bonding with other persons—one of the most central aspects of our human lives—is made possible for us through the opening to the notion of "bond" that comes to us initially because we are oral beings.

The second stage of the child's sexual development is the anal stage, that is, the stage dominated by the pleasures and forms of significance made available by the anus. The anus is a sphincter, a controllable gateway that regulates the outward flow of one's feces. The pleasures associated with the anus attach especially to this ability to control—to stop and start the putting forth of one's feces—and to the correlated ability to offer or withhold one's own thing—the "gift"—from another.[11] In the experience of toilet training in particular, the child-as-anus finds her- or himself to be an independent and autonomous agent with whom the parents must negotiate; the child can withhold its feces for the sake of an enhanced pleasure that will come by a subsequently more forceful and substantial release, but also for the pleasure of disobeying, that is, of asserting his or her autonomy in the face of others.[12] Such anal experience, like oral experience, is the prototype for many of our most important later experiences. Whereas orality emphasizes incorporation and bonding, anality emphasizes separation and alienation: the controlled separating of the gift from oneself and one's independence from others. Anal logic is thus the prototype for experiencing oneself as an independent self dealing with what is alien, and for experiencing oneself as both active and passive (controlling, but also responsive) in dealing with the determinacies one encounters. For this reason, anal experience is the prototype both for interpersonal power relations (sadism and masochism) and for knowledge; each sphere is a form of gaining mastery over an alien determinacy.[13]

What both of Freud's analyses here show is that the original forms of bodily experience are prototypes, that is, they provide the fundamental schemes within which our more sophisticated experiences can emerge; in other words, these figurings of the body leave their traces in our more mature experiences.[14] In our mature experience we treat ourselves as independent agents encountering a fixed alien world; that is, our mature experience is governed by what Freud sometimes calls *the reality principle*. But, according to this experience of the world, reality is independent of us, and its unyielding presence forces itself on us, requiring us to mold ourselves to it.[15] What this means is that in our mature experience of the world as "real," the originary character of infantile bodily experience has been effaced. The very nature of our bodily openness to the world, in other words, is such that it leads us to experience the world in such a way that the body's formative role is concealed. Our developed experience implicitly bears the trace of our embodiment in the very schemata for meaning that we live through, but these bodily roots are explicitly concealed within that experience.[16] Our infantile embodiment is thus the unconscious foundation of our mature experience.

What we have seen in this first section is that we are sensitive bodies whose very nature is to open up for us forms of experience that can develop beyond their own initial form. The body itself opens up forms of significance that are themselves capable of growth—it is "self-transcending"—and this process takes the form of a response to the pleasures of the body, which ultimately induce in us the experience of the world as "real." That is, a life founded in bodily pleasure precisely leads us to an experience of the world in which this bodily foundation is concealed. It is because we are such bodies that we have an experience of the world as real, but precisely because the body opens us to "the reality principle," it equally conceals itself. The body is thus ultimately the unconscious within experience, the continuing presence of our childhood in our adult lives. Let us look further at the precise nature of our childhood prototypes.

THE FAMILY AS A CATEGORY OF EXPERIENCE

Our body initiates us into significance. Its original determinacies are the "prototypes" of all subsequent experienced determinacy in that they—in their self-developing forms—provide the terms in which all subsequent experience is articulated. As we have already intimated, one of our most profound experiences is the experience of other people. Crucial to Freud's account is his integrating of this theme of our experience of others with the theme of the development of the child.

In studying orality and anality, we have been studying the forms of the child's subjective openness to its environment. To understand the child's development, however, we must also take account of the distinctive natures of the objects that characterize its environment. We have already seen that the child's environment includes food and whatever other materials it can make for ingestion, and also feces and whatever other products it can generate from its own bodily sphere. As the child develops, however, it also discovers that it must contend with that distinctive kind of reality that is another person, and it experiences this primarily in the persons of its parents.

A child's bodily reality is insufficient to support itself on its own, and thus it is always within the context of a family or its substitute that we grow and develop to maturity. The child's development is contextualized by this family life and the constant interaction with the parents that it entails. The growth of the child's experience of its world is to a very large degree the growth of the child's experience of its parents. They are the most prominent figures of the child's reality, being the agents who substantially control the ways in which reality is made to impinge on the child or the way the child is buffered from contact with the demands of the world. As the child's desiring body develops, it is the parents who define the primary terrain within which the child's desire operates. Freud's studies identify the ways in which the mother typically becomes the primary object of the child's desires—the primary site of pleasure—whereas the father typically becomes the primary agent of reality's resistance to the child's desires—the primary site of antagonism.[17] One of Freud's most famous contributions to psychology—his discussion of the Oedipus complex—is the story of the characteristic growth of the child's personality within this desire-mother-father triangle, and in particular of the ways in which the developments within this triangle determine the essential shape of one's future dealings with other people.

As previously described, the child's family relations are being construed from the outside. But this is not, however, how the family exists within the child's perspective. For the child, the family triangle is not initially experienced as a negotiation among three fully formed human substances. On the contrary, for the child, family life is precisely the way that a notion of what it is to be a person first develops.

Just as the distinctive forms of our given embodiment set for us the prototypic forms from which all subsequent forms of experiencing will emerge, so do the distinctive forms of our original objects set for us the prototypic forms from which all subsequent forms of object will emerge: it is from our original objects that we learn what it is to be an object, and the distinctive characters of these originals leave their traces in our subsequent experiences. The parents are the initial routes by which the child comes to encounter the human as such: it is through its familial experience that it becomes familiar with humanity. The child's experiencing is opening upon a new world—the human world—and what we call family life is, for the child, its initiation into this rich world of significance. Again, for the child, its mother and father are significances that come to develop within this world on the basis of the child's bodily forms of interaction: the mother, for example, is the desirable object that gradually emerges from out of the experience of the tasty flow of milk. Notice, though, that this is the opposite of how we (relying on "the reality principle") construe this: whereas for the child the mother comes to be from the milk, we treat the milk as a derivative product that comes to be from the substantial reality of the mother. Our perspective inverts the actual order of causality within experience. This is crucial for understanding what "the family" actually is. We, again relying on the reality principle, treat the family as a biological category, that is, we understand it in terms of the physiological causality of reproduction and so on. For the child, however, "the family" is rather an experiential category: the family just is those through whom the child comes to be familiar with the human. As a category of experience, the family is constituted by those who were in fact exemplary in initiating one into the sense of what it is to be a person, and there is no reason that these need be the ones whom we would designate "the biological parents." This notion that the family is not a biological reality, but is rather the experiential reality that is our initiation into human experience is the third great insight operative in Freud's study.[18]

I argued earlier that it is the notion of the prototype—the self-transcending original—that is the great insight lurking within Freud's notion of the unconscious, and it is this same notion of the prototype that is relevant here in our consideration of the family. We do not begin with a fully developed sense of what it means to be a person (indeed, we could not so begin since the human realm is the realm of freedom, which means it is a realm that defines its sense only through its own activity). On the contrary, our sense of what it is to be a person is shaped by our ongoing participation in human affairs, and it is our initial engagements with our familiar others that provide us with the prototype for our subsequent human experiences.[19] It is how we became familiar with the human world that provides the matrix for our subsequent expansion of our human relations. This means that the family—our initiation into human familiarity—gives the founding shape to our mature sense of other persons. This is the reason that we are always dealing with "father figures" when we encounter authority and "mother figures" in those who are the objects of our desire, and this is the reason why the events that transpire between parents and children are not simply equivalent to all other events that transpire in the child's life but are rather formative experiences, that is, experiences that decisively shape forever the very way in which the child will have an experience of the human world. It is not, in other words, that we are intimate with our parents, but rather that what it is to be intimate *is* being with our parents.

Just as it is the original form of our embodiment that is the matrix and the concealed foundation for our adult life, so are our familial relations— understood experientially, not biologically—the generative roots of all of our dealings with other people. The unconscious is thus the continuing presence of the child's body within our world, and it is also the continued experiencing of our family.

THE UNCONSCIOUS AND THE DESIRE OF THE OTHER

I have tried so far to show that Freud's notion of the unconscious can be defended precisely to the extent that we see it as being of a piece with a conception of the human body as the self-transcending prototype for experience and with the attendant conception of the family as the prototypical experiential process of initiation into familiarity with the human world as such. Though these descriptions of the child, the body, and the family are not to be found in Freud, I have tried to show that they are on the horizon of Freud's own descriptions, and it is by employing these notions that we can defend the Freudian conception of the unconscious as infantile, bodily, and familial; we can say, in other words, that the unconscious is precisely the continuing experience of our own childhood body and of our family within all the structures of our mature experience. In this third section, I want to shift, however, from defending Freud to criticizing one aspect of his position. In particular, I think that Freud has not adequately accounted for our experience of other people and, consequently, has not properly understood the nature of the sexual sphere. These are substantial challenges, but their force will not be to reject the Freudian unconscious but to further enrich this notion while at the same time drawing psychoanalysis in the direction of the philosophical tradition of phenomenology as practiced by such figures as Martin Heidegger and Maurice Merleau-Ponty (the subject of the final section).

For all the depth of insight into the human condition that Freud's work evinces, there remains in this work a fundamental blind spot when it comes to conceptualizing human experience. Though Freud recognizes that the distinctive character of the human as a subject requires a unique method for gaining access to its reality—namely, the method of psychoanalysis—he fails to recognize the ways in which the distinctive character of the human being as an object similarly differentiates it from any other sort of object in such a way again as to require a unique method. What I mean by this is that Freud does not recognize the need to explain how it can be that the child comes to experience other persons as persons at all. Though he relies on the experiences of one's desiring one's mother or fearing one's father, for example, he does not treat these, *qua* experiences, as different in kind from experiences of tasting milk or passing feces. But a mother—a person—is not the same kind of object as milk, for to experience an object as a person is precisely to experience that object *as another subject*. The experience of the other subject *qua* subject is definitive of, and, indeed, foundational for, our human experience, but Freud nowhere indicates that he recognizes the philosophical problems this entails ("the problem of other minds") nor does his account of the child's emerging experience address this decisive theme.

If the nature of the child's experience is solely to experience objects as objects—as alien surfaces—there could be no experience that would allow the child to recognize any object as the "outside," so to speak, of another subject. In seeing the mother's eyes, for example, it would see moving surfaces emblazoned with blue and black concentric circles, embedded in transparent containers with rounded surfaces, and so on; it would not, however, see the eye seeing, that is, it would not experience itself as falling under the gaze of another, for this corresponds to no objective feature of the situation. However, the child does experience the gaze of the other. Indeed, observation of the imitative behavior of newborn infants has shown that the recognition by the child of another person as like itself (i.e., a subject, my "other") is essentially immediate within experience: from the start, the child lives in a kind of subjective sympathy with other subjects, and, indeed, lives a bodily life that is immediately responsive to the subjective character of the other's body.[20] The fact that we experience other subjects as subjects at all indicates that we must be open to this significance by nature, for it is something we could never learn on the basis of "objective" experience, and the observation of newborns confirms that this is so.[21] Why is this important for Freud's account?

This is important for our study of the ontology of the Freudian unconscious because it shows that responsiveness to other subjects as subjects must be a facet of the original bodily sensitivities that enable the child's experience of the world to develop. The infantile body, the continuing experience of which is the unconscious in adult life, must be an intersubjective body. Along with being infantile, bodily, and familial, the unconscious must also be the presence of the other within us. This has further consequences for Freud's study.

That this is a blind spot in Freud is clear, for example, when he remarks that the child's withholding of feces can be for the sake of magnifying the strength of the feeling of release, or it can be for the sake of being disobedient, with its attendant sadistic pleasure.[22] Notice, though, that for the child to act for the sake of disobedience requires that the child experience itself as interacting with another cognitive, desiring, rule-engendering being: one can only disobey another subject. Freud, in other words, has already relied on the notion that the child's experiences are shot through with intersubjective significance without attending to the significance of this fact. We might similarly revisit Freud's example of breast feeding and ask: is the child's pleasure derived exclusively from the tastes and textures of its encounter with the milk and breast as objects, or is it already taking pleasure in the experience of the company of another person—the mother as such?

Recognizing this intersubjective significance that is already at play in the primitive oral and anal experiences suggests a reconceptualization of the sexual sphere, and a challenge to a significant aspect of Freud's interpretation of the child's sexual development. Regarding the sexual sphere as such, these observations suggest redefining the sexual sphere precisely as the bodily sensitivity to others as others, that is, the bodily desire for another desiring body as such. On this construal, sexuality would be the experience of our own bodies precisely as sites of contacts with other persons, the experience of our own bodies as intersubjective. Regarding Freud's analysis of childhood sexuality, it suggests that Freud's interpretation of pre-genital sexual experience as specifically autoerotic cannot be strictly correct.[23] These experiences are from the start experiences of taking pleasure in the contact with other persons—indeed, Freud himself acknowledges that other people are sexual objects for the child from the start[24]—and the whole notion of the auto-erotic, far from being the primitive root of sexual experience, will have to be reconceived as deriving its possibility and its significance from the original sexual experience of the other.

This modification to our understanding of the child's experience does not simply lead to the rejection of Freud's account; on the contrary, it enables us to justify one of its most central aspects in a way that Freud is not otherwise able to do. To say that our experience is defined from the start by a sympathy for or openness to other subjects as subjects is to say that our desire is inherently a desire for others. Our nature is to desire others, which means to desire other subjects, other desiring bodies. But if we desire other subjects as subjects, that is, as desirers, what we are desiring is, in fact, that we be desired by them. To desire others is to desire to be desired by them. For this reason, it is the other's desire that has the power to satisfy or frustrate us, has the power to shape the form our experience takes: it is the desire of the other (in both the objective and the possessive senses of the genitive) that is the driving force shaping our bodily entry into meaning.[25] This, then, explains why our original others—our family—

have such a profound effect on our development as persons. It is our family members who fundamentally possess *in their power to desire us* the most decisive shaping force in our sexuality.

Freud himself is strongly cognizant of the importance of this notion that our psyches are shaped by our living under the gaze of others, and he relies on it throughout his work in the notion of "fear of the loss of love." Yet Freud's conceptuality cannot sufficiently account for the emergence of this experience. Freud analyzes this phenomenon only in terms of the giving of pleasure and the threat of punishment, but, as we saw earlier, such an explanation in terms of objective properties fails to account for the distinctive experience of the other as a *subject*, which is definitive for the experience of oneself as subjected to the other's desire.[26] Once we have recognized the essential intersubjectivity of human experience, however—that is, once we recognize that our desire is precisely for the desire of the other—then we have found the missing link that explains why we are inescapably governed by the demands of living under another's gaze. How the child experiences the desires directed or not directed toward it by the mother and the father (or whoever experientially constitutes the child's family) will necessarily be the parameters for the child's sexual, that is, intersubjective human development. It is thus the desire of the familial other that fundamentally defines the infantile, bodily unconscious.

OBJECTIVITY AND METHOD

Before concluding this chapter, I want to consider one more aspect of this theme of the experience of others. I want to turn to the theme of knowledge—of objectivity—and consider the source of this value within human experience. Once again, my analysis here will draw on Freud's own insights, but will also lead to a criticism of a side of his method.

Freud identifies the pursuit of knowledge as drawing on the anal prototype, for it is an attempt at mastery. It is mastery of the given, determinate nature of the alien things of our world. According to Freud, we discover that there is such a world (the world of "the reality principle") because of the resistance we encounter from the world as we try to carry out our desires, and this especially means the resistance that comes from the wills of our parents. While these are two necessary conditions for the development of the project of knowing, they are insufficient as an explanation. The pursuit of knowledge is governed by the value of objectivity. This experience of this value exceeds the simple experience of the resistance of the object. Faced with resistance, I can adopt any number of strategies: I can refuse to acknowledge it and continue to act as if it is not there (a familiar psychological mechanism); I can change my direction so as not to have to encounter it (ditto); I can fight with it and try to overpower it, or, again, I can allow my entire way of being to collapse in a sense of defeat (yet again, a strategy well attested by Freud's own studies of psychopathology). None of these strategies amounts to know-ing: none responds to the obstacle as something to be understood on its own terms. The project of mastery similarly falls short of explaining the ideal of objectivity. Mastery of the object requires only that I be able to force it to behave according to my desires. There are many ways to accomplish this without attaining an insight into the true nature of the object (indeed, the project of mastery may well be such as to preclude in principle this attaining of insight). I have exerted my masterly control over your possessions when I have taken your books and used them to prop open my doors and fuel my fires, but I surely have not understood the nature of books in so doing, and certainly not the content of any of those books. Or, again, a parent may exert masterly control over a child by knowing how to manipulate the child into submissive behavior; here again, though, we should say—and the child cer-tainly feels—that the parent does not really understand the true nature of the child. Objectivity, then, is something beyond either the experience of resistance or the strategy of mastery.

What specifically constitutes objectivity is the demand to be answer-able to the determinacies of what is other on that other's own terms.[27] But what is answerability, and what, ultimately, are the other's own terms? Regarding the notion of "the other's own terms," we should recall that we (which means Freud as well) are precluded in principle from invoking the nature of some reality "in itself" that characterizes the things of our world, for our very study of the bodily unconscious has shown us that reality does not have such a nature but has its characteristics irreducibly rooted in the prototypic nature of the subjective body. If that is so, however, how can there ever be any resistance to the subject—that is, how can my own bodily perspective ever have to answer to anything beyond itself? To what else could I ever be answerable? It is our reflections on intersubjectivity that have given us our answer: our bodily perspectives are constituted by answerability from the start, because they are answerable to the desire of the other. It is these—the desiring perspectives of others—that are the autonomous sites of resistance that we encounter in experience, and it is because we *already* desire to be recognized from within the other's desire that we experience ourselves as answerable to the resistance of the other. This is the experience that is at the foundation of the value of objectivity and thus ultimately of knowledge. The value of "objectivity" is the value of coordinating the terms of one's own experience with the terms of every-one else's perspective in principle. The ideal of objectivity, in other words, is the ideal of universality within intersubjectivity.

Discovering intersubjectivity itself to be the definitive root of the ideal of objectivity again has implications for our interpretation of Freud's work. Even though Freud himself, through his analysis of the bodily roots of all meaning, has implied that all the significances of human experience can only be explained "from the inside," Freud nevertheless typically conducts his own analyses from the presumption of the reality of a "world-in-itself," and this is reflected by his regular reliance on the causal explanations offered by the natural sciences. His own analyses should have shown him the untenability of this approach, however. The natural sciences are themselves projects of knowledge that operate *within* the world of significance opened up by the infantile body and its sexual desires. The self-transcending body explains the natural sciences, and not vice versa. Our reflections on objectivity show up this same conclusion in a yet more powerful way. Pursuing objectivity is the way we navigate our own experience of the weight of the perspectives of others: pursuing objectivity is not demanded by reality-in-itself; rather, belief in a reality-in-itself is one strategy we use for coping with our sexual involvement with others. The description of our experience of sexuality explains the ideal of objectivity, and not vice versa. This means psychoanalytic insights are not compatible with the presumption of the ultimacy of "scientific method" as that is deployed in the natural sciences. On the contrary, the ultimate method can only be the description from the inside of our developed sexual experience. Freud's own insights should have led him to recognize the description of our intersubjective experience as the ultimate method (which is what he often *practices* in his case studies, but not what he explicitly relies on in his theoretical statements). This description of intersubjective experience as it is lived just is the method called phenomenology.

CONCLUSION

By focusing on Freud's "Three Essays," we have been able to derive and defend a notion of the unconscious as the continuing presence of the infantile and intersubjective body in adult experience. This approach has offered us a powerful conception of the human body as a determinate, self-transcending openness: it has allowed us to reconceptualize the family as an experiential reality that is our initiation into experience *qua* human, and has shown why our mature experience cannot outstrip the forms of childhood life whose traces it bears. This approach to Freud's studies has also led us to challenge psychoanalysis to recognize that this bodily unconscious must also be the presence of the desire of the other in us, and this last recognition brings with it a reinterpretation of the ideal of objectivity that shows phenomenological method to be the legitimate heir to Freud's psychoanalytic theory of the unconscious.

NOTES

1. All references to this work will be to "Three Essays on the Theory of Sexuality," trans. James Strachey, in *The Standard Edition of the Complete Psychological Works of Sigmund Freud*, Vol. 7, ed. James Strachey (London: The Hogarth Press and the Institute of Psycho-Analysis, 1953), 130–243. All other references to Freudian

THE BODILY UNCONSCIOUS IN FREUD'S "THREE ESSAYS" 47

texts will be to the *Standard Edition*, given in the form of Volume number followed by page number.

2. William Wordsworth, "My Heart Leaps Up When I Behold" (1802).

3. Compare Freud's definition of "instinct," 168.

4. On the notion of the assemblage as the form of experience, see especially Gilles Deleuze and Felix Guattari, *Anti-Oedipus: Capitalism and Schizophrenia*, trans. Robert Hurley, Mark Seem, and Helen R. Lane (New York: The Viking Press, 1977), chapter 1, "The Desiring Machines."

5. For the contrast of "the pleasure principle" and "the reality principle" see especially *Civilization and Its Discontents*, Vol. 21, 66–68. In *Beyond the Pleasure Principle* Freud endeavored to establish the insufficiency of the pleasure principle for accounting for the nature of desire; for the purposes of this chapter, the transformations that Freud introduces in this work are not essential.

6. See "Three Essays," 171–173, 191.

7. See "Three Essays,"182–183. Compare *Introductory Lectures on Psychoanalysis*, Vol. 16, 329.

8. Freud repeats this basic material from the "Three Essays" in both Lecture XX from the *Introductory Lectures* and in Lecture XXXII from the *New Introductory Lectures*. The recapitulation of the stages of oral and anal development in the latter lecture offers some helpful enhancements to the discussion; see Vol. 22, 97–102.

9. "Three Essays," 179–180, 198.

10. "Three Essays," 198, 222. For a discussion of the notion of identification, see Lecture XXXI from *New Introductory Lectures*, Vol. 22, 63. Freud here defines identification as "the assimilation of one ego to another one," and explains its relation to orality. See also *The Ego and the Id*, Vol. 19, 28–32.

11. "Three Essays," 185–187, 198.

12. "Three Essays," 186.

13. "Three Essays," 192–193, 194, 198.

14. Freud invokes the notion of prototype often. See, for example, his discussions of affective states (*Inhibitions, Symptoms and Anxiety* (Vol 20, 93), of the trauma of birth as the prototype for later anxiety (*The Interpretation of Dreams*, Vol. 5, 400, *Inhibitions, Symptoms and Anxiety*, Vol. 20, 93, 133), of transference (*The Dynamics of Transference*, Vol. 12, 100), and of repression and the unconscious (*The Ego and the Id*, Vol. 19, 15).

15. See note 5.

16. I am thus claiming that the conception of embodiment implied in Freud's "Three Essays" is of a piece with that developed by Henri Bergson in his account of "motor schemas" in *Matter and Memory*, trans. Nancy Margaret Paul and W. Scott Palmer (New York: Humanities Press, 1978), and by Maurice Merleau-Ponty in his *Phenomenology of Perception*, trans. Colin Smith (London: Routledge and Kegan Paul, 1962), Part I, Chapter 3, "The Spatiality of One's Own Body and Motility." For these concepts, see David Morris, "The Logic of the Body in Bergson's Motor Schemes and Merleau-Ponty's Body Schema," *Philosophy Today* 44 (2000): 60–69. I have developed this conception further in *Human Experience: Philosophy, Neurosis and the Elements of Everyday Life* (Albany: State University of New York Press, 2003). In *The Ego and the Id*, Freud does in fact claim that "Ego is first and foremost a bodily ego" (Vol. 19, 26). This very suggestive language accords well with the discussion of bodily prototypes I am here developing. In fact, however, Freud's specific explanation of this notion

points in a different direction. The bodily ego, he says, is "a mental projection of the surface of the body," by which he seems to mean that we initially construct a sense of "self" through our sensory image of our own bodily surface. Freud seems here to be constrained in his analysis by faulty empiricist prejudices regarding the nature of knowledge; for a critique of this approach to the "body-image," see Merleau-Ponty, *Phenomenology of Perception*, 98–101 and ff.

17. "Three Essays," 222–224, 228. See *Introductory Lectures on Psychoanalysis*, Vol. 16, 329–338, for a fuller discussion of the way in which the mother develops as the primary love-object for the child.

18. Freud himself does not fully appreciate the import of this idea, and is consequently not consistent in his analyses. At many points Freud resorts to biological explanations, as if they could easily cohere with psychological/phenomenological explanation. See, for example, *Inhibitions, Symptoms and Anxiety*, Vol. 20, 154–155, discussed in note 26.

19. Freud explicitly invokes the notion of "prototype" in this context. See, for example, *Dynamics of Transference*, Vol. 12, 100; discussing how libidinal energy comes to be directed to the therapist, Freud remarks that libidinal cathexis "will have recourse to prototypes" and gives as an example the "father imago." See also *The Ego and the Id*, Vol. 19, 31–34.

20. On the child's innate intersubjectivity, see Olga Maratos, "Neonatal, Early and Later Imitation: Same Order Phenomena?" chapter 8 of Francesca Simion and George Butterworth, eds., *The Development of Sensory, Motor and Cognitive Capacities in Early Infancy: From Perception to Cognition* (East Sussex: The Psychology Press, 1998), 145–160, and C. Trevarthen, "Communication and Cooperation in Early Infancy: A Description of Primary Intersubjectivity," in M. Bullowa, ed., *Before Speech: The Beginnings of Human Communication* (Cambridge: Cambridge University Press, 1979). See Alan Slater and Scott P. Johnson, "Visual, Sensory and Perceptual Abilities of the Newborn: Beyond the Blooming, Buzzing Confusion," chapter 7 of Simion and Butterworth, ed., *The Development of Sensory, Motor and Cognitive Capacities in Early Infancy*, 121–141. For the interpretation of Meltzoff's observations of neonate imitation, see A. N. Meltzoff and M. K. Moore, "A Theory of the Role of Imitation in the Emergence of Self," in P. Rochat, ed., *The Self in Early Infancy* (New York: North-Holland-Elsevier, 1995), 73–93, and Alison Gopnik, Andrew N. Meltzoff, and Patricia K. Kuhl, *The Scientist in the Crib: Minds, Brains and How Children Learn* (New York: William Morrow and Co., 1999). See also Merleau-Ponty, *Phenomenology of Perception*, Part II, Chapter 4, "Other Selves and the Human World."

21. Freud himself relies on an almost identical argumentative structure in the "Three Essays" to demonstrate the innate character of sexuality (191), and relies on an analogous argumentative structure to demonstrate the uniqueness of our "death" as an object of experience in *Inhibitions, Symptoms and Anxiety*, Vol. 20, 129–130.

22. "Three Essays," 186.

23. "Three Essays," 181, 207.

24. "Three Essays," 192.

25. This intersubjective dialectic of desire is best analyzed by G. W. F. Hegel, *Phenomenology of Spirit*, trans. A. V. Miller (Oxford: Oxford University Press, 1977), chapter 4, section A.

26. See p. 177 for the crucial role of shame, and therefore the experience of the other as another subject, in childhood development, and pp. 222–224 for Freud's

THE BODILY UNCONSCIOUS IN FREUD'S "THREE ESSAYS"   49

explanation of the phenomenon of fear of the loss of love in terms that are virtually identical with those used in his later works. (Note especially the description of the mother, on p. 223, as "teaching the child to love.") The clearest discussion is *Inhibitions, Symptoms and Anxiety*, Vol. 20, 136–138, 143–146 and 154–155. Here Freud explains (a) that "the reason why the infant in arms wants to perceive the presence of its mother [when she is absent] is only because it *already knows by experience* that she satisfies all its needs without delay" (p. 137, my italics) and (b) that the child's anxiety "can be accounted for simply enough biologically," because the mother was originally the source of total satisfaction to the fetus in the womb and "what happens is that the child's biological situation as a fetus is replaced for it by a psychical object-relation to its mother" (p. 138). There are further examples of Freud's reliance on biological speculation to fill the lacuna in the psychological account on p. 154. *An Outline of Psychoanalysis* (Vol. 23, 200 and 206) and *Civilization and Its Discontents* (Vol. 21, 124–128) give the clearest account of the fear of the loss of love as a roughly "Hobbesian" calculus of utility according to which the "other" is simply an objective presence, capable of delivering pleasure or pain: "The chronological sequence, then, would be as follows. First comes renunciation of instinct owing to fear of aggression by the *external* authority. (This is, of course, what fear of the loss of love amounts to, for love is a protection against this punitive aggression.)" (p. 128, italics in original). Contrast this with the discussion in *Dynamics of Transference* (Vol. 12, 100) where, while speaking of innate dispositions, Freud refers to one's "need for love."

27. What could say that this "answerability" is a version of the logic of orality, in that one must identify with the ideal of the other itself. But inasmuch as this answerability must preserve the independent autonomy of the object, it is a logic of orality that is mediated by the recognition of alienation characteristic of anality. In any case, the simple combination of these two notions alone will still be insufficient to explain how it is *possible* to recognize the ideal of an autonomous other.

FOUR

THE EGO DOES NOT RESEMBLE THE CADAVER: IMAGE AND SELF IN FREUD

STEPHEN DAVID ROSS

We have only to understand the mirror stage *as an identification*, in
the full sense that analysis gives to the term: namely, the transformation that takes place in the subject when he assumes an image—
whose predestination to this phase-effect is sufficiently indicated by
the use, in analytic theory, of the ancient term *imago*.

—Lacan, 1977, p. 2

IMAGE

WHAT OF THE ancient term *imago*? What of it remains archaic, what of it
might be relevant today? What is the image? What is archaic as the image?
What role do images play in Freud, in psychoanalysis? What is their relevance to the ego, self, or *I*? Freud's study was filled with artifacts and
images, his writing is filled with fantasies, images, and dreams. In this
chapter I hope to explore the place of images in Freud in relation to the
possibility that his writing is deeply exposed by the image with an uncanny
and archaic strangeness. I will begin with the image in Blanchot, returning
after the image to Freud.

Here is Blanchot's exposition of this haunting, familiar strangeness as
the image itself. I must begin in French.

51

L'image, à première vue, ne ressemble pas au cadavre, mail il se pourrait que létrangeté cadavérique fût aussi celle de l'image. (Blanchot, 1955, p. 344)

The image, at first sight, does not resemble the cadaver, but it is possible that the rotting, decaying, cadaverous strangeness might also be from the image. [my translation][1]

But what is the image? When there is nothing, the image finds in this nothing its necessary condition, but there it disappears. The image needs the neutrality and the fading of the world: it wants everything to return to the indifferent deep where nothing is affirmed; it tends toward the intimacy of what still subsists in the void. This is its truth. But this truth exceeds it. (Blanchot, 1982, p. 254)

The image—but is this not the self, if not the image of myself, alive or dead, conscious or unconscious; the self projected in its self-possession, its genitivity,[2] strangely exposed to others *as* the image, *through and from* the image itself, the self as self image?[3] If the image does not resemble the cadaver, if it does not insist on the genitive, is it possible that the rotting, decaying stink of the dead or living self that is the ego, the cadaverous strangeness of the specular, speculative, speculated on image of the self (*Selbst* or *Seele*) that Freud names the *Ich*, known to us less familiarly as *the ego* after two centuries of specula- tion after Kant, that this strangeness of the image, the imaginariness of the mortality of the self, might also be that of the ego, who insists on having what it needs in the genitive? I think, therefore I imagine, the *I* as image— figure, copy, shade, cadaver—of *itself*. The ego—the *I* itself—at first sight, does not resemble itself, the unconscious *it* itself, but it is possible that the rotting, decaying cadaverous strangeness might also be from the self itself, in the genitive.

What, I ask, is the difference between the cadaver and corpse, at least in English (and, perhaps, in Danish: for we know that something—is it the corpse?—is rotten in Denmark), but the rot and stink of decay in the carcass that is held at bay, for the most part, in the cadaver, under our gaze? The stench that pervades the world is surely not the cadaver's *smell*. Yet if Lazarus arose on the third day from within his mortality, would he not reek under the nose of his wife and children? What do we know from the story of Philoctetes but that the stench of decay, living or dead, is awful—unlike the cadaver that allows us to see but not to smell? Blanchot speaks of the cadaver [*cadavre*] and of the corpse [*dépouille*: skin, mortal remains]; I would remind you of the carcass [*charogne*], living or dead.

I read Blanchot as presenting repeated images, betrayals, of exposi- tion and betrayal:[4] the image, which reveals and distorts the thing, almost certainly another image, conscious or unconscious; the cadaver, which positions the carcass under the gaze so as to mask the odor; the perhaps and possible—and indeed, the impossible—that returns again and again to the thing; the cadaverous strangeness, which is neither the cadaver's strangeness nor the stranger's cadaverousness, but the odor that—perhaps—haunts both the image and the corpse; the perhaps that cannot be a possibility without betrayal. Let me betray it right here: the appearance, the image, whose appearance always betrays itself and the other *as, as itself, as the other; as if: as as as*. This endless succession of images, figures, is exposition and betrayal, betrays the abundance of the earth, overflows every exposition, double-crosses every identification, crosses over every crossing, crossing out, weaving over and under, an endless succession of images or shadows. The cadaverous strangeness is the betrayal that overflows the abundance, giving beyond having, beyond gathering, beyond disappearance and nonbeing, always present as absence, lack, which is always more, in abundance.

> When beings lack, being appears in the depth of the concealment in which it becomes lack. When concealment appears, concealment, having become appearance, makes "everything disappear," but of this "everything has disappeared" it makes another appearance. . . . This is exactly what we call an *apparition*. It is the "everything has disappeared" appearing in its turn. And the *apparition* says precisely that when everything has disappeared, there still is something: when everything lacks, lack makes the essence of being appear, and the essence is to be there still where it lacks, to be inasmuch as it is hidden. (Blanchot, 1982, p. 253)

This is exposition. The thing—including its disappearance—appears as the image, is the thing inasmuch as it is—but does not resemble—the image, is exposed as the thing where it is not, is the image projected beyond itself. Shall we say *of the thing?* That returns us to the genitive. The cadaverous strangeness of the image, of the corpse: does it belong to either or both? Or may we read Blanchot as expressing the *as* in the image without genitivity?— the *passage of* as the cadaverous strangeness that haunts the passage, the perhaps unconscious *apparition* that cannot be eluded. The image does not resemble the cadaver, does not belong to the cadaver, is not of the cadaver, but it is possible that a cadaverous strangeness, reeking of the corpse, may betray the image as *apparition*; the strange cadaverousness *as* the image, betraying and betrayed in the rotting image. The image, in the depths of its lack, betrays the abundance of lack in the exposition of being, betrays the corpse in the cadaver, helps us remember the corpse in the forgetting of image and cadaver. Every knot and split at the heart of exposition open the abundance at the heart of the living self, exposed beyond (or *as not beyond*) the self image.[5]

> The image, according to the ordinary analysis, is secondary to the object. It is what follows. We see, then we imagine. After the object comes the image. "After" means that the thing must first take itself off a ways in order to be grasped. But this remove is not the simple displacement of a moveable object which would nevertheless remain the same. Here the distance is in the heart of the thing. (p. 255)

Here the betrayal is at the heart.

I would imagine the cadaver as image of the corpse as the corpse is image of the self: as exposition. I would then imagine one image after another of a self that proliferates itself in images, the self who—or what—is inseparable from the image. "Psychoanalysis maintains that the image . . . seems to deliver us profoundly to ourselves. The image is intimate. . . . Outside of us, in the ebb of the world which it causes, there trails, like glistening debris, the utmost depth of our passions" (p. 261). I postpone the thing that remains outside of us, with which we remain deeply intimate: still the image, and the debris, of ourselves:

> The image speaks to us, and seems to speak intimately to us of ourselves. But the term "intimately" does not suffice. Let us say rather that the image intimately designates the level where personal intimacy is destroyed and that it indicates in this movement the menacing proximity of a vague and empty outside, the deep, the sordid basis upon which it continues to affirm things in their disappearance. Thus it speaks to us, à propos of each thing, of less than this thing, but of us. And, speaking of us, it speaks to us of less than us, of that less than nothing that subsists when there is nothing. (p. 254)

A less than nothing of astonishing abundance. The image speaks to us, seems to speak intimately to us of ourselves. Could this be because the image is ourselves, is ourselves speaking intimately?—and in this speaking of and to and from ourselves—we and the image that are nothing, nothing but exposition—the image (and we) speak of the thing, of less than and more than this or any thing, thereby speaking to us intimately of less than us and more than us, together with the thing.

Face to face with the image beyond itself, I myself and every thing itself are exposed intimately to themselves beyond themselves, as double-crossing themselves. "But when we are face to face with things themselves—if we fix upon a face, the corner of a wall—does it not also sometimes happen that we abandon ourselves to what we see?" (p. 255). We abandon ourselves to the image, I would say, perhaps another step beyond.[6] We abandon ourselves to ourselves as the exposition that bears a cadaverous strangeness that might also be from the image without resembling it. *The image does not resemble!*—and in this lack betrays everything. The image overflows its lack in abundance.

> Let us look again at this splendid being from which beauty streams: he is, I see this, perfectly like himself: he resembles *himself*. The cadaver is its own image. . . . And if the cadaver is so similar, it is because it is, at a certain moment, similarity par excellence: altogether similarity, and also nothing more. It is the likeness, like to an absolute degree, overwhelming and marvelous. But what is it like? Nothing. (p. 258)

This splendid nothing is the strangely intimate embrace of image, self, and thing that I describe as giving in abundance, exposition and betrayal. But I would emphasize all the more the beauty streaming into the image, *as the image*. The image, double-crossing itself, is the streaming and the beauty.

> He who dies cannot tarry. The deceased, it is said, is no longer of this world; he has left it behind. But behind there is, precisely, this cadaver, which is not of the world either, even though it is here. Rather, it is behind the world. It is that which the living person (and not the deceased) left behind him and which now affirms, from here, the possibility of a world behind the world, of a regression, an indefinite subsistence, undetermined and indifferent, about which we only know that human reality, upon finishing, reconstitutes its presence and its proximity. (p. 257)

I would explore the possibility—one must speak in this tentative, dispossessive, disclaiming voice of the image, the cadaver, and perhaps the self, as such, itself—that the ego is the spectacle of the nothing or impossibility or image or whatever that constitutes the self—if the self is constituted or perhaps imagined: the cadaver that is the *I* itself. I insist on this *it* or *Es* that vanishes so easily into English: the unconscious *it* whose spectacle is the ego, making both the ego *(Ich)* and (now in English) *id* into an image, or dream, or for that matter into a cadaver that exposes or betrays the self. The ego is the cadaver with a rotting, fading, strangeness that might possibly be from itself. The ego reminds us, in the most vivid way, however obliquely, of Lazarus, specularly and corporeally. The ego returns, spectacularly and abjectly. "Man is made in his image: this is what the strangeness of the cadaver's resemblance teaches us. But this formula must first be understood as follows: *man is unmade according to his image*" (p. 260). Unmaking is making, at least for the image. Unmanning is manning, at least for the human self. Exposition is betrayal.

Exposition returns to haunt us repeatedly. As Blanchot says:

> The cadaverous resemblance haunts us. But its haunting presence is not the unreal visitation of the ideal. What haunts us is something inaccessible from which we cannot extricate ourselves. It is that which cannot be found and therefore cannot be avoided. What no one can grasp is the inescapable. The fixed image knows no repose, and this is above all because it poses nothing, establishes nothing. Its fixity, like that of the corpse [dépouille: not cadavre], is the position of what stays with us because it has no place. (Blanchot, 1982, p. 259)

I am especially interested in the *not* that haunts the haunting, which institutes the possibility of the self; the insistence in the unity and continuity of the conscious and unconscious self. I am concerned with the gender of the corpse, but that will come later. For the moment, I would remind you of dreams, returning as vividly as possible to images and their images, worrying for the moment about their decay, their smell, and their resemblances. I return to Freud.

IMAGE AND SELF

I begin again with a borderline case between dreams and reality—the exposition where I insist that life takes place and images show themselves. The case is described by Freud in extreme terms in relation to the images beyond the words:

> In a patient of about twenty-one years of age the unconscious mental activity expressed itself consciously not only in obsessive thoughts but also in obsessive visual images.... At one particular time, whenever he saw his father coming into the room, there came into his mind in close connection with each other an obsessive word and an obsessive picture. The word was "father-arse"; the accompanying picture represented the lower part of a trunk, nude and provided with arms and legs, but without the head or chest, and this was the father. (Freud, 1916, p. 42)[7]

Freud describes this image as "obsessive" and the concatenation or condensation as an "unusually crazy symptom-formation." I would describe Freud as more than usually obsessed with the image as an image, contrasted with the words. " 'Father-arse' was soon explained as a jocular Teutonizing of the honourable title 'patriarch' [Vaterarsch/Patriarch]. The obsessive picture is an obvious caricature" (pp. 42–43). It is as if the play on words was somehow normally abnormal in the conscious life of an obsessive, but the play in images was abnormally abnormal, especially derogatory and offensive. Yet in his wisdom, Freud concludes this very short paper with a reference to Demeter, evoking the story of Baubo who made the goddess laugh in her sorrow for her daughter by lifting up her clothes, presenting herself as a spectacle. Freud notes the terracottas—more images—in the excavations at Triene representing Baubo: "the body of a woman without head or bosom, and with a face drawn on the abdomen: the lifted clothing frames this face like a crown of hair" (p. 43). Somehow the dead figures come back to life in exposition.

The symptom formation is unusually crazy because of the presence of images together with the words, or because of the craziness of the images, or because of the craziness of images—which nevertheless bear responsibility for the world, perhaps because of their smells. Freud evokes all these possibilities. And indeed, there is something strangely evocative in the difference between the wordplay Vaterarsch/patriarch and the image of the father, something much more offensive or rude or disfiguring in the image. The image here does resemble the corpse while the name of the father does not kill the father. Freud imagines that the image has an ancestral quality, evoking Greek mythology. I imagine that the image has an ancestral or demonic or disturbing quality as an image, even a stench, that images can be profoundly disturbing and take us on mythological and erotic journeys as words may not (except as images). Even more interesting, perhaps, is the presence of this image together with the father, right there before the father, not in a dream. Though both word and image are projections of primary processes, Freud passes off the violence of the word as a pun but cannot similarly pass off the reek of the image.

We may be reminded of Freud's description elsewhere (Freud, 1959) of the "imaginative writer" who is too similar to "the child at play" for Jung, who returns the poet in one avatar—the visionary—to the mythological without explicitly addressing the question of the image. Yet it is unavoidable that the writer who transcends the everyday, beyond the child at play, be "imaginative" and "visionary." That is our language, however unusually crazy or obsessive. We are obsessed with images, as is Freud, in the presentations of the boundaries of our self.

Notice, then, how the image disrupts the tranquility of the body image. That is the point I am pursuing, the way in which images in Freud have more to do with body and self at their borders than words, however uncanny. For the crucial figure for the poet as daydreamer is vested in the image: "He builds castles in the air and creates what are called day-dreams"; fantasies. "Instead of playing he then begins to create phantasy" (Freud, 1959, p. 46). He builds, creates, projects fantastic castles in the air as images. Always images, not words or sounds or smells or bodily impulses. One might imagine that images provide the means whereby material reality takes on the contrast with play that make both art and the ego possible. The ego does not resemble the (real) self, but its strangeness is that of the self itself.

This returns us to the uncanny, which should certainly be dealt with, however strangely, before we pursue the image as the self. For the uncanny brings us back to the cadaver, as if to suggest that the corpse and its resemblances are vividly present wherever meanings are unfamiliar, strange. Freud's examples are taken from Hoffmann, who he describes as "a writer who has succeeded better than anyone else in producing uncanny effects" (Freud, 1910, p. 132). All are images: waxwork figures, artificial dolls, and automatons. Little Nathaniel, who does not believe that the Sand-Man puts the children's eyes in a sack and carries them off to the moon, "is determined to find out what the Sand-Man looked like" (p. 134). As if getting the look right might resolve the fear and apprehension of the image: images with the imagery of their images, redoubled in the fear that one might lose one's sight. Freud sums up this situation in relation to literature; I hope to persist in the image, still perhaps literature: "The somewhat paradoxical result is that *in the first place a great deal that is not uncanny in fiction would be so if it happened in real life; and in the second place that there are many more means of creating uncanny effects in fiction than there are in real life*" (p. 158). I imagine that the uncanny is the image, or if not the image, then the resemblance, real or imagined; that the imagery is the uncanny, and that it is this uncanniness that brings Blanchot back to the cadaver, sleeping or awake. "The dream [the image?] is that which cannot 'really' be" (Blanchot, 1982, p. 268).

> The dream touches the region where pure resemblance reigns. Everything there is similar; each figure is another one, is similar to another and to yet another, and this last to still another. One seeks the original model, wanting to be referred to a point of departure, an initial revelation, but there is none. The realm is the likeness that refers eternally to likeness *[semblable]*. (p. 268)

I myself as image, dream, apparition; *I myself* as dream of myself inhabit the realm of eternal likeness. Here I suggest we may come face to face with the uncanny, that which—the image—cannot be except as likeness of itself: the ego as fetish of the *it* itself.

DREAM

And so we come back to the uncanniness of the ego, if it is the image or spectacle of the *it*. We are led back to the decay and fading if not rotting and stinking of the spectacle: the ego—the *Ich* as spectacle of the *It*, the unavoidable spectacle of image and dream, always exposed beyond itself. "The dream does not merely reproduce the stimulus, but elaborates it, plays upon it, fits it into a context, or replaces it by something else. . . . The scope of a man's production is not necessarily limited to the circumstance which immediately gives rise to it" (Freud, 1953, p. 100); "Our dreams for the most part take the form of visual images" (p. 101): as dreams, images as images beyond themselves. " 'I could draw it,' the dreamer often says to us, 'but I do not know how to put it into words' " (p. 94). Our task here is to understand this relation as pertaining to the ego in the mode of fading, decaying, and *perhaps*.

Freud's questions of the image are: "Can these be explained by the stimuli? Is it really the stimulus that we experience? If so, why is the experience visual, when it can only be in the very rarest instance that any stimulus has operated upon our eyesight?" (p. 101). Good questions, one might say, though they betray from the start, especially in the almost unnoticed "if so," an odor of decay. Of the stimulus? Really the stimulus? Not perhaps the stimulus? The non-imagistic, invisible stimulus? The odor or trace of the stimulus? As Jung insists repeatedly, the stimulus haunts Freud's image of the artistic image. Freud might appear to be asking a different set of questions, perhaps: what is the meaning of the dream? What meaning is given by images? How might these differ from the meanings of words? Can there be meaning without the image? Can the image be anything but hypothetical, ambiguous, contingent? In this way, Freud would exemplify the subjunctive modality of the image *as* the cadaver, *as* the corpse, *as* the strange cadaverous meaning of the image *as image*: in other words, the strange archaic semblance of the image, the strangeness of the *as*, *as if*, and *perhaps*.

Freud continues down this line of descent toward the decaying taint of the image. "Dreams are often meaningless, confused, and absurd, yet there are some which are sensible, sober, and reasonable. Let us see whether these latter sensible dreams can help to elucidate those which are meaningless" (p. 101). Order will help us to explain disorder; sanity will help us to explain madness; reality will help us explain dreams; stimuli will help us explain images; meaning will help us explain meaninglessness. This is a familiar line of thought, related to the decaying of the image, that leads from Freud to a certain view of science and explanation. Freud's appeal, at least for some of us, lies in the madness and meaninglessness themselves. What if dreams, meaninglessness, and madness were the conditions of the possibility of reality, meaning, and sanity? What if the dream were the thing itself?

As Freud suggests, in connection with "prosaic dreams" in which there occur "recollections of daily life or of matters connected with it"; "In most dreams we find no connection with the day before, and no light is thrown from this quarter upon meaningless and absurd dreams" (p. 102). We cannot find the truth of such dreams in the reality that surrounds them, but in something else, perhaps themselves. Shall we pursue this line of thought to the image, from images of daily life to meaningless and absurd images? Both, perhaps, images themselves of fading, decaying, cadaverous strangeness; both, perhaps, strange beyond any original, any stimulus—images beyond themselves *as images*; the image *as beyond* itself, any *it* and any *self*.

In the face of this cadaverous strangeness, Freud imposes a principle, epistemological or methodological, reminiscent of his insistence on the stimulus: "all the interest in the world will not help us with a problem unless we have also an idea of some path to adopt in order to arrive at a solution" (p. 102). One might wish to hear this in a familiar way: we cannot find knowledge if we do not know how to seek it, reminiscent of Plato and *Meno*, of which I have elsewhere given a more radical reading:[8] learning, knowledge, truth all presuppose going beyond any familiar truth; the form in which we understand and learn is beyond any prior truth. One might then insist on hearing this in an unfamiliar way, reminiscent of the ego as well as the image. Freud will not release the ego from its ties with the *it*, the cadaverous strangeness by which the ego or the *it* may resemble itself. I have finally said it openly. If the ego is the spectacle or image, then that of which it is the image is the ego as image of itself. The *it* itself—the only self—produces or is itself an image *as beyond* itself, in the cadaverous strangeness whereby each of these images might resemble themselves, but do not resemble. It is important again to emphasize the putrefaction and decay of this resemblance, the recurrent presence of the corpse, whether of the no longer living *it* or of the shattered *it-self*.

I have said nothing so far of hallucinations and little of daydreams—fantasies—of which Freud comments that "we simply imagine something; we recognize that they are the work of phantasy, that we are not seeing but thinking" (p. 103). He almost suggests that daydreams are fantasies without images, despite his suggestions elsewhere and what I might insist on as the testimony of evidence. Fantasies are surely images, but perhaps he means—this is sheer speculation—without rotting and decay, or at least without confusion as to their taint. We know, when we daydream, that our daydreams are fantasies. We do not know, are not sure, when we dream at night that our dreams are merely images. We must know; we insist; we must be able to recognize the images as themselves.

I briefly left behind the way Freud insists that we must know in order to arrive at a solution—to a problem he insists on defining: not the meaning of the image but its explanation. He returns to tell us the way:

> [I]f the dream is a somatic phenomenon it does not concern us; it can only be of interest to us on the hypothesis that it is a mental phenomenon. . . .
>
> In that event, they are a performance and an utterance on the part of the dreamer, but of a kind that conveys nothing to us, and which we do not understand. Now supposing that I give utterance to something that you do not understand, what do you do? You ask me to explain, do you not? Why may not we do the same—*ask the dreamer the meaning of the dream?* (Freud, 1953, p. 105–106)

This is a famous point of dislocation in Freud, between an explanation of an event in terms of a stimulus and an explanation of the meaning of an utterance and performance. One might see here the cadaver again, for the image as an event is that event, somatic or otherwise; its meaning is something else, cadaverously strange. The fading, rotting decay of the cadaver has something to do with the meaning, with the performance or utterance of the image, the image as utterance, the image as performance: staging the self.

I conclude my discussion of dreams as preliminary to a return to the ego as spectacle or fantasy with two additional citations. One is in the opening to the Eighth Lecture, where Freud suggests retracing our steps a little from the distortions of dreams to confine "our attention to dreams in which distortion is absent or occurs only to a very slight extent, if there are any such dreams" (1953, p. 132). If there are such images: an explicit *perhaps*. Even so, the undistorted image must be confronted face to face if we are to face the contortions of images. As always—and against all the evidence again—purity is found in children: "The dreams we are looking for are met with in children—short, clear, coherent, and easy to understand, they are free from ambiguity and yet are unmistakable dreams" (p. 132). Yet it is Freud's delightfully ambiguous sense of this purity that arouses my interest here. "You must not think, however, that all dreams in children are of this type"—even that any are, I would say: "Distortion in dreams begins to appear very early in childhood" (p. 132). The point is that even if all dreams were distortions, Freud would insist on the possibility or intelligibility of dreams in which distortion is absent. Distortionless images are crucial if we are to examine distorted images.

But this puts us at the point at which to make the transition to the spectacle of the ego. For the image, the dream, may perhaps always be distorted, may perhaps be distortion; moreover, this distortion is perhaps not the defining characteristic of the image, but the cadaverous strangeness of its imagery. The image does not resemble the cadaver but, perhaps, is an image in virtue of the cadaverous strangeness of both, the recurrent putrefaction of the image as an image—exposed beyond itself.

On this reading, or picture, the ego expresses or is the image of some *it itself* that is always exposed beyond itself: as an image, as something else, even *as it itself*: the self exposed *as beyond itself*. Most of all, I insist, in relation to the *as*, the *as* as image, *as if* an image, always *as if beyond* itself. My question, finally, is how this pertains to the ego, the *it* itself that appears as or whose image is the ego—and, of course, not only the ego. Images multiply too rapidly to contain. That is the point of dreams: their multiplication. But I will not pursue the dream much further though I cannot avoid the image.

In the *General Introduction to Psychoanalysis*, the ego does not come on stage until one hundred pages after dreams—one might say, after the image, in the section on repression and resistance. Moreover, the ego arrives after the patient (here, perhaps, not the ego) "has said to himself something of this kind: 'This is all very pretty and very interesting. I should like to go on with it. I am sure it would do me a lot of good it if were true. But I don't believe it in the least, and as long as I don't believe it, it doesn't affect my illness' " (p. 300). These are words famously said about *mere* images, *mere* fiction, art. If it were true, it would be wonderful; it seems to be true and is certainly pretty, even beautiful, and very interesting and provocative. But it cannot truly or seriously be believed. What if resistance were the relation to the image? What if the ego, formed in resistance, took on the cadaverous strangeness of the image? Is that not a compelling hypothesis with respect to both the ego and the image?

> What is noteworthy is that this material always serves at first as a resistance and comes forward in a guise which is inimical to the treatment. Again it may be said that they are character-traits, individual attitudes of the ego, which are thus mobilized to oppose the attempted alterations. One learns then how these character-traits [resistances and images] have been developed in connection with the conditions of the neurosis and in reaction against its demands, and observes features in this character which would not otherwise have appeared, at least, not so clearly: that is, which may be designated latent. (p. 301)

Latency and *appearance* are Freud's words for what I am exploring, after Blanchot, as the corpse and the cadaver. The cadaver is the image of the corpse, I suggest, and the ego is the image of the *it*, which remains in latency. Resistances are oblique, indirect, imagistic; yet they retain an inner coherence and intelligibility—their cadaverous strangeness. The strangeness is not unintelligibility but intelligibility; the cadaverousness is the strange way in which the image and resistance pertain to what is hidden, what must remain hidden, yet comes to light through the image. "[W]e know that these resistances are bound to appear: we are dissatisfied only if we cannot rouse them definitely enough and make the patient perceive them as such" (p. 302). The resistance bears the strangeness of the image that exists in latency yet insists on appearing. Moreover, the image proliferates itself into other images, appearances, and observations: "In what way can we now account for this fact observed, that the patient struggles so energetically against the relief of his symptoms and the restoration of his mental processes to normal functioning?" (p. 304). The cadaverous strangeness of the image is not least that the image proliferates into images, and images of images, in an inescapable relation to the corpse, the latent decaying, rotting, putrefying *it*. I have not begun to smell the corpse or for that matter the fruits and flowers, which are very pretty and appealing but not perhaps serious and truthful enough.[9] What if the cadaverous strangeness of the flowers resembled that of the corpse, so that fruits and flowers were never mere ornaments and corpses were never unornamental but latent?

THRESHOLD

Freud takes us into another image, this time of a place:

> The crudest conception of these systems is the one we shall find most convenient, a spatial one. The unconscious system may therefore be compared to a large ante-room, in which the various mental excitations are crowding upon one another, like individual beings. Adjoining this is a second, smaller apartment, a sort of reception-room, in which consciousness resides. But on the threshold between the two there stands a personage with the office of door-keeper, who examines the various mental excitations, censors them, and denies them admittance to the reception-room when he disapproves of them. (p. 306)

An image of excitations, themselves images, but cadaverously strange. "When they have pressed forward to the threshold and been turned back by the door-keeper, they are '*incapable of becoming conscious*'; we call them then *repressed*. But even those excitations which are allowed over the threshold do not necessarily become conscious; they can only become so if they succeed in attracting the eye of consciousness" (p. 306).

In the context of Freud's emphasis on temporal processes and development, his recurrent interposition of spatial images may seem strange, or at least indicative. The unconscious system is—he suggests that we imagine it as—a spatial system: an anteroom crowded with mental excitations—almost certainly images with forceful vitality—separated by a threshold from another apartment in which consciousness resides. At the risk of getting carried away, I would like to dwell on this figure of dwelling as a picture or image. The consciousness has a place to dwell, is pictured as dwelling in a spatial realm. One might say that up to this point, images pervade Freud's image. Beyond this point, unintelligible perhaps, except as an image, the doorkeeper acts by examining, censoring, and denying the images admittance to the reception room. Images return repeatedly in an agitated as well as a practical state, making something happen to other images. Moreover, if these are images, some are incapable of becoming conscious even as Freud presents his image of them on the hither side of the threshold.[10]

I am fascinated by these images of images, not so much to be able to say, and so the unconscious system is *merely an image*, as that the system would be unintelligible *except as images and their images*, except *as if*. Here the ancient term *imago* for dreams begins to haunt the specter of ego and self and their development. Space begins to unravel time as if the diachrony of time were its spatiality—that is, its *imago*. The copy that is the dream is anything but the same again, is always on the move. The *imago* is the nonrepetitive repetition; the image of the image is the exposition whereby the ego can express the *it* as if *not beyond* itself. In the same way—leaving the image aside—repression is a silencing in which the music can still be heard, however cacophonously. The image transposes the excitations so that they do not cease to be excited or exciting.

Imagine, then, returning to the image whose decay may resemble that of the corpse, the cadaver that is not the corpse and does not resemble it but whose excitation, vitality, energy, even fading and death, all may resemble the strangeness from the corpse. So many *perhapses*, *maybes*, and *as ifs*: the specter of the image is *perhaps*. Perhaps the ego resembles the *it* itself, *as if* itself, the self in the *it* that cannot be itself without the *it*; resembles it *as* the image or copy—but not necessarily the visibility—of what is always something and somewhere else, perhaps, beyond the glossiness of the image: its cadaverous, decaying, reeking strangeness. Who has ever been fascinated by psychoanalysis who has not been obsessed by decay, not to mention smell?

Another example, still from the *General Introduction*, still obsessed with the development of the ego—and for that matter the girl as image. Freud tells us of two little girls, divided by class—and we must wonder, what makes Freud insist on differences in class but not differences in gender, why must little girls bear the mark of the cadaver? The two are drawn to masturbation—one assumes in private, perhaps invisibly (or it might be another story), but certainly, though Freud does not recall it, not without odor. In any case, the caretaker's daughter is a free spirit; the other is convinced that masturbation is wrong—*resembles the cadaver*, one might say:

> The differences which ensure in these two destinies in spite of the common experiences undergone, arise because in one girl the ego has sustained a development absent in the other. To the caretaker's daughter sexual activity seemed as natural and harmless in later years as in childhood. The gentleman's daughter had been "well-brought up" and had adopted the standards of her education. Thus stimulated, her ego had formed ideals of womanly purity and absence of desire that were incompatible with sexual acts; her intellectual training had caused her to depreciate the feminine role for which she is intended. This higher moral and intellectual development in her ego has brought her into conflict with the claims of her sexuality. (pp. 362–363)

I will leave aside the feminine role for which a girl is intended—by and for whom? I will regret with Freud the conflicts women experience around their sexuality—possibly not entirely absent from lower-class girls. Here I am interested in the formation of ideals of womanly purity and absence of desire, taking the ideals in their form as *imago*. Images haunt us with images, filled with sexuality and corporeality, still as images, that cannot help resembling but which may never resemble anything but images. The development of the ego is the formation of images, almost certainly images of itself.

Almost certainly images of oneself, one might say: the self who is constituted by the image. Yet this self or ego, constituted by images—of womanly purity and absence of desire—does not imagine images of herself but of other women, impossible women, even of desire itself. The *it* is inseparable from itself, the ego is constituted by images of itself as if another. The image is the image of nothing, or perhaps another image, or perhaps of the self, of itself, its self-image. We come, then, to the *it* whose self has composed both the ego and the image, the *it* whose cadaver has been rotting in the anteroom from the beginning of this exploration, the body image whose integrity and coherence has been in question from the start. Let us pursue the possibility that integrity and coherence and wholeness do not pertain to, do not resemble, the ego or body image, but that it is possible that their rot and decay, the reek of their return, also resembles that of the body image or ego. Another way to put this is to wonder if things smell enough even in Nietzsche and Freud, if the stench does not make the image visible, does not constitute the ego. What if the ego were nothing but an image, whose decay constituted itself? What decay, what stench, taints the development of the ego, in Freud or those who follow?

IDENTIFICATION

I will restrict the rest of my discussion to the short work Freud entitled *Das Ich und das Es*, translated in the Standard Edition as *The Ego and the Id*, but which I will translate, or read, perhaps more cadaverously or strangely, as *The I (myself) and the It (itself)*, or, perhaps, as *The Self who am I and the Self who is It*. For my purposes, the point is that this self is both itself and divided, and that it is both myself and itself, where the *I myself* is the image of and strangely may resemble the self *itself*.

Freud's first discussion of the self is "as a psychical id [*Es*], unknown and unconscious, upon whose surface rests the ego [*Ich*]. . . . If we make an effort to represent this pictorially, we may add that the ego does not completely envelop the id. . . . The ego is not sharply separated from the id, its lower portion merges into it" (Freud, 1960, p. 17). A diagram follows on the next page in which the ego merges with the id, so that we may say several things immediately: the ego and id, the *I* and the *it*, are pictorially or psychically or ontologically the same, inseparable; that "the ego is that part of the id which has been modified by the direct influence of the external world" (pp. 18–19), and that this relationship is a pictorial one, illustrated by Freud himself—who is famously imagistic—but perhaps also, the thesis of this discussion, that the relationship between *I* and *It* is as an *imago*, a mental picture or copy that is more than any picture or copy. It is worth adding that this mental picture is derived from *imago* as figure or portrait, especially as the *shade or ghost of a dead man*. We will not be able to escape the cadaver, nor, perhaps, may we wish to do so. The *I* is inseparable from the *It*; indeed, each may strangely resemble the strangeness of the other as well as the strangeness of the image that each itself is, of the other, as itself.

I will spare you the picture, though you might like to see it. Freud offers many others throughout his works. He comments here that "The ego is first and foremost a bodily ego; it is not merely a surface entity, but is itself the projection of a surface" (p. 20). One reading of this striking passage is that the *I* is first and foremost body, corporeal—the *I* as *it*—as an image of a surface, an image perhaps of an image, if the surface is not only bodily, not only material, or more likely, is body as image and image as body. If we recall the passage where he sharply distinguishes dreams from somatic phenomena, and suppose that he has not changed his mind, we would have to understand surface here as *imago* rather than as *soma*, *I* and *it* and the surfaces of their projection all as images and projections—or, put another way, as identifications. Only a page or so later, in the context of the superego, that other image, not *of* but *as*; the *I* itself *as* the ideal, Freud speaks of melancholia as the lost object "set up again inside the ego—that is, an object-cathexis has been replaced by an identification" (p. 23). Inside the *I*, desire is replaced by an identification—or, perhaps, can be understood from the first as an identification or image. "At the very beginning, in the individual's primitive oral phase, object-cathexis and identification are no doubt indistinguishable from one another" (p. 23). The *I*, the object, and identification are indistinguishable from each other, images of each other, what they are as images and identifications: images of images and identifications of identifications.

> When it happens that a person has to give up a sexual object, there quite often ensues an alteration of his ego which can only be described as a setting up of the object inside the ego, as it occurs in melancholia; the exact nature of this substitution is as yet unknown to us. . . . It may be that this identification is the sole condition under which the id can give up its objects. (pp. 23–24)

Here the cadaver is unmistakable, decaying right before our eyes, rotting and stinking under our nose. The person—*I myself, it itself*—gives up an object under an identification inside the *I*, *as* and *as if* the *I*, altering the *I*, in a substitution or copying or representation that remains unknown but which, perhaps, may be the sole condition under which the *it* can give up its objects into the copies that compose the *I*. This is more than the ego as image of the *it*, but the ego, the *I*, as an identification of other alterations and identifications, recollections of lost objects, images, and figures of such objects, of desire, recollections that may be the sole condition under which the *I* may constitute itself. The *I* and the *It*, defenses and drives, all are *imago*: images of images, recollections of recollections, identifications of identifications.

Freud presents this as a digression:

> Although it is a digression from our aim, we cannot avoid giving our attention for a moment longer to the ego's object-identifications. If they obtain the upper hand and become too numerous, unduly powerful and incompatible with one another, a pathological out-come will not be far off. It may come to a disruption of the ego in consequence of the different identifications becoming cut off from one another by resistances; perhaps the secret of the cases of what is described as "multiple personality" is that the different identifications seize hold of consciousness in turn. Even when things do not go so far as this, there remains the question of conflicts between the various identifications into which the ego comes apart, conflicts which cannot after all be described as entirely pathological. (p. 25)

> This leads us back to the origin of the ego ideal, for behind it there lies hidden an individual's first and most important identification, his identification with the father in his own personal prehistory. (p. 26)

The ego, at first sight, does not resemble the father, but it is possible that the rotting, decaying, cadaverous—pathological?— strangeness might also betray the father and his image. The identification as the ego ideal betrays the father. And, of course, the mother, who is betrayed from the first in the image of the father *as beyond* father and son.

> In its simplified form the case of a male child may be described as follows. At a very early age the little boy develops an object-cathexis for his mother, which originally related to the mother's breast and is the prototype of an object-choice on the anaclitic model, the boy deals with his father by identifying himself with him. . . . His identification with his father then takes on a hostile colouring and changes into a wish to get rid of his father in order to take his place with his mother. (pp. 26–27)

The key to the Oedipus complex lies in the identifications around which the boy (and still in this essay, shortly before Freud abandoned it, "in a precisely analogous way," the girl) identifies himself, forms an image of himself, in terms of images of his mother and father. Images upon images, images of images as further images: identifications upon identifications as the cadaverous strangeness of the *I* and perhaps *It*. But first the precisely analogous way, another image and identification: "In a precisely analogous way, the outcome of the Oedipus attitude in a little girl may be an intensification of her identification with her mother (or the setting up of such an identification for the first time)—a result which will fix the child's feminine character" (pp. 27–28).[11]

I have passed too quickly over the ideal, for it is not enough that the ego forms through multiple identifications as images of images. The height of the ego, "the higher, moral, supra-personal side of human nature" (Freud, 1960, p. 31), is achieved in another identification:

> [H]ere we have that higher nature, in this ego ideal or super-ego, the representative of our relation to our parents. When we were little children we knew these higher natures, we admired them and feared them; and later we took them into ourselves.
>
> The ego ideal is therefore the heir of the Oedipus complex, and thus it is also the expression of the most powerful impulses and most important libidinal vicissitudes of the id. . . . Whereas the ego is essentially the representative of the external world, of reality, the super-ego stands in contrast to it as the representative of the internal world, of the id. (p. 32)

The ego is the representative, identification, image of reality—a reality formed as the play of images; the ego ideal—another image—is the representative of the *it itself*, another identification, another image. "Through the forming of the ideal, what biology and the vicissitudes of the human species have created in the id and left behind in it is taken over by the ego and re-experienced in relation to itself as an individual" (pp. 32–33). This gives another meaning to humanity created in the image of God: God himself, *It itself*. As I keep insisting, the self itself as the image and the cadaverous or angelic strangeness. It is by no means irrelevant that Freud ends this discussion of the superego with an image in a painting. "The struggle which once raged in the deepest strata of the mind, and was not brought to an end by rapid sublimation and identification, is now continued in a higher region, like the Battle of the Huns in Kaulbach's painting" (p. 36). Just how much higher is this region in general and Kaulbach's painting in particular may remain open to disagreement. But the identifications identified through images recur repeatedly in Freud and the self, in the ego as itself.

The ego as itself is distinguished from the *it* in terms of perception and drive, in terms of reality and the pleasure principle. "For the ego, perception plays the part which in the id falls to instinct" (p. 19). Perception, in its glorious insistence on reality, is the reappearance of the image. The instincts or drives appear to be another matter.

This is a famous story, begun in this text and continued in *Civiliza-tion and its Discontents*: On the basis of theoretical considerations, supported by biology, we put forward the hypothesis of a death instinct, the task of which is to lead organic life back into the inanimate state; on the other hand, we supposed that Eros, by bring-ing about a more and more far-reaching combination of the par-ticles into which living substance is dispersed, aims at complicating life and at the same time, of course, at preserving it. . . . The prob-lem of the origin of life would remain a cosmological one, and the problem of the goal and purpose of life would be answered dualis-tically. (1960, pp. 37–38)

I take the answer, perhaps, to be *imagistically*, the dualism as the image, revolving strangely and cadaverously around death and the corpse. Freud returns us to death, thereby to Blanchot—though we know that Blanchot writes with an image of Freud in mind. The drives do their work through images; the images do not resemble drives or things but are haunted by an uncanniness in image, drive, or thing. In this way, reality as it passes over into or is haunted by an image is haunted by the strangeness of death—and life, which is no less strange and no less cadaverous.

With Freud I am drifting toward narcissism, understood as a primary identification, one might even say the primordial image:

At the very beginning, all the libido is accumulated in the id, while the ego is still in process of formation or is still feeble. The id sends part of this libido out into erotic object-cathexes, whereupon the ego, now grown stronger, tries to get hold of this object-libido and to force itself on the id as a love-object. The narcissism of the ego is thus a secondary one, which has been withdrawn from objects.

Over and over again we find, when we are able to trace instinc-tual impulses back, that they reveal themselves as derivatives of Eros. (1960, p. 45)

They reveal themselves as images of desire. Image and desire come together in narcissism, the image the ego imagines for itself, as itself, pervaded by love. Narcissus holds up the image of himself to himself in the limitlessness of his desire, strange and uncanny.

The ego, at first sight, does not resemble itself, but it is possible that the rotting, decaying, strangeness of love and death might also be from the ego as image of itself.

I am drifting toward narcissism with the reek and stench of life and death, love and sacrifice, in my nostrils. Learn to smell, Nietzsche says—or should have; learn to give others the smell. The smell of the image, the image as the smell of—no, not the cadaver or the corpse, and not the perfumed, glowing body inclining toward another, but life itself in its profusion of fragrances, odors, and aromas, including the stench of the corpse and the scents of love.

Before returning to Blanchot with the smell of the image in our nostrils, it might be worth a glance at the way the image does its work not so much in Freud as in Strachey's reading of it in one of his appendices. The issue is whether the ego or the id "remains the great reservoir of his libido" (p. 69). Strachey comments:

> The analogy of the "reservoir" is from its very nature an ambiguous one: a reservoir can be regarded either as a water storage tank or as a source of water supply. There is no great difficulty in applying the image in both senses both to the ego and to the id, and it would certainly have clarified the various passages . . . if Freud had shown more precisely which picture was in his mind. (1960, pp. 69–70)

One might say that Strachey acknowledges the duplicity of the image and insists that it be undone, whereas the image may be said to be duplicitous as itself, thereby retaining the strangeness that Strachey wants Freud to eliminate. What if, in speaking both of the image and of the libido, source and storage were both pertinent, however strangely? Or for that matter, magically? I am bringing the image back to Blanchot:

> Thus the image has two possibilities: there are two versions of the imaginary. And this duplicity comes from the initial double meaning which the power of the negative brings with it and from the fact that death is sometimes truth's elaboration in the world and sometimes the perpetuity of that which admits neither beginning nor end. (p. 261)

> Magic gets its power from this transformation. Its aim, through a methodical technique, is to arouse things as reflections and to thicken consciousness into a thing. From the moment we are outside ourselves—in that ecstasy which is the image—the "real" enters an equivocal realm where there is no longer any limit or interval, where there are no more successive moments, and where each thing, absorbed in the void of its reflection, nears consciousness, while consciousness allows itself to become filled with an anonymous plenitude. . . . Thus, behind things, the soul of each thing obeys charms which the ecstatic magician, having abandoned himself to "the universe," now controls. (p. 262)

On this reading, psychoanalysis is magic. That is not, however, the point on which I would insist. I am taken more with the soul of each thing to which we magicians—exposed *as beyond* ourselves, beyond any self—abandon ourselves. I give over control to the magician, keeping the *Sorcerer's Apprentice* in mind.

AMBIGUITY

Blanchot closes his essay on the image with a gesture toward ambiguity, another name, perhaps, for exposition and betrayal, even madness. This, perhaps, is what I have been saying of the image, of the thing, and of the self: the image exposed *as not beyond* itself; the self exposed *as not beyond* the image and itself; the self image *as not beyond* itself; each double crossing itself and the others; always another crossing, another exposure. But first and last Blanchot and three images, three meanings, each double-crossing the others. "On the worldly plane it is the possibility of give and take: meaning always escapes into another meaning . . . we never come to an understanding once and for all" (p. 263).

This is, perhaps, a familiar understanding of contingent truth. Blanchot's second and third images are far stranger, more archaic.

> Here it is no longer a question of perpetual double meanings—of misunderstandings aiding or impeding agreement. Here what speaks in the name of the image "sometimes" [*tantôt*: presently, soon, in a little while, yet to come, maybe someday, ever; deferring, postponing—all *as if, perhaps*] still speaks of the world, and "sometimes" [perhaps someday] introduces us into the undetermined milieu of fascination. . . . However, what we distinguish by saying "sometimes, sometimes," [« *tantôt, tantôt* »: presently, presently, later, later, soon, soon, come, come, someday, someday, ever, ever, perhaps, perhaps] ambiguity introduces by "always," [*toujour* without quotation marks] at least to a certain extent, saying both one and the other. . . . Here *meaning* does not escape into another meaning, but into the *other* of all meaning. Because of ambiguity nothing has meaning, but everything *seems* infinitely meaningful. Meaning is no longer anything but semblance; semblance makes meaning become infinitely rich. It makes this infinitude of meaning have no need of development— makes meaning immediate, which is also to say incapable of being developed, only immediately void [*vide*: empty].[12] (p. 263)

I would say that this fascination—soon, presently, later, to come, as if, perhaps—haunts the image and thereby—again, perhaps later, perhaps always in immemorial time—disperses as a fragrance or apparition throughout the things themselves, above all in the identification of the self or ego or it *as if beyond* itself, always and everywhere, double-crossing, betraying betrayal—perhaps, soon, presently, later, to come, always, immemorially. I would say that this emptiness is perhaps so close to fullness and abundance, this to come perhaps so close to always, this later so close to forever, so near and far, though they do not resemble, as to share in their ambiguous strangeness, the strange immemorial and archaic semblance of the image. *As as as this image, as this perhaps, as the other image or identity, and as the other of all images and identities; images and identifications and meanings as not beyond themselves, as abundance, as if.*

At the center of the principle, always, the One does violence to itself, and guards itself against the other. (Derrida, 1997, p. ix)

I betray myself in betraying the others; I double-cross myself in double-crossing the others. I overflow myself in giving to the others. I present my identity as image in betraying the abundance in the earth.

Always another crossing; always other crossings, in abundance.

NOTES

1. Ann Smock's translation (Blanchot, 1982, 256) leaves out too much, omits the decay, fading, rot, and stink of the corpse, as if the cadaver were doubly preserved, and insists on the genitive: "The image does not, at first glance, resemble the corpse, but the cadaver's strangeness is perhaps also that of the image."

Whatever the translation, we may recall Hegel, speaking of the image, God, and law—and of a girl, to whom I will return:

> The religion of art belongs to the spirit animating the ethical sphere. . . . But this self, through its being empty, has let the content go; this consciousness is Being merely within itself. Its own existence, the legal recognition of the person, is an unfulfilled empty abstraction. . . . It is consciousness of the loss of everything of significance in this certainty of itself, and of the loss even of this knowledge or certainty of self—the loss of substance as well as of self; it is the bitter pain which finds expression in the cruel words, "God is dead."
>
> The statues set up are now corpses in stone whence the animating soul has flown, while the hymns of praise are words from which all belief has gone. The tables of the gods are bereft of spiritual food and drink, and from his games and festivals man no more receives the joyful sense of his unity with the divine Being. . . . They are themselves now just what they are for us—beautiful fruit broken off the tree; a kindly fate has passed on these works to us, as a maiden might offer such fruit off a tree. Their actual life as they exist is no longer there, not the tree that bore them, not the earth. . . . But just as the maiden who hands us the plucked fruits is more than the nature which presented them in the first instance . . . since in a higher way she gathers all this together into the light of her self-conscious eye, and her gesture in offering the gifts; so too the spirit of the fate, which presents us with those works of art, is more than the ethical life realized in that nation. (Hegel, 1910, pp. 751–754)

The girl gathers the images into her life and memory as if they might be preserved as cadavers in her self-conscious eye, as if to make them her own. See note 2.

2. Ann Smock's translation marks this genitivity: "the cadaver's strangeness is perhaps also that of the image" (p. 256). My translation does not insist that the strangeness belong to the cadaver or image.

3. My chapter addresses the identification of self as image as multiplication and proliferation rather than as identification and integration: self image rather than self-image.

4. Two terms from Levinas:

Truth can consist only in the exposition of being to itself, in a singular inadequacy with itself which is also an equality, a partition in which the part counts for the whole, is the image of the whole. (Levinas, 1978, p. 61)

The beyond being, *being's other* or the *otherwise than being*, here situated in diachrony, here expressed as infinity, has been recognized as the Good by Plato. . . . The beyond being, showing itself in the said, always shows itself there enigmatically, is already betrayed. (p. 19)

I include the showing, the image, in the betraying.

5. Blanchot speaks of the step (*pas*) not (*pas*) beyond (*au-delà*) (and not a step) (*Le pas au-delà*: the step *as not beyond*). I speak of *beyond* as incessantly traversing this *not*, this impossibility.

6. Or *as not beyond*. See note 5.

7. All Freud citations are given by page numbers in the volumes cited with the complete works in the *Standard Edition* listed in the following References.

8. See my Ross, *Learning and Discovery*.

9. See note 1.

10. I stay here with the image. But I must allude, however briefly, to the cadaverous strangeness of the doorkeeper who guards the entrance to the reception room of consciousness from the anteroom *as not beyond*, especially as he appears in Kafka's parable, where the time is never right for K. to enter but the door is open only for him. Only for him yet never, to be discovered upon his death. Is this not the decay and fading of the image, not to mention the cadaver?

11. Later, in another precisely analogous way, Freud insists that the little girl undergoes symbolic castration. "So we must admit that THE LITTLE GIRL IS THEREFORE A LITTLE MAN," Irigaray responds, "A little man who will suffer a more painful and complicated evolution than the little boy in order to become a normal woman! A little man with a smaller penis. . . . A little man who would have no other desire than to be, or remain, a man" (Irigaray, 1985, p. 26). So the little girl is an image of a little man, I would respond. The *I* is formed—little man indeed, man or woman—in the imaginary. Of which Irigaray says:

We can assume that any theory of the subject has always been appropriated to the "masculine." When she submits to (such a) theory, woman fails to realize that she is renouncing the specificity of her own relationship to the imaginary. Subjecting herself to objectivization in discourse—by being "female." (Irigaray, 1985, p. 133)

She does not resist the specificity of a woman's relationship to the image whereby she may identify herself: woman as image as herself, in the angelic strangeness that haunts, or reeks of, the imaginary.

I do not mean to imply that women are angelic where men are cadaverous, but to relieve the gloom and stench of death that haunts the image and identification.

12. In French: "Ici, ce qui parle au nom de l'image, « tantôt » parle encore du monde, «tantôt» nous introduit dans le milieu indéterminé de la fascination, « tantôt » nous donne pouvoir de disposer des choses en leur absence et par la fiction, nous retenant ainsi dans un horizon riche de sens, « tantôt » nous fait glisser là où les choses sont peut-être présentes, mais dans leur image, et où l'image est le moment de la passivité, n'a aucune valeur ni significative ni affective, est la passion de l'indifférence. Cependant, ce que nous distinguons en disant « tantôt, tantôt », l'ambiguité le dit en disant toujours, dans une certaine mesure, l'un et l'autre, dit encore l'image significative au sein de la fascination, mais nous fascine déjà par la clarté de l'image la plus pure, la plus formée. Ici, le *sens* ne s'échappe pas dan un autre sens, mais dans l'*autre* de tout sens et, à cause de l'ambiguité, rien n'a de sens, mais tout *semble* avoir infiniment de sens: le sens n'est plus qu'un semblant, le semblant fait que le sens devient infiniment riche, que cet infini de sens n'a pas besoin d'être développé, est immédiat, c'est-à-dire aussi ne peut pas être développé, est seulement immédiament vide."

REFERENCES

Blanchot, Maurice. *The Space of Literature.* Trans. Ann Smock. Lincoln: University of Nebraska Press, 1982. Translation of *L'espace littéraire.* Paris: Gallimard, 1955.

———. *The Step Not Beyond.* Trans. and Int. Lycette Nelson. Albany: State University of New York Press, 1992. Translation of *Le Pas Au-Delà.*

———. *The Writing of the Disaster.* Trans. Ann Smock. Lincoln: University of Nebraska Press, 1995.

Derrida, Jacques. *The Politics of Friendship.* Trans. George Collins. London: Verso, 1997.

———. "The Politics of Friendship." *The Journal of Philosophy* 85 (November 1988): 632–644.

Freud, Sigmund. *Civilization and its Discontents.* Trans. Joan Riviere. London: Hogarth Press, 1953. *Standard Edition,* vol. 21, 59–145.

———. *On Creativity and the Unconscious: Papers on the Psychology of Art, Literature, Love, Religion.* Ed. Benjamin Nelson. New York: Harper & Row, 1958.

———. *The Ego and the Id.* Trans. Joan Riviere. Rev. and ed. by James Strachey. New York: W. W. Norton, 1960. *Standard Edition,* vol. 19, 3–65.

———. "Femininity." In *New Introductory Lectures on Psychoanalysis. Standard Edition,* vol. 22, 112–135.

———. *A General Introduction to Psychoanalysis.* Trans. Joan Rivière. Garden City, NY: Doubleday, 1953. Rev. ed. of *Introductory Lectures on Psycho-Analysis,* 1915–1917. *Standard Edition,* vols. 15–16, complete.

———. "A Mythological Parallel to a Visual Obsession." Trans. C. M. J. Hubbock. In *Creativity and the Unconscious.* First published in *Zeitschrift,* Bd. IV, 1916. *Standard Edition,* vol. 14, 337–338.

———. "The Relation of the Poet to Day-dreaming." Reprinted in S. D. Ross, ed., *Art and Its Significance.* In Sigmund Freud, *Collected Papers,* vol. 4. Article trans. I. F. Grant Duff. New York: Basic Books, 1959. "Creative Writers and Day-Dreaming" in *Standard Edition,* vol. 9, 141–153.

———. *The Standard Edition of the Complete Psychological Works of Sigmund Freud*. Ed. James Strachey, 24 vols. London: Hogarth Press, 1953–1974.

———. "The Uncanny." In *Creativity and the Unconscious. Standard Edition*, vol. 17, 217–256.

Hegel, G. W. F. *The Phenomenology of Mind*. Trans. and int. James Baillie. London: George Allen & Unwin, 1910.

Irigaray, Luce. "Any Theory of the 'Subject' Has Always Been Appropriated by the 'Masculine.'" In *Speculum of the Other Woman*. Trans. Gillian C. Gill. Ithaca, NY: Cornell University Press, 1985.

———. *An Ethics of Sexual Difference*. Trans. Carolyn Burke and Gillian C. Gill. Translation of *Speculum de l'autre femme*. Paris: Minuit, 1974. Ithaca, NY: Cornell University Press, 1993. Translation of *Éthique de la Différence sexuelle*. Paris: Minuit, 1984.

Lacan, Jacques. *Écrits: a Selection*. Trans. Alan Sheridan. New York: W. W. Norton & Co., 1977.

Levinas, Emmanuel. *Otherwise than Being or Beyond Essence*. Trans. Alfonso Lingis. The Hague: Martinus Nijhoff, 1978. Translation of *Autrement qu'être ou au-delà de l'essence*. The Hague: Martinus Nijhoff, 1974.

———. *Totality and Infinity*. Trans. Alfonso Lingis. Pittsburgh: Duquesne University Press, 1969.

Ross, Stephen David. *The Gift of Beauty: The Good as Art*. Albany: State University of New York Press, 1996.

———. *The Gift of Kinds: The Good in Abundance*. Albany: State University of New York Press, 1999.

———. *The Gift of Property: Having the Good*. Albany: State University of New York Press, 2001.

———. *The Gift of Touch: Embodying the Good*. Albany: State University of New York Press, 1998.

———. *The Gift of Truth: Gathering the Good*. Albany: State University of New York Press, 1997.

———. *Learning and Discovery*. New York: Gordon and Breach, 1981.

FIVE

THE 'ALCHEMY OF IDENTIFICATION': NARCISSISM, MELANCHOLIA, FEMININITY

EMILY ZAKIN

IN "BLIND SPOT OF AN OLD DREAM OF SYMMETRY," Luce Irigaray's long essay on Freud's writings on femininity, she takes a momentary detour to briefly consider his "Mourning and Melancholia." Already we might take this as an indication that melancholia, along with the arguments and concepts deployed in Freud's essay, is deeply imbricated with the sexual theories developed in Freud's explicit speculations on women. In her initial foray into the territory of melancholia, Irigaray suggests that there might be good reason to believe that "women have no other recourse than melancholia" (Irigaray, 1985, p. 66), only to retract this claim a few pages later, claiming to the contrary that woman "does not have a capacity for narcissism great enough to allow her to fall back on melancholia" (Irigaray, 1985, p. 71), and is instead likely to fall prey to a hysteric structure. We are thus left with two tantalizing possibilities in considering the relation between femininity and melancholia: that femininity is structurally isomorphic with melancholia, or that femininity is structurally incapable of melancholia due to narcissistic deficiencies. I propose in this chapter to approach these alternatives through close readings of three related concepts—narcissism, melancholia, femininity—with a final concept, identification, as their hinge. The relations among these terms, and within them, will prove to be paradoxical, reflecting a paradox at the heart of psychic life.

In developing my analysis, I will rely on two crucial insights provided by Julia Kristeva: first that we should distinguish a "narcissistic melancholia" that would be nonobjectal, from an ambivalent,[1] or objectal, melancholia (Kristeva 1989, p. 12); and second that a proper understanding of the death drive, especially as it appears in Freud's theory of primary masochism, which depends on the preobjectal operation of Thanatos, elucidates the distinguishing features of melancholic loss (Kristeva, 1989, p. 16). The sadness of narcissistic melancholia, Kristeva writes, "would point to a primitive self—wounded, incomplete, empty . . . afflicted with a fundamental flaw . . . the most archaic expression of an unsymbolizable, unnameable narcissistic wound"[2] (Kristeva, 1989, p. 12). This thanatic element of narcissistic melancholia entails, as we will see, a kind of masochistic unfounding of the ego.

Freud's claim that melancholia is a sadistic expression of revenge against a lost object will hence also be critically interrogated. His argument depends on two other claims: first, that in melancholia a strong attachment to an object is transformed into an identification with the object on the part of the ego; and second, that the ego is thereupon beset by the superego, which assails, berates, and tortures it. Revenge, in other words, takes the form of an attack on the ego that now, through identification, has come to resemble the lost object, with the latter the proper target. According to Freud, "hate comes into operation on this substitutive object [i.e., the ego], abusing it, debasing it, making it suffer and deriving sadistic gratification from its suffering" (1917, p. 251). On this account, a strong and sadistic superego would be intent on purging the ego of its identificatory organization in order to reestablish the ego in its illusory unity with itself. By comparing Freud's account here with his somewhat different formulations of identification in *The Ego and the Id* and *Group Psychology and the Analysis of the Ego*, I will contest both of these earlier claims. While something akin to identification is clearly at work in the melancholic operation, this 'identification' (as we will see this is an unstable, even vacillating, term) is on the part of the ego ideal and refers back to a preobjectal loss. As a result, we should think not of a sadistic, vengeful superego, but of a masochistic, self-punishing ego. Here already we might find a hint of the melancholic bond with femininity, in a loss that is encountered first and foremost as a loss within.

NARCISSISTIC IDENTIFICATION

In understanding Freud's introduction of the concept of narcissism, we must remember that Freud himself understands it as an "extension of the libido-theory" (1914, p. 75). As Freud's essay, "On Narcissism," makes clear, the ego is initially formed in being sexualized, erotically cathected; narcissism is ego libido, "the libidinal complement to egoism" (1917, p. 417): ego-cathexis is, in fact, the "original libidinal cathexis" (1914, p. 75). Narcissism, in its initial conceptual formation, is the hinge between the ego and Eros, between drive and identification. The structural-topographical model therefore does not dispense with the drives but relies on libidinal forces as the basis of ego erotism, hence ego formation. Though, as we will see, this picture is complicated in *The Ego and the Id*, where narcissism is said to enact the desexualization of libido; this revision follows the modification of the theory of the drives in *Beyond the Pleasure Principle*, such that desexualization refers henceforth to the contrast between Eros and Thanatos and not to a rejection of the drives as formative. Freud never abandons the idea that sexuality is at the root of psychical (dis)order. If melancholia, as will be discussed later, is endured as a failure of self-regard, this failure is to be understood narcissistically, as simultaneously libidinal and egoic. It thus makes sense to examine melancholia in this dual way, in terms of the topographical relations within the psyche, and in terms of the vicissitudes of drive, so that we might convey the complex interweaving of economic, dynamic, and structural relations and causes.

As already noted, in its most general form, narcissism is simply the subject's libidinal cathexis of its own ego. But, more specifically, this cathexis is, in the first instance, a founding cathexis, generative of its object. Freud writes that "we are bound to suppose that a unity comparable to the ego cannot exist in the individual from the start; the ego has to be developed . . . so there must be something added to auto-erotism—a new psychical action— in order to bring about narcissism" (1914, pp. 76–77). As Julia Kristeva ascertains, this can only mean that narcissism is supplementary (Kristeva, 1987, p. 22), the result, as Freud claims, of "a new psychical action." We cannot consider narcissism to be the primordial state of the psyche in its incipient form,[3] for narcissism implies that the existence of the ego has been initiated, and the ego is, of course, a unity whose self-differentiation provides the preliminary binding that makes possible the organization of the psyche.

Kristeva maintains that this additional element, this supplement, testifies to "an already ternary structuration" (Kristeva, 1987, p. 23) of narcissism, to an "*emptiness*" that "appears as the first separation between what is not yet an *Ego* and what is not yet an *object*" (Kristeva, 1987, p. 24). Narcissism, in other words, insofar as it inaugurates the distinction between proto-ego and proto-object (first and foremost, of course, the ego itself as object), has already moved beyond a dyadic relation, since a third term is operative precisely *between* the two, in the gap that separates them. This emptiness, Kristeva avers, is on the side of language, preventing the dissolution of borders and the confusion of limits (the regressive collapse into primordial unity or autoerotism), while also sheltering an abyss that narcissism must defend against (Kristeva, 1987, p. 42). Split in this way, both promise and threat, the interval of thirdness bespeaks a rupture laden with tension, a frontier whose guardian must both bind and keep at bay. There is therefore a "solidarity between emptiness and narcissism" (Kristeva, 1987, p. 24) that it is the work of identification to preserve.

This identification is of a quite specific form, what Kristeva calls a "nonobjectal identification" (Kristeva, 1987, p. 25), an identification prior to object-cathexis. As Freud himself points out, "identification is known to psycho-analysis as the earliest expression of an emotional tie with another person" (1921, p. 105), adding a few pages later in the same text that it is the "original form of emotional tie with an object" (1921, p. 107). While these passages from Freud both refer to an other or an object, if taken in conjunction with Freud's claim in *The Ego and the Id* that identification with the father is "apparently not in the first instance the consequence or outcome of an object-cathexis; it is a direct and immediate identification and takes place earlier than any object-cathexis" (1923, p. 31), we can infer that the references to an object in *Group Psychology* are grammatical prolepses and do not represent Freud's theoretical commitment. This nonobjectal identification, preliminary to any differentiated other, is paternal in character, representing the beyond to the mother–child relation of bodily symbiosis. The father (of prehistory) is thus the shelter of emptiness (Kristeva, 1987, p. 27), but also the agent of loss. With this initial split (a split within the psyche as well, since it produces the first differentiation within the id), we are led inexorably into the "alchemy of identifications" (Kristeva, 1987, p. 3), the transformative mode by which the external is alchemized into the internal, and thus by which the ego develops its singular character. Such alchemy foretells the possibility of both love and language, and thereby procures a subject susceptible to loss because it is immersed in a world of others. But we must not forget the threat of emptiness, the abyssal breach of infantile union that might overwhelm the ego in a melancholic void.

In shattering the preobjectal bliss of the infant, primary identification tears a space in which both the ego and its objects might emerge.[4] In this sense it initiates and propels (rather than responds to) the loss of the mother by creating her as an object. Primary narcissism thus marks not the loss of an object, but the loss of objectlessness, that is, of autoerotism, of nondifferentiation. Crucially, this means that the loss of the maternal is correlated with and even activates primary (rather than secondary) narcissism since the maternal is not, first and foremost, an object.[5] Identification with the father procures the loss of the maternal *non-object* inaugurating a primary narcissism in which the first proto-distinction between ego and object, actually ego as object, brings the not-yet ego into being as a cathected, and therefore distinct or differentiated psychical entity. As a primitive, but also permanent, stage of libidinal organization, primary narcissism sets the stage for future developments. In the subject's relation to its formative identifications, it becomes its own object. Only when the child becomes capable of taking itself as an object (to be lost) can the ego properly be said to have formed.[6] This originary narcissistic attachment, prior to all other objects, transforms not only the infantile id, but the maternal body as well, a transformation that might best be characterized as a sacrifice. It is precisely here, in this traumatic moment of simultaneous dissolution (of unity) and generation (of ego), that Kristeva situates the promise of the father, whose role it is to repair, with language, what language has torn asunder, to bequeath the possibilities of a future with others.

Since language is the very force of ternary structuration, the site of difference, it is language that the father as third embodies. It is only in language, through signification, that we can grapple with the differences of others, their being apart from us, always already gone. As Kristeva describes identification with the paternal figure, "when the object that I incorporate is the speech of the other—precisely a nonobject, a pattern, a model—I bind myself to him in a primary fusion, communion, unification" (Kristeva, 1987, p. 26). This process is one of "nourishing oneself . . . with words" (Kristeva, 1987, p. 26), enabling one to compensate for the loss of nourishment associated with the mother's body. Since "the subject exists only inasmuch as it identifies with an ideal other who is the speaking other" (Kristeva, 1987, p. 35), we must conclude that the primary identification with the father produces the first psychic differentiation, and that the ego ideal thereby established is thus constituted prior to both the ego itself and the ideal ego; the ego ideal would then provide the aggravating kernel[7] of each, mobilizing their subsequent development. As that without which "the child and the mother do not yet constitute 'two'" (Kristeva, 1987, p. 40), the ego ideal appears at the very juncture of incipient organization. By "transferring" or "displacing" its "not-yet-identity . . . to the site of Other who is not libidinally cathected as an object but remains an Ego Ideal" (Kristeva, 1987, p. 41), the child renders possible its own coming into being.[8] The ego ideal is the witness of the ego's birth. Though the father bestows this gift, it is always, incontrovertibly and irretrievably, a gift of loss.[9]

If this minimal differentiation, the space of difference itself, provides the contours of primary narcissism, we must also remember that "the development of the ego consists in a departure from the primary narcissism" (1914, p. 100) in which cathexis onto other, non-ego, objects makes possible the ego's enrichment. The object is a kind of intermediary between primary narcissism and the ego's further development. As Freud describes it, "if one has lost a love-object, the most obvious reaction is to identify oneself with it, to replace it from within, as it were, by identification" (1940, p. 193). Here we can recognize the emergence of secondary identification, in the return from an object predicated on its loss. If love is an "encroachment upon the ego" (1921, p. 103), then, as with primary identification, secondary identifications (premised on the loss of love) are both consoling and threatening. Identification in this instance operates as a kind of anti-cathexis; the ego paradoxically defends itself against loss by losing itself in, assimilating itself to, the external other who has "been abandoned as an object and has instead, by identification, been taken into the ego and thus become an integral part of the internal world" (1940, p. 205). Secondary narcissism is then libido that has been withdrawn from objects and returned to the ego via identification. According to Freud, "a limitation of narcissism can . . . only be produced by one factor, a libidinal tie with other people . . . love for others, love for objects" (1921, p. 102). We could say, therefore, that (primary) narcissism produces its own limit, since it alone makes possible a world of others to whom libidinal cathexis may be displaced. The moment an object is discovered, however, the self is refound as lacking (desiring), less than complete; if object-love fails, and the ego is compelled to return to itself, it will find something missing.

As we have seen, Kristeva's elaboration of primary identification and its support for primary narcissism decisively renders the latter's distinction from secondary narcissism, which necessitates a return from objects via the pathway of identification (a process particularly notable in, for instance, the Oedipal complex,[10] but one that persists throughout life). While this subsequent process describes the mournful propensity that Freud, in *The Ego and the Id*, will associate with ego development per se, we will see that it is primary narcissism that actually sets the stage for the advent of melancholia proper, and moreover that this distinction between primary and secondary narcissism is wholly bound up and imbricated with sexual difference, with the respective place of the father and the mother in the organization of the psyche, a parental/sexual difference that can be situated along the axis of loss. Melancholia, as I will discuss in upcoming sections, returns to the initial trauma of narcissism as a site of loss, repeating its violence but without the promise of love. Already we can see that the narrative of identification provides a hint as to the link between melancholia and femininity. If identity is eventuated through the foundational identifications that precede and constitute it, defining its contours, we must attend to the way in which the identificatory pathways of sexual difference also provide a history of loss that traces the route of melancholia. If secondary narcissism expresses itself in a fantasy of recovering lost unity, in the desire to return to what was lost in the advent of primary narcissism[11] and to close the gap[12] instituted by the father, this attempt at return can also catalyze the disruptive force of primary identification for which no compensation can be found.

MELANCHOLIC IDENTIFICATION I:
THE SHADOW OF THE OBJECT

In "Mourning and Melancholia," Freud famously declares that "in mourning it is the world which has become poor and empty; in melancholia it is the ego itself" (1917, p. 246). The melancholic endures an acute, seemingly bottomless, loss of self-regard. We can trace the route of melancholia from the moment "the shadow of the object fell upon the ego, and the latter could henceforth be judged by a special agency as though it were an object, the forsaken object" (1917, p. 249). Assimilated to the ego, the forsaken object is, according to Freud, berated and tortured by the superego, in an attempt to brutally annihilate it. Melancholia, Freud tell us, can thus be characterized as "a conflict between the ego and the superego" (1924, p. 152), a conflict that is visible in the harshness of its most prominent symptom.

Though both are expressions of grief, melancholia is distinguished from mourning, beyond the symptom of self-loathing, by virtue of the intrapsychic processes that govern the experience of loss. We can make some general claims about this distinction: the loss of a loved object for one susceptible to mourning inaugurates a psychic activity intent on working through the loss in order to reestablish a relation to the world of others; through a process of hyper-cathexis and detachment, the libido arduously labors until it has withdrawn its libidinal cathexes and freed itself from the object (1917, pp. 244–245), thereby reestablishing a coherent ego identity capable of interacting in and with the world. Melancholia, by contrast, converts object loss into a loss internal to the self: "an object-loss was transformed into an ego-loss" (1917, p. 249). There are two constitutive moments to this conversion: identification and narcissism, both ascribed by Freud to regression.

The melancholic succumbs to a regressive ploy in which the libido establishes "an *identification* of the ego with the abandoned object" (1917, p. 249), an identification that is regressive, according to Freud, precisely because it returns the ego to narcissism. Freud contrasts this mechanism with "the normal one of a withdrawal of the libido from this object and transference of it to a new one" (1914, p. 249); his implication here is that a healthy libido is capable of substituting objects one for another, while the melancholic libido lacks this capacity, though, in fact, as we will see shortly, his later writing revises the assumption, allying the melancholic turn to identification with the very rule of ego formation. In any case, because identification splits the ego from within, a conflict erupts within the psyche, an alienation within and of the self whose energy is thus withdrawn from the world. Melancholic subjects can be characterized by their inability to work through their loss and hence to maintain a coherent ego identity in the face of loss. The melancholic ego is fragile, fragmented, sustained in the mode of disintegration. Nonetheless, the perpetual self-loathing of the melancholic, experienced as an "impoverishment of his ego on a grand scale" (1917, p. 246), or an "inner travail consuming his ego," must be characterized as narcissistic, since the libidinal cathexes are withdrawn within and turned on the ego. Here we find the ego at its own limits, shaken by its own constitutive founding.

Keeping in mind our previous discussion of narcissism, the melancholic regression to narcissism cannot, obviously, be seen as a return to a unified ego, but to the very root of internal differentiation, the condition that permits life among a world of others. The inner cleavage aggravated by object loss has been there all along, from the narcissistic inception of the ego. There are two immediate sources of this regression and cleavage: because the melancholic responds to the loss of an unconscious object, so that he knows, perhaps, "*whom* he has lost but not *what* he has lost in him" (1917, p. 245), and because this "object-choice has been effected on a narcissistic basis" (1917, p. 249), narcissistic attachment does not resolve the dilemma of difference, but exaggerates and exacerbates it. The object is loved in an attempt to return to a lost unity, to undo the disruption inscribed by primary narcissism. This explains why, although it first appeared that the melancholic had "suffered a loss in regard to an object, what he tells us points to a loss in regard to his ego" (1917, p. 247), a loss within the self that the lost object only intensifies. Intolerant of absence, which is borne home most acutely by abandoned love, the melancholic ego is unstable.

An object that is cathected for its narcissistic promise (as opposed to an anaclitic attachment), its promise of unity or completion, induces a paradox, for this unity is sought without, in an externalized ideal. The loss of the object exposes this paradoxical lack within, disrupting the narcissistic fantasy that conceals the otherness of the other, rendering visible the ego's severe wound, and disposing it to aggressive self-loathing. We can conclude that the melancholic's return to narcissism from object-cathexis repeats an earlier dissolution, the ego as ideal unity again rendered impossible, an impossibility contained in the very mechanism of identification that brings the external inward, marking a site of permanent disunity. Yet surely, given that narcissism is a fundamental moment of all ego formation, this disunity cannot be localized to those who are pathologically melancholic, or even those who tend toward narcissistic object choice. Why is melancholia particularly destabilizing? How has narcissism gone awry? To address these questions we must make an extended detour through *The Ego and the Id*, the text in which Freud most fully elaborates the universal nature of melancholic identification.

MELANCHOLIC IDENTIFICATION II: THE EGO

As many scholars have noted, the model of identification that Freud sets forth in his essay on melancholia is expanded in the later work *The Ego and the Id* to become the very basis of ego formation. There Freud advances the claim that the "the character of the ego is a precipitate of abandoned object-cathexes and . . . it contains the history of those object-choices" (1923, p. 29), a claim that reverberates with our earlier discussion of narcissism as the site not of unity but of differentiation. If the ego is formed as a remnant of its lost objects, then it is loss itself that makes possible the preliminary organization of the psyche. Thus, for instance, Madelon Sprengnether can proclaim the ego to be a fundamentally "elegiac formation" whose very structure "internalizes an absence[13]" (Sprengnether, 1990, p. 229). The ego is born as a memorial to loss, and each of us is the effect of what we have lost. While Freud discerns that in melancholia, "an object which was lost has been set up again inside the ego . . . an object-cathexis has been replaced by an identification" (1923, p. 28), he now also determines this to be a "common" and "typical" process: "this kind of substitution has a great share in determining the form taken by the ego" (1923, p. 28). Insofar as identification is the pathway of identity formation, all identity is melancholic work.

This quasi-universal, "normal," nonpathological form of melancholic identification is clearly objectal, and its return from objects must therefore be related to secondary identification and secondary narcissism, given that primary identification is a preobjectal mode of ego formation. Loss not only inaugurates the ego, but keeps its development in motion and never complete, sustaining the permeability of the ego.[14] Melancholic identification in this expanded sense is thus precisely the resource that sustains the subject, however paradoxically, both supporting and threatening the ego. Although Freud, in the earlier "Mourning and Melancholia" identified mourning as a process that allows substitution of objects rather than regression to a identification, perhaps here we can see that these processes are not so opposed as they at first appeared. In this instance, it is precisely the ego's identifications that permit the de-cathexis and working-through that opens the way to new objects. It will therefore be useful to designate the identificatory mechanism at work in the ego's formation as one of mourning, in order to distinguish it from melancholia proper and its rigid identifications.

This process of mourning both constitutes, and never constitutes, ego identity, acting as both its condition and its peril. Just as narcissism both opens up a world of others, and menaces that world with emptiness, the ego is constitutively diminished, disrupted by the very form of its enrichment, that is, identification. While the ego is enriched when "it withdraws libido from the id and transforms the object-cathexes of the id into ego-structures" (1923, p. 55), assimilation of objects is also and always a differentiation that disrupts whatever unity is sought or has been established. Loved objects therefore potentially endanger the ego, luring it to dissolution.

The Ego and the Id demonstrates the inherently alienated nature of the ego, founded in acts of identification that commemorate what it is/was not. Narcissism manifests the insertion of the other at the very heart of the ego, whose existence is marked by the form of self-loss that brings it into being. To understand the consequences of this revised theory of identification, we must follow more closely the contours of Freud's argument in "Mourning and Melancholia" and its relation to The Ego and the Id. It will be useful for us to develop an analysis based on "the topographical point of view" (1917, p. 255), a task that Freud relinquishes almost as soon as he suggests it, so that we might compare melancholia with "common" and "typical" ego development: "in and between what psychical systems" (1917, p. 255) does the respective work of each occur? What, finally, distinguishes melancholia from the work of mourning that sustains ego formation generally? We must understand the conjunction of love and idealization to address this question.

MELANCHOLIC IDENTIFICATION III:
EROS AND IDEALIZATION

Group Psychology and the Analysis of the Ego both elucidates the relation between love and identification and resolves a central conundrum of the above discussion—namely, how we might characterize the specificity of melancholia given the universality of its identificatory mechanism in ego formation. In writing about love, Freud elaborates the effect of an object capable of overwhelming the ego. Freud claims that the loved object might "consume the ego," a danger that "happens especially easily with love that is unhappy and cannot be satisfied" (1921, p. 113). The ego is submerged in love, immersed in the beloved other, rendered destitute by Eros. Although "the ego remains the great reservoir from which libidinal cathexes are sent out to objects and into which they are also once more withdrawn," this reservoir cannot be contained within, for "when a person is completely in love . . . the main quota of libido is transferred on to the object and the object to some extent takes the place of the ego" (1940, p. 151). Even more drastically, in the case of the ego captivated by love, "the functions allotted to the ego ideal entirely cease to operate" because *"the object has been put in the place of the ego ideal"* (1921, p. 113, Freud's emphases). If, in identification, the object is taken in by the ego, here it is an aspect of the ego that is impelled outward, assimilated to an idealized object. Thus, Freud calls this colonization of the ego ideal " 'fascination' or 'bondage' " as a way of distinguishing it from straightforward identification. We can also call it idealization, as Freud defines it earlier in the essay, writing that in idealization, "the object serves as a substitute for some unattained ego ideal" (1921, p. 112). Idealization exalts the object for "we love it in on account of the perfections which we have striven to reach for our own ego and which we should now like to procure in this roundabout way as a means of satisfying our narcissism" (1921, p. 112–113). Just as the ego ideal acts as a "substitute for the lost narcissism"[15] (1917, p. 94), we can conclude that the loved object that takes its place, usurping and externalizing a psychical *topos*, also acts as a substitute, and is loved for the promise of an impossible fullness that cannot, of course, be regained.[16]

The differences between idealization and identification are striking, as are their similarities. While identification "enriches" the ego (since an object is introduced into it, whose properties are now the ego's), idealization "impoverishes" the ego since the ego in love "has surrendered itself to the object, it has substituted the object for its own most important constituent" (1921, p. 113). But can this difference between idealization and identification be sustained? As we saw earlier, in our discussion of narcissism, enrichment and impoverishment are two sides of the same coin, together constituting the risk of the ego's elegiac, alchemical formation. Freud himself has doubts that the two processes can adequately be delineated, maintaining that their opposition is "an illusion of contradistinctions that have no real existence. Economically there is no question of impoverishment or enrichment; it is even possible to describe an extreme case of being in love as a state in which the ego has introjected the object into itself" (1921, p. 113–114). Uncomfortable with this conclusion, Freud proposes another distinction: perhaps "in the case of identification the object has been lost or given up; it is then set up again inside the ego . . . in the other case the object is retained, and there is a hypercathexis of it by the ego and at the ego's expense" (1921, p. 114). The distinction Freud proposes here is that between keeping and giving up an object, a distinction that is itself unstable given that identification might well rely on an unconscious retention of the object: "But here again a difficulty presents itself. Is it quite certain that identification presupposes that object-cathexis has been given up? Can there by no identification while the object is retained?" (1921, p. 114). Freud now arrives at the crux of the distinction, one he will not later dispute: "the real essence of the matter," Freud writes is "whether the object is put in the place of the ego or of the ego ideal" (1921, p. 114, Freud's emphases). While identification effects alterations in the ego, the bondage of love displaces the ego ideal.

We should not suppose, of course, that identification is not also a pathway of love. We might instead view it as a divergent pathway, one less likely to lend itself to capture. We could mark "the distinction between identification of the ego with an object and replacement of the ego ideal by an object" along the axis of respect: "a soldier takes his superior . . . as his ideal, while he identifies himself with his equals" (1921, p. 134). When we discriminate in this way, we can foresee already how idealization might intersect with a form of feminine love oriented by what one can never be.[17] Returning to our reading of Kristeva, we can also see in this desire for the unattainable a "twisted mingling of sexuality and ideals that make up the experience of love" (Kristeva, 1987, p. 1). "Love," claims Kristeva, "reigns between the two borders of narcissism and idealization" where the ego potentially "shatters into pieces and is engulfed" (Kristeva, 1987, p. 6). The displacement of the ideal by the loved other risks "the tyranny of idealization" (Kristeva, 1987, p. 30) in which the ego cannot sustain itself against, or feel adequate to, the ego ideal, now represented by a cathected object whose abandonment might then throw the ego into an "archaic vortex" (Kristeva, 1987, p. 33) wherein the ego seeks to preserve love even at risk of its own annihilation.[18] Where my desire was, there I shall lose myself, cease to be.[19]

Here we might wonder about Freud's earlier formulation of melancholia as a systemic relation in which the superego rages against the ego that has taken the place of the forsaken object. In his essay on melancholia Freud never considers the possibility that the forsaken object has occupied the place not of the ego but of the ego ideal, in which case we might consider that it is the object doing the raging. This prospect would not simply invert, but rearticulate the meaning and structure of melancholia. We could well agree with Freud that "the misery of the melancholic is the expression of a sharp conflict between the two agencies of his ego" (1921, p. 132), but investigate whether it is the object "unworthy of love" (1921, p. 133) that is reproached and attacked, or if instead it is the ego that takes itself as unworthy of love and is thereby condemned and abused by the idealized object. This is not, of course to displace aggression onto an external source and render the ego an innocent victim; rather this reading would situate aggression more firmly in its self-destructive, or masochistic, roots, noting that the conflict between the ego and the superego that is the essence of melancholia is in the first place experienced as a need for punishment, and the triumph of disaggregation over unity. As Freud reminds us again and again, the ego itself is first and foremost an object, and remains so even as it develops: "the ego now enters into the relation of an object to the ego ideal which has been developed out of it" (1921, p. 130). This self-objectification renders the narrative of self-debasement plausible; if idealization is the melancholic form of identification, that which distinguishes it from mournful ego formation generally, we might then conclude that the identificatory/idealizing mechanisms of melancholia and the concurrent fragmentation of the self are rooted in egoic masochism rather than sadism of the superego. In this masochistic abdication,[20] suffering is inflicted not on but by the lost object that has taken up residence in and as the ego ideal. Melancholia is hence characterized by Kristeva as a "shadow" cast on "bright and fragile amatory idealization" (Kristeva 1989, 5). Rather than mourning the loss of an object, the melancholic refuses this identificatory release and remains ensnared.

MELANCHOLIC IDENTIFICATION IV: THANATOS AND DESEXUALIZATION

As already discussed, Freud contends that "the melancholic's erotic cathexis in regard to his object has thus undergone a double vicissitude: part of it has regressed to identification, but the other part . . . has been carried back to the stage of sadism" (1917, pp. 251–252). To further challenge Freud's second claim, and clarify the first, we will need to look more closely at the process of desexualization or defusion of the instincts, said to characterize, in differing ways, both sublimation and idealization.

In describing identification, Freud explicitly links its mechanisms to the trajectory of sublimation: "the transformation of object-libido into narcissistic libido which thus takes place obviously implies an abandonment of sexual aims, a desexualization—a kind of sublimation, therefore. Indeed, the question arises . . . whether this is not the universal road to sublimation, whether all sublimation does not take place through the mediation of the ego, which begins by changing sexual object-libido into narcissistic libido and then, perhaps, goes on to give it another aim" (1923, p. 30). Freud, moreover, refuses to confound "the formation of an ego-ideal . . . with subli-mation" (1915, p. 94), writing instead that the two might often be in tension and that a high ego ideal need not favor sublimation. While exaltation of the object might well demand a redirection of libidinal instincts, "it cannot enforce it" (1915, p. 95) with the result that idealization may well lead to repression of the libido, rendering the desired object unconscious, and "the satisfaction of love impossible" (1915, p. 99). If amatory idealization, unlike identification, is not allied with sublimation, it is nonetheless clear that both incur a desexualization. If the aim cannot be converted, then the ego desexu-alizes in a different way, one that may actually threaten sublimation, since the object unconsciously retained appears, because it is desexualized, in its most aggressive, thanatic aspect. This release of Thanatos defines the melan-cholic conflict between the ego and its ideal.

Freud's account of melancholia is limited because at the time of its elaboration, he did not yet have an account of either the death drive or primary masochism. These later theorietical developments enable us to see that melancholia represents a defusion of instinctual energy, a decomposition of Eros and Thanatos. In place of self-preservation, the melancholic pre-serves the loved object, idealizing it at the risk of the ego's own disintegra-tion. As Freud writes, "the more a man (sic) controls his aggressiveness," for example, aggression against a lost object, "the more intense becomes his ideal's inclination to aggressiveness against his ego" (1923, p. 54). This re-fusal to turn against the abandoning object elucidates the superego's partici-pation in melancholia as one initiated by the ego's invitation.

Freud claims that in melancholia, "a pure culture of the death instinct" is "holding sway in the superego" (1923, p. 53), and later calls the superego "a kind of gathering-place for the death instincts" (1923, p. 54). Consistent with this latter view, he holds that melancholic self-torments are "without doubt enjoyable," since they represent "a satisfaction of trends of sadistm"[21] (1917, p. 251). Yet, a quarter of a century later he writes that "satisfaction of the death instinct remaining in the ego seems not to produce feelings of pleasure[22]" (1940, p. 154). This apparent contradiction can be resolved if we disentangle the death drive from the superego, and remember that masoch-ism, unlike sadism that fuses Eros and Thanatos, represents an instinctual defusion. Freud argues that "the essence of a regression of libido . . . lies in a defusion of instincts" (1923, p. 42), that is, in generating an unadulterated death drive by sundering the union with Eros that permits its release. If we can now correlate Freud's depiction of masochism with his theory of melan-cholia, this will also support the view that the latter is anchored to the bondage of the ego ideal rather than identification of the ego.

In "The Economic Problem in Masochism," Freud writes of the death instincts that they may "refuse to be tamed . . . by being bound to admixtures of libido" (1924, p. 164). Thanatos, that is, may refuse fusion with Eros, a refusal Freud calls desexualization. Freud explains the origin of erotogenic masochism by pointing toward an original drive toward disintegration, a drive that is displaced outward by libidinally binding it and directing it toward mastery. When placed "in the service of the sexual function," this drive is "proper sadism" (1924, p. 163). That which "does not share in this transposition outwards," but is nonetheless bound libidinally is "the original, erotogenic masochism" (1924, pp. 163–644), the "residuum" as well as "evidence of, and a remainder from the phase of development in which the coalescence . . . between the death-instinct and Eros took place" (1924, p. 164). This series reveals not only that sadism always represents a fusion of aggression and sexuality, but also that even a primary masochism is preceded by an unbound death drive, an originary drive to destruction in which sadism and masochism cannot be distinguished (1924, p. 164). Only moral masochism, "having loosened its connection with . . . sexuality" (1924, p. 165) harks back to this unamalgamated death drive. Here, Freud is tempted to declare, "the destructive instinct has been turned inwards again and is now raging against the self" (1924, p. 165). Notice that this description is remarkably similar to the language Freud employs to describe melancholia. Freud, however, reminds us that the term masochism is properly connected with "erotism" and so does not fully endorse this conception of moral masochism as a total desexualization.

Freud also refers moral masochism to an "unconscious sense of guilt" or "need for punishment," which expresses "a tension between ego and superego" (1924, pp. 166–167), again employing language similar to that used to describe melancholia. Masochistic guilt is founded in the ego's "perception that it not come up to the demands made by its ideal" (1924, p. 167). The superego, of course, is the psychical agency formed through identification with the parents and allied with the id. The superego emerges by binding the libido "to the alteration of the ego produced by means of identification. The transformation [of erotic libido] into ego-libido . . . involves an abandonment of sexual aims, a desexualization" (1923, p. 46). We can thus characterize the superego as the desexualized (even sublimated) representative of the id.[23] Freud emphasizes that we cannot understand desexualization as a "transformation" of instinct where one "turns into the other" (1923, p. 43). Instead he conceives of a "displaceable energy" that "proceeds from the narcissistic store of libido—that it is desexualized Eros" (1923, p. 44) or *"sublimated energy"* (1923, p. 45) that is, energy divested of Eros and yet retaining its purpose, "that of uniting and binding" (1923, p. 45). Narcissism, still understood as "ego-libido," acts as a kind of de-cathexis, one that by releasing the ego from its objects makes sublimation possible. This narcissistic "mediation of the ego" and the identificatory formation of the superego are both routes of sublimation (1923, pp. 45–46), although the latter appears to be more dangerous[24] as "the 'defusion' of the instincts which takes place along with this incorporation [of parents] into the ego" can lead the superego to "become harsh, cruel, and inexorable against the ego" (1917, p. 167).

It will be useful, before moving forward with this discussion, to make some distinctions. While Freud sometimes uses the terms *ego-ideal* and *super-ego* interchangeably,[25] they can be distinguished. For instance, in the essay "Dissection of the Psychical Personality," Freud refers to the superego as having three distinct functions, "of self-observation, of conscience, and of [maintaining] the ideal" (1933, p. 66), which might correspond with three different psychical agencies or at least with three modifications of the same agency. The superego would be prohibitive, representing law, conscience, and the sense of guilt. The ego ideal would be exhortative, presenting idealized versions of the ego toward which it might strive and through which its identity could be forged (but thereby also representing a permanent schism within). Both would operate through modes of self-observation. Whether we see the ego ideal as simply the obverse side of the superego, or as a distinct agency, it is nonetheless clear that it cannot simply be assimilated into the proscriptive role usually assigned the superego and is linked instead to a narcissistic promise. In the essay "On Narcissism," for instance, Freud writes of an agency of "conscience" (1914, p. 95), which we might now call the superego, whose work it is to compare the ego with the ego ideal; inevitably this comparison will expose not only the ego's inadequacy, but its essential vacuity, the emptiness hidden by sustaining ideals. This explains conscious guilt as "the expression of a condemnation of the ego by its critical agency" (1923, p. 51), a guilt that Freud links to conscience generally, or morality. Unconscious guilt[26] also expresses this criticism, but in inverted form: the ego not only submits to but needs its punishment.

In large part on this basis, Freud distinguishes between morality proper and moral masochism, noting that "in the former, the accent falls on the heightened sadism of the superego to which the ego submits; in the latter, it falls on the ego's own masochism which seeks punishment hidden" and "remains as a rule concealed" (1924, p. 169). Although "the sadism of the superego and the masochism of the ego supplement each other and unite to produce the same effects" (1924, p. 170), moral masochism can also interfere with moral sensibility, which may vanish into or become swallowed by the resexualization of the Oedipal complex out of which feminine masochism emerges. While morality itself has an inherently sadistic quality, expressed in the satisfaction the superego takes in the "glaringly conscious" sense of guilt (1924, p. 169), moral masochism expresses the ego's masochistic need for punishment, a need that desexualizes insofar as it is regressive, and resexualizes insofar as it returns to the Oedipal complex. Although melancholia bears traces of masochism, the two should not be confounded. While masochism can be said to reactivate the Oedipus complex, melancholia returns to a prior, pre-Oedipal, loss, a state prior to the Oedipal identifications of the superego and allied with the ego's narcissistic formation.

If the two routes to sublimation are narcissism (the formation of the ego) and morality (the formation of the superego), moral masochism disrupts the latter, while melancholia disrupts the former. Both disruptions are a kind of excessive perversion of the very process they undermine and intensify. Freud warns of the ego's activity that "through its work of identification and sublimation it gives the death instincts in the id assistance . . . but in doing so it runs the risk of becoming the object of the death instincts . . . the ego's work of sublimation results in the defusion of the instincts and a liberation of the aggressive instincts in the superego" (1923, p. 56). The libidinal movement toward unity and binding is imperiled by the very sublimations it demands and requires. Perhaps we could say that melancholia does not, after all, represent the antithesis of sublimation, but its absolute realization, so divested of Eros that it is no longer fulfills the latter's purpose of uniting and binding, instead tearing apart unities. This tearing apart, however, seeks to return to a preobjectal state prior to differentiation, to a unity before unity—a unity prior to the narcissistic break that presents objects with which the ego might libidinally bond. Moving from the object to the ego, and from love to aggression, melancholia attests to the narcissistic paradox of ego formation, displaying Eros at its own limit; the very forces that allow the ego to form structures, to develop and enrich itself are also those that initiate its decomposition.

FEMININE IDENTIFICATION I:
AN ESPECIALLY INEXORABLE REPRESSION

We can now return to our point of departure, and consider how the narcissistic decomposition of the ego, intensified by melancholia, might be homologous with femininity. Basing her remarks on the three essays by Freud devoted specifically to women's sexuality ("Some Psychological Consequences of the Anatomical Distinction Between the Sexes," "Female Sexuality," and "Femininity"), Luce Irigaray explores the familiar trajectory of the girl's Oedipal complex, performing an immanent critique that takes Freud's concepts to their very limit. Freud describes the girl's pre-Oedipal "pre-history" as "so grey with age and shadowy and almost impossible to revivify, that it was as if it had succumbed to an especially inexorable repression" (1931, p. 226). What is inexorably repressed, of course, is the mother, repudiated but nonetheless retained. If forsaking the mother marks the end of the girl's prehistory, then the Oedipal complex marks an historical period that never fully comes to a close. As Freud writes, the girl's acquiescence to Oedipalization is "more difficult and more complicated" than it is for boys (1933, p. 117) and is "the outcome of a long and difficult development; it is a kind of preliminary solution, a position of rest which is not soon abandoned" (1933, p. 129). Since the Oedipal Complex provides "a haven or refuge" (1933, p. 129), girls will "demolish it late and, even so, incompletely" (1933, p. 129). Freud cautions, however, that given the import of the Oedipus complex, "the manner in which one enters and leaves it cannot be without its effects"

(1925, p. 257), and its most critical effect for girls lies in the composition of their superego. While the repression of the Oedipus complex in boys "smashes it to pieces" and provides "the nucleus of the superego" (1925, p. 257) that opens the path toward sublimation, no such relentless destruction occurs in girls, with the consequence that "their superego is never so inexorable" (1925, p. 257). Less severe, the girl's superego is correlatively less amenable to the pathways of sublimation.[27] We might conclude that the hysterical disposition will manifest itself at just this juncture, expressing a love of law (allied with the still-loved father), rather than identification with it.

Taken together, however, these two aspects of the girl's feminine development, her inexorable repression of the mother and her fragile, unsteady, superego, might instead produce a disposition to melancholia. We saw above that the narcissistic "mediation of the ego" and the identificatory formation of the superego are both routes of sublimation (1923, pp. 45–46). Here Freud tells us that the latter pathway is blocked for girls, and that the former can only manifest as regression to a wounded narcissism. With the girl's path to sublimation obstructed, love[28] or melancholia seem the only options. To the ego, Freud asserts, "living means the same as being loved—being loved by the superego" (1923, p. 58), and this will be especially true for the girl who has not fully introjected the superego inside herself. The superego, of course, is the psychical substitute for the lawgiving father, who we saw at the beginning of this chapter is also the origin of the ego ideal. Irigaray describes hysteria as a relentless inquiry into the other's love, the unremitting concern with whether I am loved. Melancholia, we could say in a preliminary formulation, is the obverse of hysteria, a form of unrequited love for the superego, representing less a fear of conscience (morality) than an embrace of conscience that fears its loss of love. The melancholic, like the hysteric, wants to be the loved object; when she is not loved, she is not. Thus, Kristeva characterizes melancholics as inhabiting a 'living death' (Kristeva, 1989, p. 4). If the girl's ego is depleted by object loss, she will suffer again the originary schism between self and object.

FEMININE IDENTIFICATION II: INCORPORATING THE THING

In *Black Sun*, Julia Kristeva correlates narcissistic melancholia with an originary matricidal loss, a loss that, for women, is both impossible and necessary. What Freud has called *inexorable repression*, Kristeva describes as a kind of destitution in which "the disappearance of that essential being continues to deprive me of what is most worthwhile in me" (Kristeva, 1989, p. 5). Narcissistically wounded by this disappearance of what is "not an Object but the Thing" (Kristeva, 1989, p. 13), that is, a preobjectal attachment prior to object-cathexes and identifications, the melancholic's future is rendered barren, a site where "any loss entails the loss of my being" (Kristeva, 1989, p. 5), and no loss can be mourned. Yet, Kristeva claims, "matricide is our vital necessity" (Kristeva, 1989, p. 27), the founding separation that enables the ego to be born and grow. She does not conclude that all women are melancholic: for some women, the lost object may be or "transposed" through "unbelievable symbolic effort" (Kristeva, 1989, p. 28), the effort defined by the Oedipus complex. For others, however, this matricidal drive is inverted, in an effort to avoid an "*impossible mourning*" (Kristeva, 1989, p. 9). This inversion holds the death drive inside, directed against the self: "the melancholy woman is the dead one that has always been abandoned within herself and can never kill outside herself" (Kristeva, 1989, 30). Without the Oedipal, effort of renunciation, and without the identificatory support of the father, "the lost object remains, throbbing in the 'crypt'" (Kristeva, 1989, p. 30). Locked within, this undead mother is after all "not so fully lost" (Kristeva, 1989, p. 30). Since one cannot mourn what is not lost, it is instead retained, so that neither the other nor the self exists, but only the Thing: "the depressed subject has remained prisoner of the nonlost object (the Thing)" (Kristeva, 1989, p. 47). Not having lost the mother, the melancholic retains "a Thing buried alive" that "will not be translated," that is, represented in language, "in order that it may not be betrayed" (Kristeva, 1989, p. 53). Irigaray employs similar language, detailing "a 'loss' that radically escapes any representation. Whence the impossibility of 'mourning' it" (Irigaray, 1985, p. 68). Both would agree that the feminine risk of Oedipalization is that the mother, "walled up within the *crypt* of inexpressible affect" (Kristeva, 1989, p. 53), will remain a disquieting phantom[29] haunting the girl's psyche.

In their essays "The Illness of Mourning and the Fantasy of the Exquisite Corpse" and "Mourning *or* Melancholia: Introjection *versus* Incorporation," Nicolas Abraham and Maria Torok advance a comparable hypothesis, arguing that melancholia represents a refusal to mourn, a "refusal to acknowledge the full import of the loss, a loss that, if recognized as such, would effectively transform us" (Abraham & Torok, 1994, p. 127). Comparing this refusal to the work of mourning, entailing as it does "the painful process of reorganization" (Abraham & Torok, 1994, p. 127), they claim that the melancholic is engaged in the forlorn attempt to "safeguard his topography" (Abraham & Torok, 1994, p. 131); if every loss potentially reconfigures the terrain of the psyche, altering its contours through identification, it is precisely this transformation that the melancholic resists and guards against, in favor of psychical homeostasis. Abraham and Torok call this rigid safeguarding *incorporation* to distinguish it from the more difficult but more nourishing process of introjection that permits of psychical transformation. Incorporation,[30] they claim, erects "a commemorative monument" or "tomb" (Abraham & Torok, 1994, p. 114) in the psyche at the very site where the psyche might otherwise have flourished; it thereby performs a kind of "recuperative magic" (Abraham & Torok, 1994, p. 114) that "simulates profound psychic transformation" (Abraham and Torok, 1994, p. 126), without actually undertaking its difficult labor. In attempting to foil the inevitability of loss, incorporation maintains "a *secretly perpetuated* topography" (Abraham & Torok, 1994, p. 125) that exempts the subject from real psychical change. In thus refusing to take in the loss and be changed by it, melancholic incorporation converts object loss into loss in the ego. Mourning, of course, also confronts the subject with a loss, paradigmatically for Abraham and Torok, the loss of the breast, but here the empty mouth can be "filled with words" (Abraham & Torok, 1994, p. 127), a process that they take to be "the initial model for introjection" (Abraham & Torok, 1994, p. 128). Undergoing "the passage from food to language in the mouth presupposes the successful replacement of the object's presence with the self's cognizance of its absence" (Abraham & Torok, 1994, p. 128). This absence can be tolerated when the replacement of food by language promises a future beyond the boundaries of the infantile world. Introjection, like mourning, provides the possibilities of sublimation, and of new objects. The melancholic, however, reverts this process, treating words as things to be digested, ideals to be swallowed; since the word is indigestible it remains pristine and unsullied, but also unamenable to the movement of signification.

The crucial factor, according to Kristeva, that determines the choice between melancholia and mourning is identification with the primal father. Primary identification, she contends, "would be the means, the link that might enable one to become reconciled with the loss of the Thing. Primary identification initiates a compensation for the Thing and at the same time secures the subject to another dimension" (Kristeva, 1989, p. 13), a dimension in which the ego might be bound to language and form connections with others. While words exile the Thing, they also provide the resources to mourn the Thing and promise a future in which there will be others to love. It is not that words replace the mother, but that in not replacing her, they allow her to be lost. Kristeva praises the child, the "intrepid wanderer" who "leaves the crib to meet the mother in the realm of representations" (Kristeva, 1989, p. 41). By renouncing her, the child might also find a new, mediated, path to her, recover her in altered form or in another figure, although this task is clearly easier for the boy. Even so, "the child," Kristeva writes, "becomes irredeemably sad before uttering his first words; this is because he has been irrevocably, desperately separated from his mother, a loss that causes him to try to find her again, along with other objects of love, first in the imagination, then in words" (Kristeva, 1989, p. 6). With these "signifying bonds" (Kristeva, 1989, p. 10), the subject can enter the world, finding a "way out of the states of withdrawal in which the subject takes refuge" (Kristeva, 1989, p. 10). Primary identification is thus considered by Kristeva as a kind of prophylactic against melancholia, enabling further identifications that convert loss into growth, and, like introjection, making possible the loving work of mourning.

Thus, she determines that "with those affected by melancholia, primary identification proves to be fragile, insufficient to secure other identifications" (Kristeva, 1989, p. 14). Others will henceforth be only supplements, idealized in an attempt to recuperate what cannot be regained. The loss of such ideals will then "easily collapse" the psyche, since "the experience of new separations, or new losses, revives the object of primary denial" (Kristeva, 1989, p. 64), overwhelming the subject with sorrow: "the loss of the erotic object breaks up and threatens to empty her whole psychic life. The outer loss is immediately and depressively experienced as an inner void" (Kristeva, 1989, p. 82). Since one can only love oneself in the object, in a detoured narcissism, one will perpetually hold on to idealized others in an attempt to evade abandonment. Here we might see how melancholic identity is homologous with a certain form of femininity, promoting an emptiness within the self that language can neither cover over, compensate, nor signify. Since the subject can neither relinquish the lost object nor admit of its loss, where the paternal signifier flounders, where also that "words fail to fill the subject's void" (Abraham & Torok, 1994, pp. 128–129). The object is instead preserved in an attempt at "narcissistic reparation" (Abraham & Torok, 1994, p. 131) directed toward eradication of the void within. The incorporation of the mother, however, is thereby also an exile from language: in ingesting the loss, a boundary is erected that resists the movement of signifiers.

Of course, melancholics still speak although they are "foreigners in their maternal tongue" (Kristeva, 1989, p. 53), emerging into a language heterogenous to their non-loss. Kristeva compares melancholic speech to a mask, "a beautiful facade carved out of a 'foreign tongue' "[31] (Kristeva, 1989, p. 55). By preserving the object in its pristine state of "total innocence" (Abraham & Torok, 1994, p. 136), the melancholic shelters an "undisclosable idyll" that never was, "pure and devoid of aggression" (Abraham & Torok, 1994, p. 136). Thereby exalted, the ideal is rigidly devoured in an all-consuming and hence self-diminishing fury, releasing the aggression that is the secret kernel of the maternal crypt.

If there is a feminine propensity for this bondage, if women are more susceptible to burying the mother alive, we must relate this to the development of their femininity. Little girls[32] are asked to identify with the lost object (the mother) without thereby being able to signify that loss. The loss is thus incorporated as a remnant of the earlier bond, but is excluded from access to language and representation. Expelled from the symbolic universe, the Thing nonetheless persists in the psyche. Amatory idealization, temporarily promising release from the hold of the Thing, might act as a catalyst for melancholia insofar as this later love appears as an avatar of a more primordial loss and makes prominent the lack within, the very lack the ideal other is meant to banish or dissolve. Activating the fantasy that one can compensate for lack,[33] that the other can complete me, this love is precarious, both a continuation of narcissism, and its limit, witnessing the impossibility for (re)birth and threatening to preclude egoic agency.

Women are perhaps more prone to melancholic incorporation pre- cisely because of the two aspects of the Oedipal complex discussed earlier. On the one hand, the girl's initial loss is inexorably repressed, inaccessible to language, and thus inconsolable. The maternal bond is rendered uncon- scious, and cannot be mourned. On the other hand, the subsequent deficiency of the girl's superego renders her prone to idealizations that diminish rather than expand the contours of the ego, locking objects within. If the rule of ego formation is an identificatory mourning, girls are more likely to fall prey to melancholic idealization. Melancholia can be seen as a longing for the self, a self that never was, since its bondage to the Thing precluded the enrichment of identification. Without a strong identification with a primal father who would facilitate separation from the mother, and fill the now- empty mouth with words, the matricidal origins of subjectivity remain with- out symbolic recompense, and the subject might never fully emerge, marking a primitive failure in the creation of an external world in which I might exist, exist as capable of signifying both it and me. For such a melancholic, the signifier is only violence and not promise, recapitulating the narcissistic trauma of matricide. Feminine melancholia is a response to this trauma, circling around a phantasmatic wholeness, and denying the void it conceals.

CONCLUSION

Here we can finally arrive at a more conclusive answer to the stark choice with which we began: whether femininity is better correlated with hysteria or melancholia. While hysterical symptoms will be tied to an ambivalent identification with the mother, and hysteria is therefore rooted in secondary narcissism, staying within the realm of objects, melancholia, to the contrary, presents less an ambivalence than an absence or lack of an object that never was (the Thing), returning to the founding disturbance of primary narcis- sism. Psychical structure might bend one way or the other depending on the specifics of the Oedipal complex. The alternative, according to Kristeva, is between being "prisoners of the archaic mother" (Kristeva, 1987, p. 42) or being among those who "seduce this 'father of individual prehistory' " (Kristeva, 1987, pp. 42–43).

Freud's account of melancholia attributes its suffering to the ego's identification with the lost object; the superego indirectly avenges itself against the object by denigrating the ego now identified with it. I have here advo- cated a view that instead lends melancholic weight to the ego ideal's assimi- lation of the lost object and thereby understands this assimilation as a masochistically driven one. The melancholic loses herself first in the face of an irredeemable absence (that is kept present) and later in confronting an unattainable ideal. We can thus see how the structure of sexual difference contributes to the melancholic formation. Since the ego ideal is founded in a primary identification with the father,[34] who provides access to language at the expense of a preobjectal union with the maternal body, feminine subjects are particularly vulnerable to the loss of the maternal Thing. Feminine melancholia enacts a particularly deathbound form of nostalgia, expressing the unrelenting desire to recuperate what has always already been lost, a loss that cannot be mourned because the object never existed, and because the language of mourning is incommensurate with what it exiles. Feminine development hence highlights the mechanism by which the alchemical logic of identification, which might otherwise warrant the ego's growth, in melancholia displaces its own founding.

NOTES

1. Freud's texts support this distinction insofar as the conflict of ambivalence is highlighted in "obsessional states of depression" (1917, 251) that retain the object, and in which "there is no regressive drawing-in of libido" (1917, 251) as in narcissistic melancholia.

2. Kristeva is here echoing Freud's description, when he writes that "the complex of melancholia behaves like an open wound, drawing to itself cathectic energies . . . from all directions, and emptying the ego until it is totally impoverished" (1917, 253).

3. Freud's writings lend themselves at times to an alternative reading that would name what I am here calling autoerotism as primary narcissism. In this case, Freud's readers, and sometimes Freud himself, forget the "new psychical action" here articulated. To keep autoerotism conceptually distinct from primary narcissism enables us to attend to a moment of psychical transition that we might otherwise lose sight of.

4. As Freud writes, "a child's first erotic object is the mother's breast that nourishes it . . . there is no doubt that, to begin with, the child does not ditinguish between the breast and its own body; when the breast has to be separated from the body and shifted to the 'outside' because the child so often finds it absent, it carries with it as an 'object' a part of the original narcissistic libidinal cathexis" (1940, 188). Objects carved out of the child's body by their absence retain a narcissistic trace. The border between inside and outside is thus slippery and unstable, since not only is the external father the core of the ego (an interior exteriority), but the breast that was body becomes externalized as an object (an exterior interiority).

5. Kristeva calls the maternal 'abject.'

6. The father thus enables this first differentiation of the ego from the id, a differentiation that might also demarcate the emergence of a distinction between conscious and unconscious. It is at a point prior to this latter distinction, however, that a discrete, individuated body emerges that is not coterminous with the mother's body, a body-ego whose contours achieve some preliminary boundary. The ego as premised upon a perceptual image of coherent bodily borders thus arises first as a perceptual apparatus, that is, as a distinction between inside and outside or as a divergence of the self from the external world, whose very condition lies in the father's intervention. It is thereby through the father that the body becomes organized, so that one could almost say that not only is the ego "first and foremost a body-

THE 'ALCHEMY OF IDENTFICATION'   99

ego" (1923, 27), but also 'the body is first and foremost an egoic body,' prior to which there is no proper body at all. This unity is of course illusory, garnered from a surface image ("the projection of a surface" [1923, 26]), that is projected onto a disorganized organism, but it is an illusion that sets in motion further organization. Another way of saying this is that the ego and the body proper emerge simultaneously.

7. Lacan is of course the first to make this point. By providing "the origin of the ego ideal" (Freud, 1923, 26), the father also supports the ideal ego, the ideal unity arrived at. Lacan describes the moment of looking in the mirror through the "reference-point of him who looks at him" so that through this intermediary, "the subject sees appearing, not his ego ideal, but his ideal ego, that point at which he desires to gratify himself in himslf" (Lacan, 1977, 257). Both the ego ideal and the ideal ego of course comprise aspects of the ego, providing imaginary and symbolic sites of identification, but here Lacan gives priority to the ego ideal, the symbolic retroactively constituting the imaginary. Lacan makes similar claims even earlier, in his first seminar.

8. This transference also reveals that the loss of the mother is one that the child desires and is relieved by. The child wants to abandon its mother, to be released from her overwhelming hold. Exile from the maternal is the condition for the child's regeneration. Of course, that the child desires this separation does not render it less traumatic, but precisely defines it as trauma.

9. As Freud puts it "each of the mental differentiations . . . represents a fresh aggravation . . . increases its instability" (1921, 62). Even in "being born" we have taken a step from "absolutely self-sufficient narcissism" into a world with its objects, entering a state difficult to endure, and from which we are tempted to revert, that is, to return to an earlier undifferentiated state.

10. Though Freud questions whether this process is in fact active in the resolution of the Oedipal complex.

11. What is lost, is what is excluded from language (the maternal/feminine) in order to make language possible.

12. We can call this the ideal ego, insofar as attempts at recuperation invoke a kind of illusory or imaginary unity. As noted earlier, (note 7), the ideal ego follows from the ego ideal, which makes possible a unified body ego that returns from identification with aspecular image.

13. I disagree, however, with Sprengthener's characterization of mourning for lost object for two reasons. First, she claims that "the mother's body itself [is] a focus of mourning" (9) whereas I argue here that it is precisely the site of the impossibility of mourning, and hence the advent of melancholia. Second, she at times (as in the instance just noted) conflates mourning with melancholia, situating their common origin in a primordial loss rather than a primary identification.

14. Though, of course, the ego is also a rigidity.

15. Kristeva also describes the ego ideal as "a revival of narcissism, its abeyance, its conciliation, its consolation" (Kristeva, 1987, 22).

16. In this love we can see two opposing tendencies toward repetition at work, the tendency to return to primary narcissism, and the tendency to return to the moment before primary narcissism, in an attempt to undo its disruption, the moment prior to its originative dispensation of the ego. If we conceive of narcissism as founded in the intervention of an ideal other, then clearly it already entails a drama of misrecognition; in reaching for this ideal, we disturb its presence, render it absent.

17. According to Kaja Silverman, the power of "unrequited love . . . is predicated on the impossibility of loving the self" (Silverman, 1996, 34). Narcissistic object choice is thus "love for the one who is able to love the subject in a way that compensates for the impossibility of self-love" (Freud, 1914, 34). By putting "a man in the place of her ego-ideal" (34), a woman might gain self-love, but only through the detour of the other's love. Since the narcissist loves as a "sexual ideal . . . whoever possesses an excellence which the ego lacks for the attainment of its ideal" (1914, 81), what is idealized is that which fills in for lack and remedies or counteracts self-loathing. At the same time, however, "self-regard has a very intimate connection with the narcissistic libido . . . not being loved lowers the self-regarding feelings . . . to be loved is the aim and the satisfaction in a narcissistic object-choice . . . he who loves has, so to speak, forfeited a part of his narcissism, which can only be replaced by his being loved" (1914, 78). In this way love demands being loved, and "the narcissistic (active) subject is exchanged by identification for another, extraneous ego" (1915, 96), and narcissism appears not at all as self-sufficiencey, but as a wholly dependent passivity.

18. Freud writes that "by taking flight into the ego love escapes annihilation" (1917, 178).

19. If, in Freud's model, what I can't have I become and hence I am hated insofar as I am this lost object, that is, insofar as my ego is identified with it, in this model, what I can't have I idealize as that which I ought to be and hence I am hated insofar as I fail to be the lost object, that is, insofar as my ego fails to identify with the lost object, insofar as I am myself. Possessed by nostalgia for a past that never was, an object that never came to be as such, the melancholic can only repeat the impasse of identity.

20. If melancholia is thus formed in the bondage of the ego to its ideal, we can see why "separation of the ego ideal from the ego" might result in a kind of mania, in which release from the ideal's hold is experienced as a psychical "festival": "the abrogation of the ideal would necessarily be a magnificent festival for the ego" (1921, 64).

21. Since, "for purposes of discharge the instinct of destruction is habitually brought into the service of Eros" (1923, 39), we might recognize that sadism and masochism are always adulterated Thanatos, amalgamated with Eros, and that this is the source of their pleasure.

22. It makes sense that the peculiar satisfactions of the death drive would not be pleasurable if we consider that unadulterated thanatos would be beyond the pleasure principle.

23. If the ego comes to take pleasure in, eroticize, this movement, this resexualization is feminine masochism.

24. In fact, as we will see, it might well be the former that is more fundamentally dangerous.

25. While the ego ideal might generally be seen as a "residue" of parental identifications, the superego specifically is a memorial to the aggressive dependencies of infantile life.

26. Freud claims, oddly, that melancholia displays "over-strongly conscious guilt" (1923, 52), a thesis that not only runs counter to his analyis of melancholia elsewhere, but is also contradicted in a footnote on the previous page, where melancholia is clearly associated with a "borrowed" and unconscious guilt.

27. The superego might protect one from melancholia by enabling identifications that appropriate aggression for cultural products.

28. As Irigaray points out, love will fail, because the father cannot accede to the girl's desire to please him; he offers her not love but law, to which the daugher responds by attempting to please the law, to love it in the father's place, and even to desire law instead of love.

29. Abraham and Torok develop the concept of phantom in reference to the passing on and inheritance of encrypted secrets.

30. Freud also describes the melancholic ego as incorporative "in accordance with the oral or cannibalistic phase of libidinal development" in which the ego wants to devour the object (1917, 249–250). Incorporation thus seems to be a "dispositional point in the development" of melancholia, providing a moment of fixation to which the melancholic might regress, but even more significantly, which always "persists alongside of and behind the later configurations and obtains a permanent representation in the libidinal economy and character of the subject" (1933, 100).

31. This notion of the foreignness of language brings Kristeva's position closer to Freud's, who claims that the melancholic cannot stop talking, and that the melancholic speaks the truth, giving form to a self-knowledge that is displaced or obscured in the nonpathological functioning of the psyche. Although Kristeva argues that the melancholic is exiled from the signifying economy, her claim here is that the melancholic nonetheless presents the facade of signification, a facade that might well support a strange and alien truth.

32. For little boys, on the contrary, the loss of the mother represents an entry into the symbolic universe and identification with the paternal function

33. We could say that in hysteria the fantasy is about completing the other, being that which the other is lacking, while in melancholia, the fantasy is about the other completing me, filling my lack. We might venture further that the the difference between hysteria and melancholia reflects not only that between bodily symptoms and self-hatred, but also differing roots in Oedipal or pre-Oedipal conflicts.

34. Since, as Freud writes, "the ego is formed out of identifications which take the place of abandoned cathexes by the id" and "the first of these identifications always behave as a special agency in the ego and stand apart from the ego in the form of a super-ego" (1923, 48), we can conclude that, although the ego ideal is originally formed through an identification on behalf of the ego, as a special and distinct agency that separates from the ego, it becomes henceforth capable of sustaining its own capacity for identification (or idealization). While a strong superego will resist continuing influence, a weak superego will be susceptible to, and even encouraging of, continuing modification by idealization, thus maintaining a site of vulnerability to otherness.

REFERENCES

Abraham, Nicolas and Torok, Maria. (1994). *The Shell and the Kernel*. Ed. and Trans. Nicolas T. Rand. Chicago: University of Chicago Press.

Freud, Sigmund. (1914). "On Narcissism: An Introduction." In *The Standard Edition of the Complete Psychological Works of Sigmund Freud*. Ed. James Strachey. London: Hogarth Press. Vol. 14.

———. (1915). "Instincts and Their Vicissitudes." In *Standard Edition*. Vol. 14.

———. (1917). "Mourning and Melancholia." In *Standard Edition*. Vol. 14.

———. (1920). "Beyond the Pleasure Principle." In *Standard Edition*. Vol. 18.

———. (1921). "Group Psychology and the Analysis of the Ego." In *Standard Editon*. Vol. 18.

———. (1923). "The Ego and the Id." In *Standard Edition*. Vol. 19.

———. (1924). "The Economic Problem in Masochism." In *Standard Edition*. Vol. 19.

———. (1925). "Some Psychical Consequences of the Anatomical Distinction Between the Sexes." Vol. 19.

———. (1931). "Female Sexuality." In *Standard Edition*. Vol. 21

———. (1933). "Femininity." In *Standard Edition*. Vol. 22.

———. (1940). "An Outline of Psychoanalysis." In *Standard Edition*. Vol. 23.

Irigaray, Luce. (1985). *Speculum of the Other Woman*. Translated by Gillian Gill. Ithaca: Cornell University Press.

Kristeva, Julia. (1987). *Tales of Love*. Translated by Leon S. Roudiez. New York: Columbia University Press.

———. (1989). *Black Sun: Depression and Melancholia*. Trans. Leon S. Roudiez. New York: Columbia University Press.

Lacan, Jacques. (1977). *The Four Fundamental Concepts of Psychoanalysis*. Trans. Alan Sheridan. New York: Norton.

———. (1988). *The Seminar of Jacques Lacan. Book I. Freud's Papers on Technique, 1953–54*. Trans. John Forrester. New York: Norton.

Silverman, Kaja. (1996). *The Threshold of the Visible World*. New York: Routledge.

Sprengnether, Madelon. (1990). *The Spectral Mother*. Ithaca: Cornell University Press.

SIX

THE ONTOLOGY OF DENIAL

WILFRIED VER EECKE

IN THIS CHAPTER I will present Freud's analysis of the puzzling phenomenon of denial, which consists in simultaneously denying and revealing the truth. Thus, when a patient answers that the female figure in his dream is not his mother, Freud interprets the answer as revealing that it really is his mother. Or when a patient boasts that it is pleasant not to have had her headaches for so long, Freud interprets this as signaling that the attack is not far off.

I will start by delineating the problem as Freud treated it. Next, I will show that the phenomenon of denial is part of a larger process. I will also point out that Freud refrains from fully analyzing that whole process, leaving a promising task for this project. Third, I will describe and elaborate on three metapsychological insights of Freud, one of which I will show implies that realizing the truth hidden in a denial is more than an epistemological problem: it involves hard emotional work. Fourth, I will show some limitations in Freud's analysis of the phenomenon of denial. In particular, I will demonstrate explicitly that realizing the truth hidden in a denial requires more than epistemological work, it also requires acts of separation from intimate others and the mobilization of powerful aspects of language. Finally, I will present and analyze an autobiography in which the author describes the undoing of a profound denial related to the death on the battlefield of his father when he was a two-month-old infant. This case will illustrate my theoretical claim that undoing a denial requires acts of separation and skillful usages of metaphors.[1]

DEMARCATION OF THE PROBLEM

By the examples he gives, Freud demarcates the problem he intends to discuss by means of the concept of *Verneinung*, which the authors of the *Standard Edition* of Freud's works translate as "negation," but which I prefer to translate as "denial."[2] Freud's demarcation is at the same time restrictive and expansive.

Let us first look at the restrictions imposed on the domain of the concept *Verneinung* by Freud's examples. The first example is the rejection by a patient of an emotion that might be imputed to the patient given what the patient intends to say. Freud presents the case in this way: "Now you'll think I mean to say something insulting, but really I've no such intention" (Freud, 1925, p. 233). Freud continues by presenting what he thinks goes on in the patient: "We realize that this is a rejection, by projection, of an idea that has just come up" (ibid.). Typical for a denial is the fact that the patient labels a phenomenon—in this case an emotion—but that the labeling in a denial is incorrectly rejected as untrue.

The second example concerns a patient who has told Freud about a dream in which there is a female figure. Freud reports the case as follows: "You ask who this person in the dream can be. It is *not* my mother." Freud then continues: "We emend this to: 'So it is his mother.' In our interpretation, we take the liberty of disregarding the negation and of picking out the subject-matter alone of the association. It is as though the patient had said: 'It's true that my mother came into my mind as I thought of this person, but I don't feel inclined to let the association count' "(ibid.). In his comments on this second example Freud is very explicit about the two dimensions he seems to consider constitutive of the phenomenon of denial. On the one hand, there is an activity of labeling. Freud describes it as an act of associating a known figure (mother) with the unknown figure in the dream. Describing what happens in the first constitutive moment of denial as an association seems to me to underplay the role of linguistically identifying the unknown phenomenon. In a denial, one does not so much associate two images—the unknown figure in the dream and the figure of the mother—as one labels a previously unknown phenomenon. The other constitutive element of a denial is the negation of the labeling activity performed by the patient. Freud interprets the negation in a denial to mean, in the first example, a rejection of an idea that has come up, and, in the second example, a disinclination "to let the association count" (ibid.).

Freud's third example is that of a neurotic who has already been informed by Freud of the workings of unconscious processes. Freud describes his patient as telling him: " 'I've got a new obsessive idea' . . . 'and it occurred to me at once that it might mean so and so. But no; that can't be true, or it couldn't have occurred to me.' " Freud interprets the statements of his patient as follows: "What he is repudiating, on grounds picked up from his treatment, is, of course, the correct meaning of the obsessive idea" (ibid.). In this example we have again two moments. There is what Freud calls "the repudiation" and there is the description of the meaning of a new obsessive idea.

In the third paragraph of his article, Freud starts to conceptualize what he thinks to be the phenomenon he wants to study. He writes: "Thus the content of a repressed image or idea can make its way into consciousness, on condition that it is negated. Negation is a way of taking cognizance of what is repressed" (ibid.). Freud here introduces explicitly a third constitutive element of denial: repression. The first constitutive moment was the correct labeling of the repressed. The second constitutive moment was the refusal of the revealed truth. A denial is then understood as a mechanism whereby an unknown repressed phenomenon "makes its way into consciousness" (ibid.). Freud finds the mechanism of negating so essential for the result of a denial—letting the repressed make its way to consciousness—that Freud proposes a new technique for treating patients who have difficulty in revealing a piece of information about something that is repressed and thus unconscious. Freud writes: " 'What,' we ask, 'would you consider the most unlikely imaginable thing in that situation? What do you think was furthest from your mind at that time?' If the patient falls into the trap and says what he thinks is most incredible, he almost always makes the right admission" (ibid.). In order for Freud to invent this new technique and, even more, for this technique to be effective, it must be the case both that there are two centers of meaning creation and that the meanings created by these two centers are not compatible. Freud addresses this incompatibility between the two systems of meaning creation by giving consciousness a face-saving device. Freud asks what the most unlikely imaginable thing is or what was furthest from the patient's thought. Freud provides consciousness with a form of distance from the truth it is invited to discover or, formulated differently, he provides consciousness with the opportunity to deny what it sees. Freud observes that when consciousness accepts the face-saving device and describes what it thinks is the furthest from its mind, consciousness *almost always* describes the unconscious correctly. In one of the next paragraphs, Freud calls the negation in a denial "the hall-mark of repression, a certificate of origin—like, let us say, 'Made in Germany' " (ibid., p. 236).

Some authors have expanded the meaning of denial to include nonverbal activities. Thus, Edith Jacobson uses the label *denial* for such phenomena as amnesia (p. 63, 64), disavowal or undoing of castration (pp. 74, 77, 83), avoidance (p. 75), and wishful fantasies distorting reality when they are a means of defending against fearful objects (p. 78). Such an expansion of the concept of denial omits, in my opinion, a crucial element in the phenomenon Freud wants to study: that is, a denial *correctly labels the repressed phenomenon*, even though a denial denies the correctness of the labeling. Labeling and correctly labeling what is repressed are crucial aspects of the puzzle that Freud wants to study under the phenomenon called denial.

There is, however, an expanded meaning of denial that does correspond to Freud's interpretation of denial. I believe that I can argue for that expansion because Freud provided a fourth example of the kind of phenomena he was going to study. The fact that the example is mentioned not in the main text, but in a footnote, might indicate that Freud too felt that this example is a form of extension of the core phenomenon. He actually claims that the fourth example is using the same process; he does not claim that the process is identical with the process at work in the first three examples. Here is how Freud describes the new example, which he calls boasting: " 'How nice not to have had one of my headaches for so long.' But this is in fact the first announcement of an attack, of whose approach the subject is already sensible, although he is as yet unwilling to believe it" (ibid.). At first, one could argue that the patient in this new example does not make a false statement. It seems to be correct for the patient to say that he has not had the headaches for a long time. Therefore, this example could be said to be a misfit. It is not a proper example for the phenomenon to be studied by Freud, that is, denial, for in it nothing is denied. However, when one looks in the rest of Freud's oeuvre one can notice additional similar examples. Freud's explanation of these examples provides arguments for seeing the similarity between the fourth example and the other three. In the process, Freud also forces us to accept a fourth not-so-visible constituent element in the phenomenon of denial.

Freud discusses the danger of boasting in his study of Frau Emmy von N. He does so in a long footnote, having warned his readers at the beginning of his study that he will reproduce the notes that he made at night during the beginning of the treatment and will put insights acquired later in footnotes (Freud, 1895, II, p. 48). Emmy von N. regularly had "neck-cramps." Freud describes them as consisting "in an 'icy grip' on the back of the neck, together with an onset of rigidity and a painful coldness in all her extremities, an incapacity to speak and complete prostration. They last from six to twelve hours" (ibid., p. 71). In the evening session of May 17, 1889,[3] Emmy von N. "expressed her astonishment that it was such a long time since she had had any neck-cramps, though they usually came on before every thunderstorm" (ibid., p. 75). The morning of May 18, Emmy von N. "complained of cold at the back of her neck, tightness and pains in the face, hands and feet. Her features were strained and her hands clenched" (ibid., pp. 75–76). In a footnote that may have been written up to five years after the treatment, Freud writes that Emmy von N.'s "astonishment the evening before at its being so long since she had had a neck-cramp . . . [can be understood as] a premonition of an approaching condition which was already in preparation at the time and was perceived in the unconscious"(ibid., p. 76, n. 1). The patient disregards the true premonition.

Freud describes a second patient, Frau Cäcilie M., who had regularly similar premonitions. Thus, Freud writes: "while she was in the best of health, she said to me 'It's a long time since I've been frightened of witches at night,' or, 'how glad I am that I've not had pains in my eyes for such a long time,' I could feel sure that the following night a severe onset of her fear of witches would be making extra work for her nurse or that her next attack of pains in the eyes was on the point of beginning" (ibid., p. 76, n. 1). Freud provides a beginning of a conceptualization of these phenomena. He says it this way: "On each occasion what was already present as a finished product in the unconscious was beginning to show through indistinctly. This idea, which emerged as a sudden notion, was worked over by the unsuspecting 'official' consciousness (to use Charcot's term) into a feeling of satisfaction, which swiftly and invariably turned out to be unjustified" (ibid., p. 76, n. 1). These examples of boasting are therefore not strictly speaking like the other three examples of denial. In boasting, the patient does not utter a falsity. It is indeed true that the patient has not had neck-cramp, been frightened of witches, or experienced pain in the eyes. However, what the patient is re- porting is naive because it does not report the most interesting thing that could be reported. The patient does not say that she feels that an attack, or witches, or pain in the eyes is coming. Here we come to the essence of Freud's new insight. Freud claims that the unconscious has a wisdom that consciousness does not have. Freud claims that the cause for the boasting of his patients is the wisdom of the unconscious that feels that the attack or the painful crisis is coming. Consciousness, in its limited information capabili- ties, does not see the attack on the horizon. All that consciousness can report is that it is aware that these attacks have not occurred for some time. Freud thus tells us, on the one hand, that the unconscious takes the initia- tive and formulates the truth, but that, on the other hand, consciousness does not know what the unconscious already knows. Freud says as much when he explains the popular warning against boasting: "We do not boast of our happiness until unhappiness is in the offing and we become aware of our anticipation in the form of a boast" (ibid., p. 76, n. 1).[4]

The similarity with the other examples of denial is that in boasting also an all too real but frightening truth is denied. The real truth is that the unconscious is aware of a coming attack. Thus, things are bad. Consciousness, on the other hand, looking only to the past, says that things are good. But notice, boasting is not without epistemological value. Just as is the case with the other examples, boasting hits the nail on the head by correctly labeling the problem. Only, just as in the other examples, boasting wrongly evaluates the problem. One can therefore formulate the similarity of the example of boasting with the other examples of clear-cut denial as follows: an unknown unpleasant truth has been correctly labeled but wrongly evaluated.

Let us make a further observation about Freud's explanation of boast- ing. In a last attempt to clarify the superstition that boasting is bad Freud writes: "[In boasting] the subject-matter of what we are recollecting emerges before the feeling that belongs to it—that is to say, because an agreeable contrasting idea is present in consciousness" (ibid., p. 76, n. 1). We here have in Freud's analysis of boasting the first hint that the unconscious and consciousness systems obey a different logic in creating statements. The unconscious is able to present something to which unpleasant feelings are attached. Consciousness seems inclined to turn to pleasant feelings. Freud will explain later in the article that the ego as the seat of consciousness is, at some point in its development, unable to accept anything unpleasant associated with itself. He writes: "the original pleasure-ego wants to introject into itself everything that is good and to eject from itself everything that is bad" (ibid., p. 237). The ego is thus at that point of its development a narcissistic, imaginary construction.[5]

PHENOMENOLOGICAL ANALYSIS OF THE PROCESS OF DENIAL

Having delineated the phenomenon that he wants to analyze (i.e., verbal denial), Freud then proceeds to unpack the background of that phenomenon. Freud teaches us that a verbal denial is part of a larger process.

First, there is a postulated prior phase: repression. Freud points out that a *Verneinung* (denial) has the effect of "taking cognizance of what is repressed" (ibid., p. 235). This idea is so important to Freud that he formulates it three more times. He writes: "Thus the content of a repressed image or idea can make its way into consciousness, on condition that it is *negated*" (ibid.). Or: "it [*Verneinung* (a denial)] is already a lifting of the repression" (ibid.). Or finally: "[by *Verneinung* (a denial)] one consequence of the process of repression is undone—the fact, namely, of the ideational content of what is repressed not reaching consciousness" (ibid.). As already pointed out in the analysis of the examples given by Freud, a necessary precondition for a denial thus seems to be the existence of repression. When the mechanism of repression is successful, then consciousness is faced with a blank. For the patient who dreamed about a female figure a successful repression would have resulted in her saying: "You ask me who that figure is in my dream? I do not know." We have an example of Freud's patient Emmy von N., when Freud asks her "what the stammer came from" (1895, II, p. 61). Freud reports that the patient reacted by silence, by giving no reply. When Freud insisted and asked: "Don't you know?" she replied "No." When Freud pressed her by asking "Why not?" the patient angrily replied: "Because I *mayn't*" (ibid.).

Second, there is the actual phase of denial. By contrasting the phenomenon of denial with the postulated state that preceded it, Freud is able to emphasize the novelty in the phenomenon of denial. The novelty is that consciousness is now aware of a phenomenon that it was not aware of before. Further on in his reflections, Freud describes this contribution of denial as contributing to the freedom of thinking because it provides consciousness with content that it lacked, insofar as consciousness is now aware of what it previously was not. Furthermore, repressed thoughts are important—Freud even claims that they are indispensable—to the patient. Freud puts it this way: "With the help of the symbol of negation [in a denial], thinking frees itself from the restrictions of repression and enriches itself with material that is indispensable for its proper functioning" (1923, p. 236). Again: "But the performance of the function of judgement is not made possible until the creation of the symbol of negation has endowed thinking with a first measure of freedom from the consequences of repression and, with it, from the compulsion of the pleasure principle"(ibid., p. 239).

Freud, however, points out that one should not be too enthusiastic about the presumed victory of a denial over repression. He describes that victory then also in a variety of ways. He writes that a denial is "a way of taking cognizance of what is repressed . . . though not, of course an acceptance of what is repressed" (ibid., pp. 235–236). Or: "With the help of negation only one consequence of repression is undone" (ibid., p. 236). And finally: "The outcome of this is a kind of intellectual acceptance of the repressed, while at the same time what is essential to the repression persists" (ibid.). A denial is thus a very ambiguous performance. It undoes one crucial aspect of repression in that a denial labels the repressed. A denial lets a careful listener know precisely what the object of an effort of repression is. On the other hand, a denial makes it clear to any listener that the patient does not accept the truth as it is labeled and thus revealed in a denial. Freud knows that the female figure represented—let us suppose as domineering—in the dream of the patient is in truth the patient's mother. But the denial of the patient states the contrary: that female figure is not my mother. Freud describes the ambiguity of this denial quite well when he writes: "It is as though the patient had said: 'It's true that my mother came into my mind as I thought of this person, but I don't feel inclined to let the association count" (ibid., p. 235). In a denial, a patient thus rejects or refuses to accept a true proposition.

Third, Freud informs us that therapy can promote further progress. Freud reports that it is possible to conquer "the negation as well and [bring] about a full intellectual acceptance of the repressed" (ibid., p. 236). He adds, however, that in this new phase "the repressive process itself is not yet removed" (ibid.). One can imagine that Freud asked the patient who dreamt about the female figure what eyes the female figure had, what hair, what clothes, what shoes, and so forth. If the patient was forced to recognize each time that the eyes, the hair, the clothes and the shoes of the figure all resembled those of her mother, she might then have concluded: "I guess it then must be my mother." Such an intellectual acknowledgment is clearly not a full emotional acknowledgment. As in the case of denial, here too there is a split between the intellectual and the affective processes.[6]

Clearly, this latter situation suggests the expected existence of a fourth stage in the process of denial wherein what is repressed is overcome both intellectually and affectively. One can imagine that the patient who dreamt about a domineering lady and who subsequently identified her as his mother is now able to solve the emotional conflict arising from the fact that the female figure is simultaneously a domineering figure and his mother. Freud does not provide us, in his article, with any hints of the steps that will have to be taken to achieve that fourth stage. In the rest of this chapter I will articulate insights derived from studying that fourth stage.[7]

FREUD'S METAPSYCHOLOGICAL REFLECTIONS

Having observed that the emotional reaction and the intellectual attitude toward a repressed phenomenon that reveals itself in a denial are different, one would have expected that Freud would have reflected on that difference. Instead, Freud uses most of the rest of the article on denial to explain how the intellectual function, that is, judging, is similar to and possibly emerges out of the affective life.[8] He makes use of the generally accepted distinction between an attributive and an existential judgment. In an attributive judgment one is concerned with whether an object—in Freud's examples, the ego—has a particular quality. Am I a person who insults people, has bad ideas about my mother, and so forth? An existential judgment must decide whether a representation exists only in my memory or in my mind, or, on the contrary, also exists in reality. Freud gives as example the child who imagines the mother's breast. An existential judgment must make the distinction between a representation to which nothing corresponds in reality and a representation that fits the reality.

In the process of reflecting on attributive judgments, Freud reminds us of a first metapsychological thesis that will be very useful to explain a puzzling aspect of denial. It will also give us a hint of the difficult road that must be traveled to undo a denial. The piece of psychoanalytic theory that Freud reminds us of is the thesis that the ego is a narcissistic construction whose judgments, at first, follow the pleasure principle and not the reality principle. Freud writes that "the original pleasure-ego wants to introject into itself everything that is good and to eject from itself everything that is bad. What is bad, what is alien to the ego and what is external are, to begin with, identical" (ibid., p. 237).

If we apply the just-reported part of psychoanalytic theory to the person who makes a denial, one must accept the proposition that the ego of that person does not follow the logic of the reality principle in which the truth is recognized even if it is unpleasant. Rather, the ego in that case follows the logic of what Freud calls the pleasure principle.[9] That logic is described as introjecting into oneself anything that is good and rejecting from oneself all that is bad. Such an explanation fits the examples given by Freud. Having insulting thoughts about someone one is dependent on, having a bad image of one's mother, or having attacks of headaches are all undesirable things. The logic of the pleasure principle demands that each of them be rejected as belonging to the original ego—all elements admitted under the logic of the pleasure principle necessarily having the narcissistically pleasing characteristics of being good and nothing else but good.

Enlightened by this Freudian idea, one is able to predict that fully undoing a denial will involve much more than epistemological work. It will involve addressing the ego's love of a narcissistic self-image. Giving up such a narcissistic image is for the ego to accept that it is less than what it thought it was and loved thinking itself to be. The great question is then: How will the person react to such a demand? Will she react with aggression? Will she mourn? Will she look for a creative way to somehow recover what she denied? Or finally, will she select a combination of these techniques?[10]

When reflecting on the judgment of existence, Freud develops a second metapsychological idea. He starts by pointing out that a judgment of existence is necessary when a person has developed a more realistic ego, an ego that obeys the reality principle. Freud himself gives the example of the infant who must be interested in distinguishing an imagined breast from an imagined breast that also exists (1895, I, pp. 327–330). An imagined breast or more generally a representation of something is by itself already a warrant of the existence of the represented thing because "the antithesis between subjective and objective does not exist from the first" (1925, p. 237). Freud then continues his argument by claiming that the opposition between the subjective and the objective is the result of the activities of the mind. The mind can bring before itself "once more something that has once been perceived, by reproducing it as a presentation without the external object having still to be there" (ibid.). Also "the reproduction of a perception as a presentation is not always a faithful one; it may be modified by omissions, or changed by the merging of various elements" (ibid., p. 238). The judgment of existence must then verify if the object that is presented by the mind is still there in reality. Freud is now ready to make his second metapsychological comment while reflecting on the process of denial. Freud writes: "The first and immediate aim, therefore, of reality-testing is, not to *find* an object in real perception which corresponds to the one presented, but to *refind* such an object, to convince oneself that it is still there" (ibid., pp. 237–238). Or "it is evident that a precondition for the setting up of reality-testing is that objects shall have been lost which once brought real satisfaction" (ibid., p. 238). This line of thinking by Freud suggests that truth telling as it is conditioned by judgments of existence requires more than the acquisition of the linguistic function of negation. *It also requires a nonlinguistic form of negativity.*[11] It requires that something that once provided real satisfaction has been lost. But such a loss cannot just be passively undergone. It will also have to be actively created. Some act of separation will have to be made.

Freud presents a third metapsychological idea when he concludes his reflections on judgments by arguing that he has been able to show the psychological origin of judgments because they make moves similar to those of the primary instincts. In attributive judgments—so Freud tell us—a characteristic of a thing is to be accepted and thus affirmed or is to be rejected and thus denied. In judgments of existence one wants to know whether a presentation of a thing is only a presentation and is thus to be considered worthless or whether on the contrary to the presentation there corresponds something real and thus the presentation is valuable because it corresponds to something that exists. Freud writes: "The polarity of judgments appears to correspond to the opposition of the two groups of instincts which we have supposed to exist. Affirmation—as a substitute for uniting—belongs to Eros; negation—the successor to expulsion—belongs to the instinct of destruction" (1926, p. 239). Freud thus makes the connection between judgments and emotions by means of three pairs of concepts. The first pair is *affirmation* and *negation*. The second pair is *substitute for uniting* and *successor to expulsion*. The third pair is *Eros* and *instinct of destruction*.

The last pair, Eros and instinct of destruction, expresses the polarity of human affectivity as Freud sees it. From early on Freud explained neurosis by means of the notion that a human being is a battlefield for different emotional forces. Originally, he thought that the basic opposition was between sexuality and ego forces. Sexuality assured reproduction. The ego assured self-preservation and expressed itself most strongly in hunger. Freud called the sexual energy libido.[12]

When Freud analyzed the problem of narcissism he noticed that the libido was directed not only toward the sexual object but also toward the ego itself. This insight destroyed the opposition between the libido (a force for reproduction) and the "ego force." In his essay *Beyond the Pleasure Principle*, Freud explicitly accepts this conclusion and therefore reduces both the ego instincts and the libido to one force, *Eros* (1920, pp. 44–61). The force opposing the libido (or love force) is the instinct of destruction (which in its ultimate form is the death drive). Thus, Freud reintroduces psychological duality.

The second pair, substitute for uniting and successor to expulsion, is a strange one. The way Freud labels them indicates that the two elements of the pair are not coequal; there is no symmetry between the two. The German word *Nachfolge* (successor) indicates that a prior action has taken place—referred to as expulsion. Freud's understanding of the way the original narcissistic ego constructs itself is consonant with the idea that it is a "successor." Indeed, Freud claims that the narcissistic ego is the result of—metaphorically—'spitting out of itself' what is considered bad (1925, p. 237). The German word *Ersatz* (substitute), on the other hand, is used for an object or a situation. The idea that something is a substitute presupposes that something precedes the substitute either in time or thought. The idea of unity does not include that same suggestion of a prior state as suggested by the idea of substitute. Could this mean that unity is the primary situation of the child, according to Freud, whereas rejection (spitting out) is a secondary reaction?[13]

The asymmetry signaled in the choice of labels for the second of the three pairs of words relating judgments and affective forces can be clarified further by reflecting on the central problem of this chapter: negation-denial. A denial presupposes, first, a connection between two facts, that is, a form of unity. A denial also presupposes that this connection was repressed. A negative judgment—particularly a denial—is then the expression of an original connection *and* of a trace of a prior repression, that is, a negation. An affirmative judgment expresses only a relation between the two contents. Whether there was a split between them is not expressed in an affirmative judgment. Thus an affirmative judgment has less expressive potential than a negative judgment. In an affirmative judgment one only affirms a connection or a unity. What preceded the connection cannot be expressed by an affirmative judgment.

This leads us to the first pair mentioned by Freud: the affirmative and the negative judgment. This pair too must consist of parts that are not equally important. The negative judgment has more expressive potential. Thus, it is understandable that Freud finishes the paragraph by underlining the central function of the symbol of negation. Negation expresses both a connection between two concepts and a rejection of that connection. When the negative sentence is a denial, then the negation is a sign of a repression that is simultaneously overcome and maintained at a new level.

Freud uses his metapsychological speculation of the connection between affective forces and judgments and the primacy of *Eros* to explain a clinical fact: the negativism of many psychotics.[14] Freud thinks that the negative attitude of this type of psychotic results from the withdrawal of the libidinal components of the instincts such that too much destructivity remains. A normal person thus seems to need a quantity of libido. This type of psychotic is then one who lives in a degenerated situation because of a lack of sufficient libido. Psychosis is here explained as degeneration. In his essay, *The Ego and the Id* (1923, pp. 40–47, especially pp. 40–42), Freud talks about the mixing of the libido and the aggressive tendencies. Here, Freud takes a developmental point of view. The libido in the child develops, according to him, from an oral to a genital phase. This happens, says Freud, through addition of erotic components. The regression from a genital to an anal-sadistic libido is the result of the disappearance of the erotic elements. In these reflections Freud moves from his epistemological problem of denial to anthropological concerns about the development of libidinal and aggressive tendencies. It is a connection that will prove very valuable for exploring an aspect of denial that Freud did not explicitly address: the full undoing of a denial.

SPECIFICATIONS AND CORRECTIONS OF FREUD'S REFLECTIONS

However influential this short paper of Freud's has been, it is important to show its limitations. First, Freud seems to have a misconception of his own analysis. Freud claims to be analyzing the function of judgments. In fact Freud is not analyzing judgments but rather is analyzing the prehistory of judgments. Using Merleau-Ponty's terminology, one could say that Freud is sketching the preverbal history of the judgment. In that preverbal history Freud emphasizes the great importance of the acquisition of the linguistic symbol of negation. In so doing Freud either overlooks or fails to emphasize two other dimensions in a person's prehistory.[15] The first dimension hidden behind the emphasis of the importance of the linguistic symbol of negation is the fact that everything needs to be elevated to the level of language. It is not the case that the requirement of elevating something to the linguistic level is restricted to the act of repressing or negating. Lacan understood this when he interpreted Freud's concept of *"Bejahung"* (affirmation) in the pair *"Bejahung-Verneinung"* as a "saying yes" to the symbolic system in general.

Independent of the psychoanalytic tradition, Hegel also seems to have understood the requirement that human beings need to elevate needs and feeling to the level of language. Hegel does not use the word language but points to a requirement that must produce two characteristics consonant with elevating things to the level of language. Thus, Hegel writes: "as the feeling too is itself particular and bound up with a special corporeal form, it follows that . . . the subject . . . is still susceptible of disease, so far as to remain fast in a *special* phase of its self-feeling, unable to refine it to 'ideality' and get the better of it" (Hegel, 1971, #408, pp. 122–123). Bringing feelings (and needs) to the level of 'ideality' allows free subjectivity to assign feelings and needs the relative places that subjectivity wants and needs to assign them. By elevating feelings and needs to 'ideality' consciousness acquires a form of fluidity (ibid., p. 124) compatible with the requirement of freedom. Such a consciousness can then proscribe to itself "behaviour which follows from its individual position and its connection with the external world, which is no less a world of laws" (ibid., p. 123). If consciousness is unable to elevate a particular feeling to 'ideality,' then consciousness "is engrossed with a single phase of feeling, it fails to assign that phase its proper place and due subordination in the individual system of the world which a conscious subject is" (ibid., p. 123). Consequently, such "a feeling with a fixed corporeal embodiment sets [itself] up against the whole mass of adjustments forming the concrete consciousness" (ibid., p. 124).

I interpret Hegel's claim that human beings must elevate feelings and needs to 'ideality' as similar to the Lacanian claim that human beings need to insert themselves with all their needs and wishes into the world of language so as to make all and each of these needs and wishes interconnected and thus relative. Failing to do so leads, according to both Lacan and Hegel, to mental illness.[16] By overemphasizing the great importance of replacing repression by a linguistic negation, Freud neglects to bring out the important point that the whole of life needs to be elevated to a linguistic world.

The second dimension hidden behind Freud's emphasis on the importance of the linguistic form of negation is the prehistory of negation with its effort at separation and the aggression involved in it. Freud does mention that the "the original pleasure-ego wants . . . to eject from itself everything that is bad. What is bad, what is alien to the ego and what is external are, to begin with, identical" (1925, p. 237). Spitz does not just mention that prehistory of negation, he also analyzes it. In particular, he analyzes the function of aggression related to saying "no" (Spitz, 1957, pp. 51–52, 56–59, 130–133).

Spitz starts by pointing to the fact that prior to the acquisition of saying "no," at about fifteen months of age, the child's relation to its mother undergoes a drastic change. As the child begins to crawl and/or walk, the child moves away from the mother and does things that might endanger it. The mother, acting as the external ego of the child, constantly issues prohibitions in word and gesture. These prohibitions force the child into passivity and are experienced as frustrations. Among the most frequently returning means for the mother's expressing prohibitions is the use of the word "no." According to Spitz, the child responds to the frustrations resulting from the prohibitions in progressively more complicated ways. First, the child sides with the adult who prohibits and does what the adult wants—for example, not touching an electric outlet (Spitz, 1957, p. 56). However, such a reaction leads to unacceptable frustrations for the child. Furthermore, the passivity that is forced on it provokes an aggressive reaction from the child's unconscious. The child is thus put in a paradoxical situation: it is still in a very dependent relation with the maternal figure while also feeling aggression toward that same figure. Spitz believes that the child solves this tension by identifying with its mother as an aggressor (ibid., pp. 56, 133).[17] By such a move the child dynamically satisfies both contradictory feelings. In consequence, the child acquires the gesture of saying "no" and is now able to use that gesture with all the frustration and aggression attached to it. Finally, the child can make use of the newly acquired word (or gesture) either against itself or against the mother. In using the no-saying against itself the child creates a cleavage within itself between itself as an object observed and as an observer (Spitz, 1957, pp. 130, 133). In using the no-saying against a person with whom the child has "primary narcissistic dependent relations" (ibid., p. 56), the child severs its dependency relations with that other person (p. 52) and establishes its own separateness (p. 57). From then on the child will have to establish a new kind of relation with that person. Spitz calls those new relations "highly enriched" (ibid., pp. 57, 129, 131). By means of a case I will study in the next section, I will demonstrate that the acts of separation and severing involved in no-saying lead to the need to introduce metaphorical relations. The linguistic form of negation will thus lead us by means of the idea of separation and the idea of aggression hidden in acts of separation to the appearance of the phenomenon of metaphor.[18]

COMPLETING FREUD'S REFLECTIONS

By overstressing the importance of the acquisition of the linguistic symbol of negation, Freud undervalued in his study of denial the importance of two

dimensions in human growth: the acts of separation with the implied aggression behind no-saying and the many other functions of language besides the
one provided by the linguistic symbol of negation. I will now illustrate these
claims by a concrete case of denial and the person's successful efforts at
overcoming such a denial.

In *Father, Son, and Healing Ghosts*, the author, Anthony Moore, provides us with an autobiographical account of dealing with the death of his
father who perished on a battlefield in the Second World War when the
author was a two-month-old infant. The young Moore developed several
strategies to deal with that traumatic event in his life. He identified so much
with his father—the dead marine officer—and imitated him so much that
the young Moore at one point felt that "he was unable to be [himself]"
(Moore, 2000, p. 4).[19] At the same time, when asked about his feelings about
the loss of his father, Moore had the habit, from his childhood on, of answering: "You can't miss what you never had" (p. 1). This is clearly a denial, since
the statement goes together with the attempt of erasing the pain of the loss
of the father by a suffocating imitation and identification with the father. We
find traces of the pain inflicted—even self-inflicted—on the young Moore
when we discover that he developed two fantasies related to the death of his
father. Born April 16, 1944, shortly before his father's death on June 15,
1944, the young Moore developed the fantasy that there must not have been
space enough in the world for both of them together and thus he was the
cause of his father's death. He further felt that if he were to father a child
that would be his own death warrant (pp. 3, 98).

Undoing intellectually his denial that he did not miss his father was
made possible—in accord with Freud's own reported examples—by the help
of a therapist, who in the case of Moore said: "You can also miss what you
never had but know you had every right to have" (p. 4). Undoing emotionally the conflict and healing the wound behind the denial is a more complicated story.

First, Moore's efforts at distancing himself from the idealization of his
father were crucial. After having spent his high-school years with dedication
and enthusiasm in a military high school, the young Moore avoided ROTC
in college. He gives as his reason that he felt he "had had enough of the
military" (p. 2). By his senior year, Moore returned to his love for the Marines
and took the entrance exam for the Marine Corps Officer Candidate School.
Thus, the first attempt at separation from his identification with his father
did not stick. A second and new form of separation from the identification
with his father was initiated by his mother (and grandmother). When he
told them about his plans to enroll in the Marine Officer School while the
Vietnam War was taking place, the young Moore saw in their eyes either
their fear of his death or their disapproval of his risking his life. Thus, his
mother (and grandmother) put a wedge between the young Moore and his
father. The young Moore accepted the invitation of his mother and grand-

mother to make the separation from his idealized father because of his own wish to live.

Moore himself tells us that once he had separated himself from his father's identity he felt the need "to reconnect to the energy and meaning that continued to flow from the image of [his] father" (p. 5). Moore thus found himself in the contradictory situation that he wanted to be both separate from and connected with his father. He found a solution to this challenge in what in Lacanian terminology is called a metaphoric move.[20] Having refused to become a Marine because that might lead to death, the young Moore lost an important connection with his father. Moore recovered that connection with his father by becoming a Jesuit. Moore writes about this decision: "Being a Jesuit was like being a Marine. Sometimes the Jesuits were even referred to as the Pope's Marines. Furthermore, the idea of joining a religious order carried with it an image of dying, dying to the world, particularly the world of marital love" (p. 3).[21] By the metaphorical power of the words "Marine" and "dying" the younger Moore was able to reconnect with his father after having separated himself from him.

The metaphorical power hidden in being a Jesuit was not able to unify the life of the young Moore. He writes that "the life of celibacy left me feeling empty and alone. I missed the warmth and understanding of close friendships with women" (p. 3). Furthermore, he was still haunted by the two malignant fantasies that he was the cause of his father's death and that his fathering a child would lead to his death.

By leaving the Jesuits, Moore separated himself again from his father by cutting the metaphoric connection that he had established earlier. Moore then contacted the soldiers from his father's unit. He received from them two crucial pieces of information. The first piece of information was the warmly told story of how the younger Moore's father had, by gambling, lost his family's money for the remainder of the month. This information allowed Moore to de-idealize his father. Moore describes the effects of learning about his father's gambling peccadillo this way: "His human shortcomings made him more alive, more real for me. He was no longer a perfect, idealized hero, but a man of flesh and blood who could be foolish, make mistakes and get into the kind of trouble from which his wife had to rescue him. Learning about my father's peccadillos was a liberating experience. Trying to be the perfect son of an ideal father was a burden that often got in the way of my being myself. . . . Just thinking about my father in this way created a more balanced hero archetype for me to follow. Another gap in my fatherless childhood was being filled" (pp. 67–68).

The second useful piece of information that the young Moore received from the soldier friends of his father was details about what his father did in the last battle that he survived. In that battle, the battle for Roi-Namur, Lieutenant Moore's mortar platoon was positioned 125 yards from the end of the island with the remaining enemy forces in-between. Moore possessed a firing table for the 60-mm mortar guns indicating the angle of elevation for various distances. Unfortunately, the firing table did not provide the angles for distances of less than 200 yards and was therefore completely useless in the final hours of the battle for Roi-Namur (p. 94). This fact must have been very disturbing to Lt. Moore as it put his men in avoidable deadly danger. When actually resting in Maui after the battle of Roi-Namur Lt. Moore took corrective action. "Lt. Moore and Burke Dixon spent the afternoon of Easter Sunday firing a mortar and calculating the approximate angle of elevation for distances of 100, 125, 150, and 175 yards. The lieutenant then wrote the corresponding ranges and settings in blue ink at the top of the firing table" (p. 97). Easter Sunday was the last day about which the younger Moore was able to get detailed personal information concerning the activities of his father before he was killed on the first day of the attack on Saipan. Consulting his calendar, the younger Moore dated Easter in 1944 as April 9. Moore himself was born the next Sunday, April 16, 1944. Lt. Moore died June 15, 1944. The younger Moore used the information about his father's activity on Easter 1944, a week before his own birth, to undo the deadly grip of his own unconscious beliefs resulting from the temporal sequence April 16, 1944 (his birth) and June 15, 1944 (his father's death). Here is how Moore himself describes the transformation of his unconscious beliefs: "The new date, April 9, opened the possibility of an alternative temporal sequence, April 9 and April 16, a sequence that suggested a different pattern of meaning: two Sundays bracketing the First Week of Easter. Instead of associating my birth (April 16) with my father's death (June 15), I could now link my birth with a day in my father's life (April 9), an Easter Sunday celebrating our birth to new life in Christ's Resurrection. By joining our two lives together at the beginning and end of Easter Week, the dates of April 9 and April 16 provided a life-giving sequence to counterbalance the deadly sequence of April 16 and June 15" (p. 98). The life-giving time sequence resulted from the sacred time of Easter that calls on Christians to have hope. What was the hope that the younger Moore experienced or created that could counterbalance the deadly belief that his birth caused his father's death?

Moore gives us an answer himself. Meditating on the love letters of his father to his mother, the younger Moore writes: "Reading about his hopes and dreams for the future—dreams that had appeared to die on the beach of Saipan—I saw clearly that the heart of those dreams had come true in my own life. I had been privileged and blessed to live the life he had dreamed of living" (p. 105). The younger Moore now understands his deepest gifts and commitments to be both *his gifts* and commitments and at the same time the *fulfillment of his father's dreams*. Moore understands himself to be both himself and himself as a gift in the life of his father. By the metaphor of being a Pascal gift to his father, the younger Moore was able to overrule the unconscious fantasy that he had killed his father because there was no room for both of them. Now he feels that he is his father's dream come true. Moore is now able to appreciate and commit himself to the talents and values that he feels to be uniquely his own. He has thus undone his original denial, the painful experience at its root, and the malignant fantasies created to deal with the original pain.

DENIAL AND SELF-DECEPTION

The analysis of Moore's undoing of his denial can also help us clarify the concept of self-deception. One is right in saying that the younger Moore deceived himself when he was telling himself and others during his adolescence that he could not miss his father since he never had one. One is also right in saying that the younger Moore did not know that he was deceiving himself. He only knew that he had been deceiving himself after he was helped by his psychiatrist-psychoanalyst who told him that one can also miss what one never had but know that one had every right to have.[22] At that moment the younger Moore knew that he had been deceiving himself; he knew that his claim that one cannot miss a father one never had was a denial. One can therefore claim that it is possible to deceive oneself without knowing that one is deceiving oneself. Self-deception is thus, strictly speaking, not a lie. It becomes a lie only after the moment in which a denial has been intellectually undone and the person refuses to do the emotional work involved in taking the steps implied by the intellectual undoing.

Self-deception and denial require that one accept at least two layers of intentionality. In Moore's case one is able to clearly see these two layers at work. First, there is the conscious ego that ostensibly organizes Moore's life. The ego decides to go to military school or take the entrance exam for the Marine Corps Officer Candidate School, but not to enter ROTC in college. However, another layer of Moore, let us use the Freudian label—the unconscious—performed its own intentional acts. Long before the conscious ego made its adolescent decisions, Moore's unconscious had already interpreted the death of his father and had deeply identified with the dead father. This unconscious layer itself makes interpretations with a logic that Freud refers to as a primary process. One crucial feature of the logic of interpretation of the unconscious is that the child gives itself a form of omnipotence. In an illusionary way, the child feels that it causes all important events around itself. Thus, when Moore's father dies a short time after he is born, the younger Moore feels, unconsciously, that he caused the death of his father. He also feels that fathering a child will guarantee imminent death. Similarly, the younger Moore unconsciously idealizes and identifies with the dead father, who was so beloved by his mother. Moore's conscious ego deals with the paradox of unconscious ideations (unconscious guilt for the father's death, and idealization and identification with the dead father) by, on the one hand, making decisions that allow him to be like the father and, on the other hand, publicly denying that he misses the dead father. The healing work Moore performed starts the moment he accepts that he is a multilay-ered person who possesses a conscious ego that needs to listen to a voice beyond itself. Furthermore, the conscious ego accepts the humility entailed in listening to that other deeper voice. The conscious ego thereby accepts that it has to change.

Self-deception can be ascribed to a person by an outsider when that outsider can see several forms of interpretation at work that contradict each other. And this is the case even if the observed person is not consciously aware of the contradictory interpretations. Ascribing the status of self-deception to a person at a moment when that person is not aware of the self-deception is a teleological move. Implicit in the ascription is the expectation that the person with multiple layers is called on to act as a unified person.[23] However, aiding in that teleological move requires that one be artful. In order to be helpful one should not accuse the conflicted person of self-deceit. Rather, one should say the appropriate words so that the other can intellec-tually undo his or her own denial and thereby accept an invitation to differ-ently address the paradox behind the self-deceit. As we have seen, that requires psychic work including acts of separating oneself from caregivers and the creation of appropriate metaphors.

CONCLUSION

Freud praised the linguistic symbol of negation as a great instrument of freedom. It would be wrong, however, to attribute the healing of Tony Moore simply to the magic power of the symbol of negation in his fundamental denial. The healing was also based on several acts of cutting himself loose from his father and on the two great metaphors of being a Jesuit and being a Pascal gift to his father. I believe that I have been able to show that Freud's analysis of the function of negation is but the tip of an iceberg in the process of healing. The iceberg includes at least the idea that one has to cut oneself loose from others with all the aggression (and guilt) that this involves and the idea that the richness of language must be used in its many dimensions, including the metaphoric dimension made available by the cultural tradition in which one lives. I was able to rely on Spitz for pointing out the negative acts required for personal growth. I was able to rely on Lacan and Hegel to point to the requirement that the totality of human life needs to be elevated to the level of language. Clearly, correcting the epistemological mistake present in a denial requires addressing the great anthropological puzzles of human growth with its demand for aggressive separation from and creative (meta-phorical) connection with our original caregivers. Not properly dealing with the demand for separation and connection with his father was for Moore a form of self-deception even before he formulated a denial. When Moore formulated his denial, it was possible for others to see the self-deception at work. Only when Moore was able to intellectually undo his denial was Moore confronted with the choice of lying to himself or being authentic. As I see it, Moore avoided lying to himself because he was willing to face the difficult emotional demands made on him in order to deal in a different way with the need to separate himself from his father while satisfying his need to remain connected with him. Thus, although the concepts of denial, self-deception, and lying about oneself partially overlap, they are not identical and should be carefully distinguished.

NOTES

1. This chapter will therefore analyze territory not covered by the classic commentators on Freud's article on "Negation (Denial)" (Freud, S.E., 1925, 235–239): Lacan, Spitz, Hyppolite, and Ricoeur (1970, 314–318), to name a few. For a survey of the commentaries on Freud's article see W. Ver Eecke: Saying 'No,' 2–11. The above-mentioned commentators concentrate on the crucial Freudian claim that human beings discover unpleasant truths about themselves by means of a denial. By analyzing the new territory of the effort of undoing a denial, I will be able to establish a connection between the psychoanalytic concept of denial and the philosophical concept of self-deception. Curiously enough, the analytic philosophers examining the problem of self-deception do not pay attention to the function of denial as the crucial interface between unconscious self-deception and facing the truth by undoing one's self-deception as it appears in a denial. See the anthology by Brian P. McLaughlin and Amélie O. Rorty.

2. Negation is both the linguistic sign of negation and the negative judgment using a linguistic sign of negation. Denial is a negative judgment wrongly denying the truth presented in a negative judgment.

3. The correctness of this date is in doubt.

4. In discussing boasting Freud comes close to saying that the activity of the unconscious that is constitutive for a denial is the linguistic activity of labeling something unknown. Let me quote the relevant text of Freud again: "what was already present as a finished product in the unconscious was beginning to show through indistinctly [to consciousness]" (Freud, 1895, II, 76, n. 1). I take the expression "finished product" to mean that the unknown was labeled.

5. For an example see Ver Eecke (1984, 145). The patient deeply desires to be home when her son visits town. Yet she does not dare to ask from the nun who is director of the asylum for the permission to leave—a permission regularly granted—because: "What would that sister think of me?"

6. Freud writes that this intellectual acknowledgment without emotional acceptance is "a very important and somewhat strange variant" of that same split in a denial (Freud, S.E., 1925, 236). I understand the rest of the article to be an attempt by Freud to ponder the relation and the split between the intellectual and the affective. His main argument and contribution is the claim that, notwithstanding the split between the intellectual and the affective, it is possible to demonstrate the dependence of the intellectual on the affective.

7. Hyppolite indicates the complexity of such undoing by using Hegel's concept of aufheben 'to overcome' as a matrix for such undoing (Ver Eecke, 1984, 25–27). Later on, I will be able to do more than indicate the complexity of undoing a denial.

I will provide a careful phenomenological description of that process as a basis for a number of anthropological conclusions.

8. In cognitive science, one would call that an emergent property.

9. I therefore agree with A. O. Rorty when she stresses that human beings organize their psychic life at different levels. She makes that claim a precondition for the possibility of self-deception: "Relying on the details of modular theories of all kinds, the second picture (of multiple layers of self-organization) explains our hospitality to self-deception and other forms of irrationality" (Rorty, 23). Freud's thesis is one step stronger than Rorty's in that Freud argues that the different layers in a human being follow a different logic in their interpretation of events: the logic of primary processes and of the pleasure ego (like in dreams, jokes, or fantasies) or, on the contrary, the logic of secondary processes and of the reality ego (rational arguments). One can therefore expect that the effort of unification in a person will not be achieved solely by the logic used in secondary processes. The secondary process logic might be able to recognize a self-deception (Rorty, 25). However, one cannot expect that the secondary processes will have the resources to undo a self-deception or a denial since these phenomena are also controlled by the logic of primary processes. In fact, the case of Anthony Moore will teach us that undoing self-deception or denial owes a lot, among other factors that might be mentioned, to metaphoric work.

One can make a similar argument in the technical language of Lacan when he argues that the challenge to human beings is that they must master the experience of the real. They can do so by the totally different logics of the imaginary or the symbolic. The imaginary is not identical to Freud's primary processes and the symbolic is not identical to Freud's secondary processes or the philosophical concept of the rational. Since the symbolic is closely connected with language, we can understand Lacan's symbolic to subsume the rational or secondary processes of Freud. I have argued elsewhere (Ver Eecke, 2001) that therapeutic interventions with mentally ill people, such as schizophrenics, must take account of the fact that the schizophrenic has deficiencies both in the imaginary and in the symbolic register. Furthermore, a different logic applies to the two registers. Failure to respect the distinction between these two registers or failure to respect the difference in logic between them makes the therapeutic intervention ineffective or counterproductive. The Lacanian framework, just like the Freudian, confirms Rorty's idea that human beings have different layers of interpretation while making the stronger claim that these interpretations obey different logics.

10. Oedipus becomes aggressive toward Teiresias when the latter tells him an unpleasant truth. Forced to recognize at the end of the play the unpleasant truth announced by Teiresias, Oedipus mourns even his existence. In Ibsen's *Ghosts*, at the end of the play, Mrs. Alvin mourns the fact that she brought no brightness into the home of her husband and child but instead believed obstinately in duty and thus contributed to the despair of her own son (Ibsen, *Collected Works*, VII, 277–278).

11. It is curious that Freud draws explicit attention to the great importance of the acquisition of the linguistic function of negation but does not further conceptualize the negative moment postulated by his claim that the object of a judgment of existence must first have been lost. In the following pages, I will argue that acts of separation and the obvious or hidden forms of aggression accompanying such acts of separation will have to play an important role in the development of a person and thus also in undoing a denial and thereby restoring wholesomeness in that person.

12. Freud himself has given a survey of the development of his theory about this problem (Freud, S.E., 1930, 117–122). For an extensive discussion of this same problem, see S.E., 1915m 113–116.

13. One can find in the writings of Donald Winnicott (1991, pp. 86–94) confirmation of such a psychoanalytic interpretation of the development of the child. Winnicott argues that the child has the need to have the illusion or the experience of fusion with the mother. He also argues that the aggression of the child against the mother is necessary for the child to have confidence in the mother. The child, so Winnicott argues, believes in the all-powerfulness of its aggression. It thus fears that its aggression will kill the mother. If the mother responds to the aggression of the child with rejection, then the child will feel that its aggression is able to destroy the good object. If the mother continues to relate warmly to the child, the child feels that its aggression is not effective. The good object, the good mother, survives the aggression of the child. Such a mother is not the product of the imagination. Such a mother really exists. In such a view of child development, fusion precedes separation. Between the two stands aggression. This aggression can take many forms such as biting when nursing, or saying 'no' to the mother's offer of something the child obviously likes.

14. Elsewhere Freud refers to two authors who studied this phenomenon: Bleuler and Gross (Freud, S.E., VIII, 175, n. 2).

15. One can find texts in Freud's article on "Negation," where Freud seems to touch on the two dimensions I discuss later. But touching on a subject matter is not the same as emphasizing its importance.

16. I am, of course, not arguing that Hegel already discovered the Lacanian understanding that all mental illnesses can be articulated in their structure by their relative success or failure with respect to the paternal metaphor. I am arguing that Hegel's requirement of elevating feelings and needs to 'ideality' has great similarities with Lacan's requirement that human beings must accept their insertion into the world of language or into the symbolic system. Hegel gives as example of a mentally derailed person who was not able to elevate his desire to 'ideality' the case of an "Englishman who had hanged himself, [and] on being cut down by his servant not only regained the desire to live but also the disease of avarice; for when discharging the servant, he deducted twopence from his wages because the man had acted without instructions in cutting the rope with which his master had hanged himself" (Hegel, 1971, 134).

17. Spitz acknowledges his debt for this idea to Anna Freud in her work *The Ego and the Mechanisms of Defense* (Spitz, 1957, 45–48).

18. Authors other than Spitz have made us aware of the constitutive function of aggression in the development of human infants. For instance, Melanie Klein makes the paranoid-schizoid position a necessary phase in the child's development (Hanna Segal, 1989, 112–121) . Winnicott, on the other hand, points to the function of aggression in establishing the trustworthiness of the caring person. As mentioned before, Winnicott (1991) argues that the experience of one's own aggression and the experience of the benign reaction of the mother allows the child to establish that the caring mother is not subject to the effects of its own aggression, which the child feels to be omnipotent. The child feels that its aggression is not able to destroy the good mother. Such a mother acquires the status of an independent and thus trustworthy object (i.e., a person) (90).

19. The importance of this idea for the young Moore is obvious since within the space of two pages he repeats it several times. Thus he writes: "I needed to distinguish my own identity from my father's so I could live my own life"(4) and "By allowing my grandfather to assume a role within my conscious identity, I was able to establish some sense of identity distinct from my father" (4–5) and finally "Some separation from my father's identity was necessary for me to be free to lead my own life" (5).

20. A metaphoric move is a move whereby a subject accepts a different identity while still feeling to be the same person because a word is able to express the great similarity between the two identities.

21. Moore seems to understand that unconscious forces were at work in his decision to become a Jesuit when he writes: "When I entered the Jesuits, I was twenty-three years old. Only years later did I realize that was the same age my father was when he died" (3).

22. Rorty proposes a similar thesis when she writes: "We certainly think we can recognize self-deception in others, and we strongly suspect it in ourselves, even *retrospectively attributing it to our past selves*" (Italics mine) (Rorty, 1988, 22).

23. Contrary to Rorty, I see self-deception as the result of a person's having at least two layers of intentionality and these two layers following a different logic in their interpretation of experiences of the world. Rorty proposes a further condition for self-deception when she writes: "Not everyone has the special talents and capacities for self-deception. It is a disease only the presumptively strong minded can suffer" (Rorty, 1988, 25). Rorty interprets strongmindedness as the capability to superimpose on a multilayered intentionality the will to rational unity. I want to argue that the will to rational unity leads to a denial, not a self-deception. Furthermore, Moore's case, as I analyze it, demonstrates that the ability to discover the truth in a denial as opposed to simply living in self-deception should not be called strongmindedness. Rather, discovering the truth hidden in a denial is the result of the help of another, who in this case spoke the proper words so that Moore could accept the pain that had necessitated the self-deception. By relating the concept of denial to that of self-deception I am forced to disagree twice with Rorty's understanding of self-deception. To put it in a different way: for me it seems that many people can and do deceive themselves; fewer are able to articulate the deception in the form of a denial; fewer still are able to intellectually undo such denials and come to understand that they denied something and were thus subject to self-deception; fewer still are able to do the psychic work demanded to face up to the implications of the discovery of their denial or self-deception.

REFERENCES

Freud, A. (1936). *The Ego and the Mechanism of Defence*. London: Hogarth.

Freud, S. (1895). *S.E. Vol 1: Project for a Scientific Psychology* (Vol. 1, pp. 281–397). London: Hogarth.

Freud, S. (1895). *S.E. Vol 2: Studies on Hysteria* [With J.Breuer's contributions] (Vol. 2). London: Hogarth.

Freud, S. (1915). Instincts and their Vicissitudes. In *S.E.* (Vol. 14, pp. 109–140). London: Hogarth.

Freud, S. (1920). Beyond the Pleasure Principle. In *S.E.* (Vol. 18, pp. 1–64). London: Hogarth.

Freud, S. (1923). The Ego and the Id. In S.E. (Vol. 19, pp. 1–59). London: Hogarth.

Freud, S. (1925). Negation. In S.E. (Vol. 19, pp. 235–240). London: Hogarth.

Freud, S. (1930). Civilization and its Discontents. In S.E. (Vol. 21, pp. 57–148). London: Hogarth.

Freud, S. (1953–1974). The Standard Edition of the Complete Psychological Works of Sigmund Freud. Ed. and trans. J. Strachey. (Vol. 1–24). London: Hogarth.

Hegel, G. (1971). Hegel's Philosophy of Mind. Trans. W. Wallace and A. Miller. Oxford: Clarendon Press, 1807.

Hyppolite, J. (1988). A spoken commentary on Freud's "Verneinung." Trans. J. Forrester. In The Seminar of Jacques Lacan. Book I. Freud's Papers on Technique. 1953–1954. Ed. J. Miller. (pp. 289–297). New York: W.W. Norton.

Ibsen, H. (1908). The collected works. 11 Vols. Vol VII: Ghosts. Ed. W. Archer. New York: Scribner's.

Lacan, J. (1988). Introduction and Reply to Jean Hyppolite's presentation of Freud's "Verneinung." (Trans. J. Forrester). In The Seminar of Jacques Lacan. Book I. Freud's Papers on Technique. 1953–1954 Ed. J. Miller. (pp. 52–61). New York: W.W. Norton.

McLaughlin, B. P., & Rorty, A. O. (Ed.). (1988). Perspectives on Self-Deception. Berkeley: University of California Press.

Moore, A. (2000). Father, Son, and Healing Ghosts. Gainesville, Fl: Center for Applications of Psychological Type.

Ricoeur, P. (1970). Freud and Philosophy. Trans. D. Savage. New Haven: Yale University Press.

Rorty, A. O. (1988). The Deceptive Self: Liars, Layers, and Lairs. In B. P. McLaughlin & A. O. Rorty (Eds.), Perspectives on Self-Deception. Berkeley: University of California Press.

Segal, H. (1989). Klein. London: Karnac Books.

Sophocles. (1982). The Three Theban Plays. Antigone, Oedipus the King, Oedipus at Colonus. Trans. R. Fagles. New York: Penguin Books.

Spitz, R. A. (1957). No and Yes. On the genesis of human communication. New York: International Universities Press, Inc.

Ver Eecke, W. (1984). Saying 'No.' Pittsburgh: Duquesne University Press.

Ver Eecke, W. (2001). Lacan's theory, Karon's Psychoanalytic Treatment of Schizophrenics. Psychoanalysis and Contemporary Thought, 24(1), 79–105.

Winnicott, D. W. (1991). Playing and Reality. London and New York: Routledge.

SEVEN

THE *I* AND THE *IT*

JON MILLS

FREUD NEVER ACTUALLY used the words "ego" and "id" in his German texts; these are English translations into Latin taken from one of his most famous works, *Das Ich und das Es*.[1] When Freud spoke of the *Ich*, he was referring to the personal pronoun I—as in I myself—a construct that underwent many significant theoretical transformations throughout his lifetime. By the time Freud advanced his mature model of the psyche, concluding that even a portion of the *I* was also unconscious, he needed to delimit a region of the mind that remained purely concealed from consciousness. This he designated by the impersonal pronoun *es*, which he used as a noun—the *It*, a term originally appropriated from Nietzsche. The translation, *ego*, displaces the deep emotional significance tied to personal identity that Freud deliberately tried to convey, while the term *id* lacks the customary sense of unfamiliarity associated with otherness, thus rendering these concepts antiseptic, clinical, and devoid of all personal associations. The *I* and the *It* expresses more precisely the type of antithesis Freud wanted to emphasize between the familiar and the strange, hence the dialectic of the life within.

When we refer to ourselves as 'I,' we convey a meaning that is deeply personal, subjective, and known, while references to an 'It' convey distance, separateness, objectification, and abstraction. The I is familiar while the It is foreign and unknown, hence an alien presence. Because Freud wanted to preserve the individual intimacy associated with a personal sense of self, the I was to stand in firm opposition to the It, which was purely estranged from conscious awareness. But the distinction between the I and the It is not altogether unambiguous, and, as I will argue, not theoretically resolved by Freud himself. In fact, even psychoanalysis today in all its rich theoretical

127

variations has not rectified this issue. While Freud (1923, pp. 24–25, 38; 1926, p. 97; 1933, pp. 76–77; 1940, p. 145) eventually conceded that the I developed out of the It, he did not explain with any detail how this activity was accomplished; he merely declared that it just happened.

It is my contention that postclassical through contemporary psychoanalytic thought still suffers from ambiguity surrounding the ill-defined nature of the development of the I from the It that has either been taken as a mere propositional assumption within psychoanalytic theory, or has been subverted by alternative paradigms that boast to have surpassed Freud while subsuming his model within an overarching metahistorical paradigm. But a persisting, endemic problem to psychoanalysis is the absence of any *philosophical* attempt to account for genesis, namely, the origins of psychic reality. It is not enough to say that psychic experience begins as unconsciousness and progresses to consciousness, from drive to reason, from the It to the I: we must be able to show how these primordial processes *originally* transpire and sequentially unfold into dynamic patterns of organized mental life. Relational, interactionist, and intersubjective accounts focus on the interpersonally elaborated psychosocial matrix that defines, nurtures, and sustains the existence of the self (see Kohut, 1984; Mitchell, 1988; Stern, 1985; Stolorow & Atwood, 1992); and we have every reason to appreciate these exciting advances in our conceptual understanding of psychic development. However, without exception, these schools of thought have not addressed the a priori conditions that make the emergence of the self possible to begin with, that is, the ontological ground and moments of inception of psychic reality.

We have reason to believe that the I and the It are not ontologically differentiated; nor is it to be accepted at face value that the I does in fact develop from the It. What is missing in previous developmental accounts is any detailed attempt to chronicle the very processes that bring the I and the It into being in the first place. Throughout this chapter, I will be preoccupied with what I call the genesis problem, namely, Beginning—the origins of unconscious life. By way of dialectical analysis, I will trace the means in which such primitive processes acquire organization, differentiation and integration, teleological progression, self-constitutive identity, and psychic cohesion. While Freud articulated the fundamental intrapsychic forces that beset human life, he did not attend to these ontological-transmutational concerns. It is my intention to offer a dialectical account of the coming into being of the I and the It, or what I call the ego and the abyss, and show how psychoanalytic process psychology provides an adequate solution to the question and nature of unconscious maturation.

CONCEPTUALIZING THE PSYCHE

When Freud refers to the mind, he is referring to the Greek notion *psyche*, which corresponds to the German term *Seele*. In fact, Freud does not speak of the 'mental apparatus' at all but instead the 'organization of the soul' that he specifically equates with the psyche. Freud adopted this usage as early as 1905 when he emphatically said: " 'Psyche' is a Greek word and its German translation is 'soul.' Psychical treatment hence means 'treatment of the soul' " [*Seelenbehandlung*] (1905b, p. 283). Furthermore, Freud (1933, 1940) equates psychoanalysis with the science of the life of the soul (*wer die Wissenschaft vom Seelenleben liebt*), which stands in stark contrast to the biological connotations associated with the English word "mind" (see Bettelheim, 1982, pp. 71–75).

Freud was well read in ancient philosophy; Plato's notion of the soul, as well as his depiction of Eros, left a lasting impression on Freud's conceptualization of the psyche. Before we proceed, however, it is important to distinguish between what we mean by psyche, self, I or ego, and the It. Historically, psychoanalysis, like other professions, has the propensity of using highly technical jargon to capture the complexities of human mental functioning. This is patently justified, but it posses a problem in conceptual discourse and mutual understanding, especially when concepts remain murky or are presumed to have universal definitions when in fact they mean many different things to different theorists and philosophic disciplines. So that we may avoid equivocation of our terms, let us begin with a conceptual definition of the I.

The I or ego has a special significance for Freud associated with personal identity, self-reference, conscious thought, perception, mobility, reality testing, and the higher executive functions of reason and intelligence. *Das Ich* is not a common German expression used in everyday conversation: it is used only by professionals in a quasi-scientific context.[2] Neither are references to the self (*Selbst*) or the subject (*Subjekt*) common parlance. In fact, to refer to oneself as "*mein Ich*" or "*mein Selbst*" would be viewed as being exceedingly narcissistic. The term *ego* also imports negative connotations associated with inflated self-importance and self-love, such as in the words "egotistical," "egoism," and "egocentric," hence the terms *I* and *ego* have a shared meaning in both German and English. Since the word "ego" has become immortalized in psychoanalytic literature as well as popular culture, for customary purposes I will refer to the I and the ego interchangeably.

Freud realized that he could not adequately account for the I as being solely conscious, and therefore introduced a division between conscious and unconscious ego domains and their respective operations. What Freud was mainly concerned about in this division was to explain how certain ego properties, qualities, and tension states impacted on the nature of wish, defense, drive discharge, and self-preservation, and how the I stood in relation to an alien force and presence compartmentalized from the ego itself. The ego became a pivotal concept for Freud because it was the locus of agency, intention, and choice both consciously and unconsciously realized—however, an agency that existed alongside competing agencies in the mind. This theoretical move on Freud's part is not without conceptual drawbacks and has led many critics to question the plausibility of competing mental entities. While Freud used the terms *provinces, domains,* and *realms* to characterize such psychic activity, he in no way meant to evoke substance ontology characteristic of ancient metaphysics in vogue with some forms of material-ism today. Freud explicitly abandoned his earlier neurophysiological visions of the mind represented in his *Project for a Scientific Psychology* (1895), and by the time of *The Interpretation of Dreams* (1900) adopted a corpus of the soul that admonished reductionism (see Freud, 1900, p. 536;1916–1917, p. 21). Characterizing Freud's theory of agency in terms of entity or substance ontology further misrepresents his views on the active processes that consti-tute the psyche. Freud's purported agencies are active, purposeful, malleable processes—not static, fixed, immobile structures. While Freud (1900, 1923, 1933) also prefers spatial metaphors in his description of these forces, he is quick to remind us they are only heuristic devises: the question of localiza-tion becomes a meaningless proposition when we are in actuality discussing temporal mental processes.

Freud's use of the term I imports ambiguity when we compare it to a psychoanalytic conception of the self. In some of Freud's (1914) intervening works on narcissism, his concept of the ego corresponds to the self; and in *Civilization and its Discontents* (1930), he specifically equates *das Ich* with *das Selbst* (p. 65). This implies that the self would not contain other portions of the psyche such as the drives and the region of the repressed. This definition also situates the self in relation to otherness and is thus no different from our reference to the ego with its conscious and unconscious counterparts. In German, however, the 'self' encompasses the entire human being; but on a very earthly plain, it represents the core from which the ego acts and relates mostly to the conscious aspects of personal identity. While a strong case can be made for the self as a supraordinate (see Meissner, 2000) encompassing principle—what Freud calls the Soul (*Seele*)—I believe Freud is justified here in conceptualizing the I, ego, and self as synonymous constructs. The self stands in relation to its opposite, namely, the Other, as does subject to object, and hence evokes a firm point of difference. This is precisely why Freud insisted on the dialectical presence of otherness: the I is *not* the It.

For Freud, the It is *alienus*—both alienated mind and that which is alienating. We know it as conflict and chaos under the pressure, whims, and persecutory impulses of the drives, our animal nature. They emanate from within us, but are not consciously willed or desired. The It does not know and does not say no—*It* knows no negation (Freud, 1925b, p. 239; 1933, p. 74). Under the force of foreign excitations clamoring for discharge, unrest and tumult are its very nature. Yet such chaos by necessity is combated by degrees of order from the ego. Freud's introduction of the It preserves that realm of inner reality we may never directly know in itself. Here Freud insists on the Kantian *Ding an sich,* the Fichtean *Anstoss*—an impenetrable limit, obstacle, or impasse. The mind becomes demarcated by a rigid 'check' that introduces irreconcilable division and contradiction; in other words, dialectic.

We may never have direct access to the It, only to the way in which it appears. We know the It through its endless derivatives—such as dreams, fantasies, slips, and symptoms, as well as what torments us—that which we wish would remain dead and buried, forever banished to the pit—disowned, renounced, hence repressed. But things that are forgotten have a way of turning up unexpectedly. With every covering over, every concealment, there is simultaneously a de-covering, a resurfacing of the old, a return of the dead. Freud crowned the It the king of the underworld—Hades, while the I traversed the domains of its earthly surface down into the bowels of its nether regions.

Freud's final paradigm of the mind rests on a basic logic of modification. The I differentiates itself and develops out of the It; and later, the I modifies itself again and evolves into a critical–moral agency, what Freud calls the *Über-Ich*, or that aspect of the I that stands over against itself and holds itself up to a higher authority. Here the I undergoes another doubling function, in fact, a doubling of the doubling—this time turned onto itself. What is familiarly know as the *superego* is nothing other than a split-off portion of the I that stands in relation to a particular form of identification: namely, a set of values and prohibitions it internalized from familial relations and cultural experience, ideals and principles the self strives to attain. Freud's logic of modification, however, goes unexplained, the explanatory limits of which he modestly concedes (Freud, 1933, p. 77; 1940, p. 145).

While Freud makes the superego (over-I, or above-I) into a critical agency that besieges the I and defiles the It, the superego is merely an extension of the ego, both the self in its exaltation as an identification and pining for its ideal form, as well as the judgment, fury, and condemnation that inform our sense of conscience, guilt, shame, and moral reproach. The ego and superego are therefore the same agency divided yet internally conjoined. Freud spoke prematurely in making the superego a third agency of the psyche, when, properly speaking, it is not: it merely *appears* as an independent agent when ontologically the ego and the superego are the same. The ego is *supra* in relation to itself—what it wants to be, hence what it strives to become. And when the ego does not live up to itself—up to its own ideals—it debases itself with as much wrath and force as is brewing in the tempestuous cauldron of the It. It is no coincidence that the It and the superego share the same fist of fury—because both are fueled (with stipulations) by the drives, a point I will return to shortly. But for now it becomes important to emphasize that the psyche is a divided self with each division and modification remaining interdependent and ontologically bound.

In the end, Freud gives us a vision of the mind as composed of three ontically interrelated forces with varying qualitative degrees of organization and zest ranging from the most primitive, unmodulated evolutionary impulses to the most refined aspects of intelligence and ethical self-consciousness—all brought together under the rubric of soul. Bettelheim (1982) tells us that nowhere in his texts does Freud actually provide us with a direct definition of the soul (p. 77), although we may infer that he intended for it to stand as an overarching concept that enveloped the three agencies of mental life. We do know, however, that Freud had no intentions to imply that the soul is immortal, nor does it carry any religious connotations whatsoever. Freud (1927, 1933) was a vociferous atheist; thus, his use of the term is meant to reflect our shared collective humanity.

Freud's tripartite division of the soul returns us to the Greek vision of the psyche with one exceptional difference: the soul is largely unconscious. As the seat of the passions (*eros*), reason (*nous*), and moral judgment (*ethos*), the psyche becomes a dynamic organization of competing dialectical forces. Because the notion of consciousness is a modern—not an ancient—concept, Freud is able to enrich the Platonic view by showing that irrationality and emotional forces driven by unconscious processes constantly plague the intellectual and ethical strivings of the ego. Therefore, the logocentrism that is often attributed to Freud must be viewed within the context of the pervasive tenacity of irrational pressures, although there is always a logic to the interior. Left undefined by Freud, we may nevertheless say that the psyche is the composition of competing dialectical processes that inform and sustain the division of the I from the It along with its multifarious derivatives. The psyche is pure process and experiential flow composed of a multiplicity of dialectical organizations—each with varying degrees of opposition, complexity, and strands of unification—that form a temporal continuity enduring in embodied space. While the psyche consists of unifying activity, it itself is not a static unity, rather a motional-experiential process of becoming spatiotemporally realized as mediated immediacy.

This leads us to a process account of the psyche—or, for our purposes, the Self—as a supraordinate complex whole, including both conscious and unconscious parallel activities. While classical through proceeding historical and contemporary psychoanalytic models have paid great attention to the details and developmental contours of intrapsychic, interpersonal, and psychosocial life, the question of genesis—psychic Origin—and its ontological modifications, remain virtually unconsidered. In what follows, I hope to show how psychoanalytic process psychology offers a logic of the dialectic that proves useful in explaining the rudimentary development of the psyche from its most basal ontological conditions to its most robust configurations and complexifications.

THE DIALECTICS OF UNCONSCIOUS EXPERIENCE

Freud is a dialectician of the mind: in his final paradigm he envisioned the psyche as an active composition of multifarious, bipolar forces that stand in antithetical relation to one another and are therefore mutually implicative.

The I and the It, the two classification of drives, primary versus secondary process mentation, the pleasure versus reality principle, love and hate, the individual versus society—these are only a few of the oppositional processes that inform his dialectical system. However, Freud never clarified his logic of the dialectic; instead he relied on introspection and self-analysis, clinical observation, and technical judgment based on careful consideration of the data at hand, which, over time, led to radical revisions of his many core theoretical postulates. One of Freud's most modest attributes was his ability to change his mind about previous speculations when new evidence presented itself, thus showing the disciplined persistence of a refined scientific attitude he had revered as *Logos* (see Freud, 1927, 1930).

It is not altogether clear how Freud's dialectic is philosophically constituted (a topic he said nothing about), however, we may draw certain reasonable assumptions. While some dialectical forces seek unification, resolution, and synthetic integration, others do not. For example, consciousness and unconsciousness, like the I and the It, are firm oppositions, yet their distinctions become blurred in times of sleep, daydreaming, and fantasy formation. Even when we are unconscious, the mind generates impressions and representations from the tableau of images once experienced in conscious sensation and laid down in the deep reservoir of memory within the unconscious configurations of the mind. This suggests that consciousness is on a continuum of presence and absence, disclosure and concealment, with each respective appearance being merely one side or instantiation of its dual nature, a duality highlighted and punctuated by its phenomenal valences and qualities, yet nevertheless ontologically conjoined. Consciousness and unconsciousness could not be ontologically distinct by the simple fact that each context of being overlaps and participates in the other, without which such duality could not be intelligibly conceived unless each counterpart is to be viewed as having separate essences. But if this were the case, neither could participate in the realm of the other nor could they have mutual causal influence as they are purported to possess simply because what has a distinct ontology or being would by definition have a difference essence. Just as Aristotle's (1962) criticism of Plato's (1961) forms still stands as a cogent refutation of ontological dualism based on the incompatibility of different essences, so must we extend this assessment to the split domains of consciousness and unconsciousness. Conscious and unconscious life must have the same ontology, hence the same essence, by virtue of the fact that each informs the reality of the other: their respective differences point to their modified forms.

For an essence to be what it is—without which it could not exist—it must stand in relation to what it is not. Freud maintains this division of consciousness and unconsciousness from: (1) an experiential or phenomenological standpoint—what qualitatively appears, (2) from an epistemological one—what is known, and (3) as a conceptual, heuristic scheme—what is conceived. However, despite his dual classification of drives, he does not maintain such duality from an ontological framework: consciousness arises *in* the ego, itself the outgrowth of an unconscious It. I will speak more to this later, but suffice it to say that Freud's dialectic permits both integration and impasse, synthesis and disunity, universality and particularity, hence contradiction and paradox. But as Freud (1933) says, the It knows nothing, above all the law of contradiction: "Contrary impulses exist side by side, without canceling each other out or diminishing each other: at most they may converge to form compromises" (p. 73). Mental processes could only "converge" and transmute their original forms only on the condition that they participate of the same essence, hence an original ontological ground that makes the conversion of form possible.

Another example of the blurred distinctions of duality and limit in Freud's system may be witnessed in the dialectic of repression (Freud, 1915b). What is denied conscious access, negated, and banished to the pit is not totally annulled, hence not completely opposed. Rather, it is preserved where it festers and seeks discharge through another form. Thus, opposition remains contextual, yet always has the potential of being breached.

While we may observe a boundary of firm antitheses in Freud's model, there is also a synthetic function to the ego that seeks to mediate, resolve, and channel competing desires and conflicts through intentional strategies that find their way into overt behavior and conscious phenomenon. But there is also a regressive function to ego, and each is potentially mobilized given the particular contingencies that govern psychic economy. On the other hand, the process of sublimation has a unifying, transcending character that combats regression, despite the fact that both can be operative on parallel realms of development. This leaves Freud somewhere between what Kant (1781) referred to as the antinomies of reason or the paralogisms of the self, which correspond to irreconcilable contradictions within the mind that meet with no resolve, to the Hegelian (1807, 1812, 1817a) notion of *Aufhebung*—a progressive dialectical process that cancels, surpasses, and simultaneously preserves opposition within an elevating, unifying procreative self-structure. Despite Freud's lack of clarification surrounding his dialectical logic, we can nevertheless say that his model is compatible with a process account of unconscious experience that is dialectically organized and mediated by oppositional contingent forces exerting equiprimordial pressures that are contextually realized in time.[3]

The mind is dialectical, hence relational, that is, it stands in relation—in both temporal continuity and disjunction—to what is other than its current form or experience. It is important to note that regardless of the form of difference we wish to theoretically or experientially highlight, all dialectical organizations of the psyche are simultaneously operative from the vantage point of their own unique constitutions and contextualized perspectives. Therefore, the perspectivism of each inhabited domain of lived (yet at times unformulated) unconscious experience is not to negate the force and presence of competing intentional faculties within the mind. It now becomes our task to more closely examine how these psychic processes are logically constituted through dialectically mediated progression, a discussion that will prepare us to engage the question of original ground.

PROCESS PSYCHOLOGY

In several recent publications (Mills, 2000a, 2000b, 2002), I have advocated a new theoretical approach to contemporary psychoanalytic thought called *dialectical psychoanalysis* or *process psychology*. While process psychology has potential application for theoretical, clinical, and applied psychoanalysis, here I will be mainly concerned with examining its conceptual explanatory power. This approach relies largely on Hegel's (1812, 1817a) general logic of the dialectic and its reappropriation for psychoanalytic inquiry, without, however, inheriting the baggage associated with Hegel's entire philosophical system. We need not adopt Hegel's overall system to appreciate his science of the dialectic and the logical operations in which it unfolds. Furthermore, Hegel's dialectical logic allows us to examine more precisely the nature of mental functioning and explain how unconscious modification is made possible. This has direct bearing on engaging the question of the origin of psychic reality and specifically the coming into being of the I and the It.

Process psychology assumes a fundamental axiom: mind is constituted as process. This is the essence of all psychic reality and the indispensable ontological foundation for all forms of mental life. Every mental derivative—from unconscious to conscious, intrapsychic to relational, individual to collective—is necessarily predicated on process. Process underlies all experience as an activity of becoming. As becoming, process is pure event, unrest, or experiential flow. Essence is process. It is neither fixed nor static, inert or predetermined, rather a spontaneous motional flux and trajectory of dynamic pattern lending increasing order, organization, and zeal to psychic development. As process, essence must appear for any psychic event to be made actual.

Psychic reality, with all its contours and manifestations, is dialectically constituted by competing and opposing forces that are interrelated and mutually implicative. Opposition is ubiquitous to psychic reality and operative within all subjective and intersubjective experience: that which *is* is always defined in relation to what it *is not*. Hence, there is an equiprimordality to all dichotomous relations. All polarity is mutually related and inseparable, hence one pole may only be differentiated from the other in contextual thought or by experiential perspective. Polarities of similarity and difference, identity and otherness, are phenomenal encounters in time each highlighted by their respective positionality toward the other, even though their mutual relation to opposition co-constitute their existence. Identity and difference are thus formed in relation to opposition, negation, and conflict, whereby each are ontologically interdependent and dynamically composed of fluid processes that evoke, construct, and sustain psychic organization and structure. Therefore, the subject-object contrast may only be properly appreciated as an intrinsic dynamic totality whereby each event and its internal relation is emphasized as a particular moment in the process of becoming. From the mutual standpoint of shared difference, each individual subjects stands in relation to the multiply contoured intersubjective matrix that is generated when particular subjectivities collide and interact. This ensures that process multiplies exponentially.

The nature of psychic process is derived from an active organizing principle that is replete with conflict and destruction providing thrust, progression, and ascendence within a dynamically informed system, yet may revert or regress back to more archaic or primitive shapes of mental life under certain contingencies. Process is not simply subjective experience that is radically individualized (although it encompasses it), rather subjectivity unfolds within universal dialectical patterns—as *subjective universality*—(not as predetermined, reductive mechanisms, but as teleological, contextual operations) that lend actuality and structure to lived reality. It is important to reiterate that psychic structure is not fixed, static, or immobile, but is transforming, malleable, and mediating activity or flux that provides functional capacities and vivacity within a teleologically driven, purposeful process of becoming. Therefore, all particularities of conscious and unconscious experience (whether individually or collectively instantiated) are ontologically informed by the universal, motional principles that fuel the dialectic.

Hegel's dialectical logic has been grossly misunderstood by the humanities and social sciences largely due to historical misinterpretations dating back to Heinrich Moritz Chalybäus, an earlier Hegel expositor, and unfortunately perpetuated by current mythology surrounding Hegel's system. As a result, Hegel's dialectic is inaccurately conceived of as a threefold movement involving the generation of a proposition or 'thesis' followed by an 'antithesis,' then resulting in a 'synthesis' of the prior movements, thus giving rise to the popularized and crassly misleading phrase: thesis–antithesis–synthesis. This is not Hegel's dialectic, rather it is Fichte's (1794) depiction of the transcendental acts of consciousness that he describes as the fundamental principles (*Grundsatz*) of thought and judgment. Yet this phrase itself is a crude and mechanical rendition of Fichte's logic and does not even properly convey his project. Fichte's dialectic is a response to Kant's (1781) *Critique of Pure Reason* in which Kant outlines the nature of consciousness and addresses irreconcilable contradictions that are generated in the mind due to breakdowns in reason. For both Kant and Fichte, their respective dialectics have firm limits or boundaries that may not be bridged. Hegel (1807, 1812, 1817a,b,c), on the other hand, shows how contradiction and opposition are annulled but preserved, unified, and elevated within a progressive, evolutionary process.

While Hegel's *Science of Logic* (1812) has attracted both philosophical admiration and contempt (see Burbidge, 1993), we need not be committed

to the fine distinctions of his logic that is confined to the study of consciousness. What is important for process psychology is understanding the essential
structure of the dialectic as *Aufhebung*—customarily translated as *sublation*—
denoted by three simultaneous movements that at once (1) annul or cancel
opposition, (2) surpass or transcend its prior moment, while (3) preserving
such opposition within its new, transformed, and synthesized organization.
Three movements: at once they cancel or annul, transcend or surpass, retain
or preserve—aspects of every transmogrification. The dialectic as process is
pure activity and unrest that acquires more robust organization through its
capacities to negate, oppose, and destroy otherness; yet in its negation of
opposition, it surpasses difference through a transmutational process of enveloping otherness within its own internal structure, and hence elevates
itself to a higher plane. Not only does the psyche destroy opposition, but it
subsumes and preserves it within its interior. Death is incorporated, remembered, and felt as it breaths new life in the mind's ascendence toward higher
shapes of psychic development: it retains the old as it transmogrifies the
present, aimed toward a future existence it actively (not predeterminately)
forges along the way. This ensures that that dialectical reality is always mired
in the contingencies that inform its experiential immediacy. Despite the
universality of the logic of the dialectic, mind is always contextually realized.
Yet each movement, each shape of the dialectic, is merely one moment
within its holistic teleology, differentiated only by form. The process as a
whole constitutes the dialectic whereby each movement highlights a particular piece of psychic activity that is subject to its own particular contingencies. As each valence is highlighted in its immediacy or lived experiential
quality, it is merely one appearance among many appearances in the overall
process of its own becoming.

APPROACHING THE GENESIS PROBLEM

With the enlistment of the dialectic, process psychology offers philosophical
fortification to psychoanalysis, which has long been under attack for its alleged lack of scientific credibility (see Bornstein, 2001; Fisher & Greenberg,
1996; Grünbaum, 1984). Although heralding itself a science grounded in
clinical observation, practice, and empirical hypothesis-testing, much of psychoanalytic theory may be philosophically supported through dialectical logic,
an alternative, complementary methodology that further gains in descriptive
and explanatory force when empirical accounts become tenuous or questionable. The dialectic proves especially useful when understanding the logic of
modification that Freud does not adequately address, thus lending logical
rigor, deductive justification, and internal coherence to procedural inquiry
concerning, among other things, the nature of the genesis problem. Empirical science in general, and developmental research in particular, is in no
better situation to proclaim they can determine how the ego comes into

being other than by making reasonable, inductive inferences based on observable phenomenon; and this is more often accomplished through speculative inferences based on our own subjective experiences (see Frie, 1999). For example, Stern's (1985) proclamation of the "emergent self" as the earliest stage of ego development in infancy, (from birth to two months), does nothing to illuminate the ground from which the self emergences in the first place. There is a current tendency in psychoanalytic infant research to emphasize the relational, dyadic systems, and intersubjective domains that help constitute the ego (Beebe, Jafee, & Lachmann, 1992; Benjamin, 1992; Lichtenberg, 1989; Mahler, Pine, & Bergman, 1975; Ogden, 1986; Stern, 1985), but this does not address the genesis question. While these developmental paradigms are insightful and informative, the ontology of the *inception* of subjectivity is ignored: psychic activity is presumed but not accounted for.

Empirical approaches (including clinical and/or phenomenological investigations) ultimately face the same strain as do purely theoretical attempts to define the origins of psychic development because we simply do not possess direct epistemological access to the primordial organizations of the subjective mind. Put laconically, we can never 'get inside' an infant's head. Biological attempts ultimately fail because they succumb to the bane of materialist reduction, thus effacing the unique quality of the lived experience that is displaced by simple location, what Whitehead (1925) calls the fallacy of misplaced concreteness. While our physical nature is a necessary condition for psychic life, it is far from a sufficient condition to account for the coming into being of psychic reality. This is not to disavow the relevance, contiguity, and importance of the biological sciences for psychoanalytic inquiry (see Gedo, 1996), only to emphasize that process thought extends far beyond psychophysicality.

While process psychology has a favorable attitude toward empirical science, it realizes that relying solely on perceived, observable (controlled) experience can be of little help when answering the question of Beginning. To approach such an issue, we must enlist the principle of sufficient reason: what is the *ground* of psychic life—the inner world? We cannot begin to answer this question without making a priori claims about the logic of the interior, a logic of unconscious internal modification. Tabula rasa approaches, typical of early modern philosophy, claim that all knowledge comes from conscious experience while a priori judgments tell us that certain ontological conditions of subjectivity must be unconsciously operative in order to make experience possible. While the former rely on observable experience that presupposes a psychology of cognition, the latter emphasizes the ontological and logical continuity of unconscious experience that allows for the structures and functions of consciousness to arise. Tabula rasa explanations are philosophically simple, myopic, and naive—long displaced by the Kantian turn in philosophy and refined by many German idealists and postmodern thought, whereby a priori accounts are favored in logic, linguistics, and evolutionary epistemology. As we will see, the process of unconscious modification rests on the internal negations, divisions, projections, incorporations, and reconstitutive movements of the dialectic.

We must first start with the question of genesis, of Origin—original ground. If it becomes necessary to trace the origin and development of the mind in order to come to terms with first principles—the metaphysics of the soul—then we must attempt to conceptually isolate a ground in which all else arises. Like Freud and other empirically motivated theorists, we must situate this unfolding ground within the natural world, within the corporeal subject itself, and thus avoid appealing to a singular first principle or category of the ultimate in which we nor the philosophers are equipped to satisfactorily answer without begging the question or steering us down into the abyss of infinite regress. Not only must we start with the natural being of the embryonic psyche—its natural immediacy—we must inevitably begin from the inside-out, progressing from unconscious internal activity to external mediated consciousness. In what I will soon argue, as epistemologically subjective, self-attuned experiential beings, we intuit, feel, and/or know our own interiority *before* we encounter the manifold data of the sensuous outside world, although externality, biological, social, and linguistic contingencies, as well as cultural historicity are superimposed upon us a priori as part of our ontological facticity.

From a methodological account, tracing the dialectical birth and epigenesis of the psyche from the interior to the exterior is more philosophically defendable because it does not merely presuppose the existence of the object world; instead it constructs a means to engage external reality from its own internal psychic configurations. I do not wish to revive the irreparable schism between the failed realism/anti-realism debate, only to show how process is internally mediated and dialectically conditioned. From my account, the subject–object contrast must be seen as a dialectical process system that is ontologically interdependent, emergent, and equiprimordial. The inner world of subjective experience and the outer world of objective natural events are equiprimordially constituted as interpenetrable processes that comprise our fluxuational experiences of psychic reality.

For all practical purposes, we live and function in a world that we indubitably accept as real—things happen around us even if we don't adequately perceive them or understand their existence or purpose; but our subjective appreciations of what is real is radically habituated by our own internal worlds and unconscious permutations, thereby influencing conscious perception, judgment, and intersubjective exchange. This is why psychic reality is first-order experience.[4]

All we can know *is* psychic reality: whether inner or outer, self or other, presence or absence, perceived or imagined, hallucinated or conceived—reality is mediated by subjective mind. Although an enormous aspect of mind and personal identity involves consciousness, it is only a surface organ—the modification of unconscious life, a fraction of the activity that comprises the internal processes and pervasive throbs of unformulated unconscious experience. Our epistemological understanding of the real is ontologically conditioned on a priori unconscious structures governed by *intrasubjective* processes that allow the natural external world to arise in consciousness. Therefore, our encounter and understanding of psychic reality is always mediated by intrapsychic events that are first-order or first-person experiences even if such experiences operate outside of conscious awareness or are under the influence of extrinsic events exerting variable pressures on our mental operations.

While Freud frowned on metaphysics, his theory of mind is a metaphysical treatise replete with quandaries. Although Freud stated that the I develops out of the It and that consciousness arises in the ego, he did not proffer an adequate explanation of how this activity occurs. In fact, there are many problems with the relations between ego activity and the drives, the question of mediation by the drives, the distinctness of the I and the It, and whether they can be distinguished at all—and, if so, perhaps only phenomenologically, which is not to say that they share separate essences, only different appearances. For Freud, psychic origin was proclaimed to commence in that broad category of the mind labeled *das Es*, what he earlier stipulated under the rubric of the system '*Ucs.*' Now that we have prepared the context for a process account of the mind, it is time for us to return to our original task, namely, the genesis problem, and give voice to the logic of modification Freud anticipated but left unexplained. Here we must examine the psyche's most elemental pulse from its natural immediacy, what Freud reified as the indubitable primacy of the drives.

WHERE *IT* ALL BEGINS:
THE TRANSMOGRIFICATION OF THE DRIVES

In contemporary psychoanalysis, Freud is disparaged largely due to his emphasis on the drives. This is partially the result of mistranslations of his actual German texts; however, drive theory has inevitably fallen out of vogue with analysts and clinicians who value more relational approaches to theory and practice. While these mistranslations and their implications have been previously criticized (see Bettelheim, 1982; Laplanche, 1970; Lear, 1990), nowhere do we see such a gross error as in the misconception of 'drive' (*Trieb*) translated as 'instinct.' This single mistake has misinformed five generations of English-speaking psychoanalysts and clinicians who unfortunately confuse the mind with materialist reduction. Freud never used the English term *instinct* when he spoke of humans: *Instinkt* in German always refers to animals and denotes a fixed, predetermined behavioral pattern or tropism. Freud loathed that term when speaking of the human animal. *Trieb*, on the other hand, means an inner urge, impulse, or drive, which is the proper descriptor used to emphasize the notion of inner unrest, desire, and compulsion often associated with impersonal, nonintentional forces impelling the individual from within. We may initially see why Freud's concept of drive has descriptive utility: it is an unconscious process that fuels and propels the organism. But, more important, Freud conceives of a drive as a malleable, plastic, transformative activity—not a static, genetically imprinted or determined pressure that cannot be mediated or amended. For Freud, a drive can be altered and permutated, while an instinct is stagnant and unchangeable. Whereas the expression of a drive can be mitigated if not changed entirely, an instinct cannot undergo modification at all. "Instinct" in English, however, also typifies something that is innate. Therefore, to avoid duplicating confusion about the nature of drive and instinct, all references hereafter to instinctual processes should be viewed within this stipulated context of drives.

Freud's theory of the drives went through many significant transformations throughout his career, at one time focusing solely on libido (*Lust*), later to many different competing urges belonging to both unconscious and conscious processes (e.g., *die Ich-Triebe*), then finally settling on the primacy of two antithetical yet interpenetrable classifications: sex and death. Relational schools can't buy this central tenet, what Stephen Mitchell (1992) calls the "outmoded concept of drives" (p. 3); namely, that the mind is driven and influenced by multifarious, overdetermined unconscious forces that are originally biologically based pressures impinging on the conscious subject and clamoring for release. But the main objection among these schools is the concentrated refutation of the role of libido over relational and intersubjective motives. Here we see the first big turnoff and subsequent resistance by the postclassical field: everything boils down to sex.

This unfortunate attitude is a deposit based on Freud's (1905a) early work on infantile sexuality; it does not take into account his mature theoretical advances (see Freud, 1933, 1940). As said earlier, Freud was not particularly impressed with having to think the same thing all the time: by the end of his life he incorporates libido or the sex drive into his conception of Eros—an encompassing life principle, similar in fashion to the Greeks who saw the pursuit of Eros as life's supreme aim: namely, the holistic attainment of sensual, aesthetic, ethical, and intellectual fulfillment. In this sense, mind and body are contiguous. By blindly focusing on Freud's early work at the expense of his mature theory, not only is he misunderstood, but his theoretical corpus is distorted. It also leads one to presume that Freud was committed to a genetic fallacy—namely, that all psychic life can be reduced to its developmental origins—when he was not.[5] Eros is the sublimation (*Sublimierung*) of natural desire, first materializing as drive, then progressing to the cultivated activities of the ego—that is, rational self-conscious life.

For Freud (1915a), the source of a drive is unequivocally biological and somatic. This is the second big turnoff: man is viewed as a physical–instinctual machine turned on by the environment. I am of the opinion that not only do many postclassical schools of thought misunderstand the nature of drives but they ultimately misunderstand the role of biology and human embodiment. It is simply delusional to think that biology has no place in psychic economy, and those deifying relational factors through negation of the natural body are misguided. Why sex and aggression?—because they are part of our animal evolutionary past. The notion of drive underscores Freud's natural science foundation, which is inextricably bound to evolutionary currents: sex and aggression are the two fundamental forces behind the inception, course, and progression of civilization, without which there would arguably be no human race.[6]

In the historical movement of psychoanalysis we can observe a conceptual shifting away from drive theory to ego psychology, object relations theory, self psychology, and now its current preoccupation with intersubjectivity, each calling for a paradigm shift. In the early stages of psychoanalytic theory building, each postclassical movement championed a particular constituent of psychic activity (e.g., ego over object) while complementing and subsuming Freud's general psychological theory. In fact, it was Freud who launched ego psychology and the object relations movement (see Freud, 1933). Today, however, with the insistence on relational and intersubjective approaches, psychoanalysis is being plummeted into a land of false dichotomies suggesting that relation cancels drive. And even if it is conceded that the two realms coexist, we are still asked to choose sides (see Greenberg & Mitchell, 1983, p. 390). As a result, within many contemporary analytic circles, the primacy of the drives and the unconscious itself have virtually disappeared.[7] Take Mitchell (1992), for example: "There is *no* experience that is not interpersonally mediated (p. 2, italics added); and Stolorow: Intersubjectivity "recognizes the constitutive role of relatedness in the making of *all* experience" (in Buirski & Haglund, 2001, p. xiii, italics added). These proclamations clearly state that consciousness conditions unconsciousness, when they fail to account for what Freud had been so sensitive to investigate.

While interpersonal processes are an integral and necessary aspect of psychic development, they do not by themselves negate the relevance of the drives and their mutual influence over mental life. Furthermore, Stolorow and his colleagues' (Orange, Atwood, & Stolorow, 1997; Stolorow & Atwood, 1992; Stolorow, Brandchaft, & Atwood, 1987) claim that everything is intersubjective fails to consider intrapsychic experience prior to the onset of consciousness. Unconsciousness precedes consciousness, hence subjective experience is internally mediated prior to one's encounter with the object world. In fact, drive becomes an ontological a priori that cannot be annulled or denied: moreover, it precedes interpersonal interaction by virtue of the fact that drive is constitutionally predicated.

We can never escape from the fact that we are embodied. Freud's insistence that the source of a drive is biologically given is simply to accept the brute facticity of our natural corporeality. The mistake many psychoana-

lytic theorists make is interpreting biology as reduction and that drive discharge precludes relational activity, when, contrarily, Freud's conception of
drive makes reduction impossible and relatedness possible. Let me explain.

Freud has to account for embodiment—our natural immediacy—in
which urges and impulses arise, thus he focuses on the body as initially
providing form, content, and structure to internal experience. This is why
erogenous zones are corporeally emphasized. But more important, Freud has
to show how ego activity and consciousness are also sensuous processes:
attention, perception, and the greater faculties of cognition are sentient
experiential actions. This is why Freud (1923) says that the ego is a body-
ego, itself the projection of a surface: *It* projects itself *onto* its surface, the
surface of its immediate feeling and sensuous embodiment. Therefore drive
is constituted as ego, but not at first. While Freud does not say this directly,
it may nevertheless be inferred: drive becomes ego—the ego first knows itself
as a feeling, craving, desirous corporeal being. But how does this occur? Freud
says very little.

In "Instincts and their Vicissitudes," or more appropriately translated,
"Drives and their Fate" (*Triebe und Triebschicksale*), Freud (1915a) distinguishes between four constituents of a drive: a source, pressure, aim, and
object. While the source (*Quelle*) is somatically organized, Freud is very clear
that the pressure (*Drang*) or force of a drive is its very "essence" (*Wesen*).
Here he unquestionably situates the nature of *Trieb* in its activity: drive is
pulsation, unrest—pure desire. The aim (*Ziel*) or motive of a drive is to
satisfy itself, to achieve pleasure as tension reduction, to end the craving; and
the means by which a drive is sated is through an object (*Objekt*). Objects,
especially people, are coveted for the functions they serve, and these functional objects may fulfill many competing aims as psychic life becomes more
rich and variegated. In fact, drives transmogrify through many circuitous
routes and take many derivative forms: what we commonly refer to as a
defense mechanism is the teleological fate of a drive. This is an unfortunate
term because "mechanism" evokes imagery of stasis, rigidity, and fixed predetermined movements, when instead defenses are fluid, mutable, and teleologically directed expressions of desire as *process systems*. As transformed
drive, a defense is a particular piece of desire, often unconsciously intended
and differentiated by its function in relation to a competing urge, impulse,
or counterintention, internal danger, environmental threat, and/or potential
conscious realization that must be combated. There are defenses that urge
the psyche to regress while others to progress, and this is why a drive cannot
be simply seen as biological reduction or devolve back to its original state.
Because drives transform, they cannot return to their original form: we can
never know a drive in itself, only as a psychical representative, presentation,
or idea (*Vorstellung*). Furthermore, what we often experience as drive is its
aim—the craving for satisfaction. Moreover, because drives modify themselves through a process of epigenesis, they make the more sophisticated

forms of conscious and self-conscious life possible: from the archaic to the refined, unconscious drive manifests itself through relatedness to objects.

Freud's theory of *Trieb* is not without difficulty, and many critics proclaim that because his model of tension reduction was ultimately a hydraulic component of biological-homeostasis theory, the aim or *telos* of a drive overrides relational motivations. But this conclusion is not justified, especially when others become the objects of our satisfaction. Freud (1915a) specifically says that the object of a drive is the most variable aspect and that it may serve multiple motives simultaneously (p. 123). Nowhere are we led to believe that relation is subordinated to biology when a drive is mediated though object relatedness. Furthermore, Freud's (1925a) later theory of Eros ultimately speaks to the desire for love and the pursuit of our most cherished ideals that he specifically equates with the Eros of Plato in the *Symposium* (p. 218). As a result, Eros becomes a relational principle (see Reisner, 1992), a relation toward ourselves and others through the exaltation of human value. From the most primitive mind to the most civilized societies, we are *attached* to our ideals through others.

But let us return to a conceptual dilemma for Freud: how could a drive have an object? Put another way, how could a drive take an object as its aim without possessing some form of agency? As a teleological process, a drive has a purpose constituted through its aim, but how could it also be guided in its ability to *choose* objects for its satisfaction without accounting for intentionality by an unconscious agent? Here we see why Freud had to introduce the notion of unconscious agency constituted through the alien presence of the It. The It constitutes the realm of the dual classification of drives as well as the realm of the repressed. But is Freud justified in making the It into an agency? Could it be possible that unconscious actions of the ego are actually performing object choice, while the drives and repressed material merely act as a constant pressure the ego must mediate? This is particularly problematic for Freud given that he specifically tells us that the I logically and temporally proceeds from the It. Freud is very clear in his final specifications of how the psyche develops in this fashion. In *Inhibitions, Symptoms and Anxiety*, Freud (1926) states:

> We were justified, I think, in dividing the ego from the id, for there are certain considerations which necessitate that step. On the other hand *the ego is identical with the id, and is merely a specially differentiated part of it*. If we think of this part by itself in contradistinction to the whole, or if a real split has occurred between the two, the weakness of the ego becomes apparent. But if the ego remains bound up with the id and indistinguishable from it, then it displays its strength. The same is true of the relation between the ego and the super-ego. In many situations the two are merged; and as a rule we can only distinguish one from the other when

> there is a tension or conflict between them.... [T]he ego is an *organization* and the id is not. *The ego is, indeed, the organized portion of the id.* (p. 97, italics added)

Freud clearly explains that the I is a modally differentiated aspect of the It that becomes the mental organization of its prior shape. Elsewhere he says: "the ego is that portion of the id that was modified . . . tak[ing] on the task of representing the external world to the id" (1933, p. 75). This corresponds to the ego of consciousness, where the material of sensuous perception and thought are mediated, stored, and retrieved from the inner world, hence underscoring the contiguous and interdependent levels of unconscious and conscious processes. Freud's theory of mind adheres to an architectonic process: the ego develops out of its natural immediacy, then acquires increased dynamic complexity and organization as modally differentiated shapes of earlier processes assume new forms. As previously stated, Freud's recognition that organized psychic processes develop from unorganized hence undifferentiated natural determinations insulates him from criticism that his theory of mind purports three ontologically distinct agents that participate in mutual causal relations. Because the trinity of the three provinces are modally differentiated forms or shapes of its original undifferentiated being, each participates in the same essence and thus none is an independent nominal agent. Rather they are interdependent forces that *appear* as separate entities, when they in fact together form the unification of the dynamic temporal processes that govern mental life.

Although Freud admonished Jung for allegedly "watering down" libido to a monistic energy, Freud's model of the psyche conforms to a developmental monistic ontology: higher instantiations of mental order evolve from more primordial forces of psychic life through a process of differentiation and modification. Although the I and the It are modifications of the same ontology, it is only the I that appears, itself an unconscious derivative. The specific process of differentiation, however, goes unexplained. All we are told is that the ego becomes the higher organizing agency of the mind derived from primitive processes. In fact, Freud (1940) concedes that while drives find their first psychical expressions in the It, they are "in forms unknown to us" (p. 145). But why did not Freud isolate the moments of differentiation and modification within the It itself? Given that drive is the basic constituent of mind that even precedes the organization of the It as a thoroughly unconscious agent, why did he not address modification at this level? Furthermore, if the ego is a secondary modification from a primary unconscious ground, then, by Freud's account, drive mediation would have to take place before the ego emerges; but how could a drive possess such agency? Freud does not say.

From my account, the transmogrification of the drives gives rise to psychic agency and it is through a careful inspection into the process of modification that we can potentially resolve the genesis problem. I believe that Freud was mistaken about making the It into an agency without accounting for how the unconscious portion of the I performs the executive functions of object choice for the drives and competing unconscious material pressing for discharge. The It cannot be understood as an unconscious agency (if at all) without the implicit inclusion of the I unless the nature of a drive includes the capacity to choose objects, which is highly improbable given that only the ego is organized and synthetic in its executive tasks. In fact, Freud (1915a) tells us that the object of a drive is "*assigned* to it only in consequence of being peculiarly fitted to make satisfaction possible" (p. 122, italics added). If the I is ontologically undifferentiated from the It, it makes the question of unconscious agency more delicate when attempting to account for teleology and intentional object choice. Rather than the I developing from the It, the ego may be properly said to develop from drive. But even more important, as I will soon argue, we have reason to believe that drive and ego are the same.

As it stands, there are many problems associated with Freud's contrast between the I and the It. The It is impersonal, but it allegedly picks an object for the drives: how is this so? According to Freud, only the ego can do this; hence we have a problem with an executive agency, and we have a problem with the definition of a drive. Although a drive needs an object for its satisfaction, are we justified in saying that an object is a proper characteristic of a drive? This implies that an object inheres in the drive as a property of it, when this is unlikely. An object stands in relation or absence to the *telos* or aim of a drive, but it does not follow that an object is necessarily a part of a drive's constitution, only that is requires an object for its satisfaction. In order to procure an object, it requires mediation. Here enters the I. The unconscious ego mediates object choice, not drive, hence Freud introduces a contradiction in his model. He further confounds the issue by making the ego a developmental agent that does not materialize until the formative stages of early Oedipalization, a postulate corrected by Klein and many post-Kleinians, and today confirmed by developmental researchers who recognize the existence of the ego or the self at the moment of birth (e.g., see Stern, 1985).

Freud attempts to resolve his own contradiction by making the It a separate agent. But how does it have any organizing agency without the ego that lends structure and direction to it? Yet Freud (1926) equivocates the issue by saying that the I is "identical" with the It. In Freud's final tripartite model, the ego becomes the locus of mind because of its synthetic and dynamic functions that stand in mediatory relation to the other two competing agencies. Yet these other two agencies are ontologically conjoined; hence we cannot separate any one agency from the others because of their inextricability. But is it possible to save Freud from his own contradiction? Can a drive take itself as its own object? And, if so, when does drive become ego?

Why does it emerge to begin with? At what point does the I take on a formal unity? How does it effect its transition to executive agency? To consciousness? In order to answer these questions, we must increasingly turn our attention to a dialectical account of modification.

ARKHĒ

When does psychic life begin? Does the emergence of the ego properly constitute human subjectivity, or can we legitimately point toward prior ontological forces? As mentioned earlier, I do not wish to reduce this metaphysical query to a materialist enterprise, only to acknowledge that certain physiological contingencies of embodiment are a necessary condition, albeit not a sufficient condition to account for psychic origin. While process psychology is sensitive to the contiguous and compatible work within the biological and neurosciences, this need not concern us here. If one is content with a materialist approach, let one resort to discourse on ovum and sperm. But we must proceed with a careful respect for Freud's (1900, 1933) dictum and resist the temptation of reducing the psyche to its anatomical substratum. Because empirical approaches alone cannot possibly address the epistemology of the interior or the lived quality of experiential process, we must attempt to approach the question dialectically. Put more specifically, we are concerned with isolating the experiential movements that bring about the inception of lived psychical reality. Before we can address the ego of consciousness, we must first account for original ground through a process account of the coming into being of archaic structure. Although unarticulated by Freud himself, the concept of drive allows us to engage the question of genesis.

We must now return to the question of ground. Although Freud tells us that the It conditions all other forms of psychic agency, drives and the repressed condition the It. Furthermore, since repression is a vicissitude of the drives, drives necessarily become a grounding unconscious activity. Therefore, what we can infer from Freud is that the drives become primordial. But is this enough? How do the drives constitute themselves in the first place, that is, how do they function as organized unconscious life? Moreover, how do they come into being at all?

Unconsciousness precedes consciousness, hence there is a radicalization to unconscious subjective experience. In fact, consciousness is the manifestation of unconscious structure, first expressing itself as drive. While Freud emphasized the equiprimordiality of Eros and destruction, his notion of the death drive may be arguably considered one of his most important theoretical achievements. The death drive (*Todestrieb*) is not merely the innate presence of animal aggression or externalized acts of destruction, rather it is the *impulse toward death*. While the drive toward death may be observed as a *will to murder*, first it speaks to the subject as a *will toward suicide*. But, as Freud tells us, mainly due to antithetical, counteractive drives motivated by the desire for adaptation and self-preservation, self-destructive impulses are typically deflected and defended against through projective displacements that find fulfillment through many circuitous paths throughout our developmental histories. Death *appears* as aggression and destruction whether externally displaced or turned on ourselves.

Before Freud fully committed to his notion of the death drive, he gave a speculative account of the evolutionary birth and metamorphosis of animate from inanimate life. In *Beyond the Pleasure Principle*, Freud (1920) conjectures that *"the aim of all life is death"* (p. 38), and that organic life ultimately wants to return to an inorganic state of quiescence. In considering how animate activity came into being, Freud speculated that inorganic matter would have been perfectly content with its simple unity of quiescence if not for the encroachment of neighboring dangers that threatened its internal cohesion and integrity. As a result, libido or a life principle was erected as a defensive maneuver against the imminent threat of destruction from a foreign invasion. From this account, the drive toward life is a defense against a real or perceived danger that threatens to invade the organism's solipsistic world. Extending this notion to the human subject, death is paradoxically beyond the pleasure principle yet at the same time is the ultimate pleasure: death is a tensionless state. But death only becomes pleasurable to the extent that it is protracted and endured; this is why Freud says that it must be engaged through circuitous routes of self-destruction (i.e., as repetition) that bring the organism back to its original inorganic condition. In other words, violence is brought about through the subject's own hands.

Freud's bold claim has not been well received among psychoanalysis and has been outright rejected based on biological grounds (see Sulloway, 1979/1992) ; yet death is unequivocally ontologically conditioned. Death—conflict, negation, chaos—saturates psychic structure and is the motional process behind the very evolution of the dialectic. By turning our attention to a process account of the dialectic of desire, I believe we are justified in saying that death is our original drive. Negativity is our inner being that enters into opposition with itself—its own competing, antagonistic mental processes vying for expression whether consciously or unconsciously conceived. As Hegel informs us, the mere act of confronting opposition is negative and aggressive, hence a conflictual enterprise of canceling, surpassing, and preserving such negativity within the unconscious abyss of our inner constitution. Yet the destruction inherent in all dialectical relations is merely a moment within the holistic process of elevating inner states to higher forms or modes of being. Hence, there is a *positive significance to the negative* that brings about more advanced levels of psychic progression and realization. In this way, negativity is both a grounding and transcending process of mind. Extending Freud's notion of the death drive to process dialectics allows us to show how the unconscious grounds its own ground through determinate negation. Death is teleologically directed and experi-

enced as life turned outward, from the interior to the exterior, toward pro-
curing the means of returning to its previous state of undifferentiated, undisturbed peace.

In considering the inception of psychic life, however, we must take
Freud's thesis further. In conceiving of genesis—the birth of psychic activity—it makes more sense to me that mental life would have to experience
a form of upheaval from within its own interior constitution, rather than as
a response to trauma from without. Instead of a pristine, unadulterated state
of quiescence, the soul, embryonic ego, or preformed unconscious agent (what
Freud calls the It), would have to experience a rupture due to internal dis-
cord that would serve to punctuate its breach to life, a process of awakening
from its nascent self-entombed unity. But how is this possible? Hegel (1817c)
describes the process by which the unconscious soul undergoes a dialectical
evolution that eventually becomes the ego of consciousness. Hegel's method
is particularly relevant to the question of genesis. By taking a dialectical
approach to our theoretical analysis, we may speculate how unconscious
agency first materializes.

Because mind cannot emerge *ex nihilo*, we must posit the coming into
being of psychic agency as a progressive unconscious, dialectical activity; in
other words, as a determinate teleological drive. Given the brute facticity of
our embodiment—the givenness of nature itself—mind must emerge from
within its natural beginnings. In the *arkhē*, there is simple immediacy, the
mere given existence or immediate *isness* of psychical pulse, what we may
loosely call *unconscious apperception*. This is unconsciousness in its immediacy, neither cohesively constituted nor developed, rather the experiential
presence of its sentient being. Because what *is* is an unconscious, prereflective
immediacy, we may only designate it as an implicit agent or passive activity
belonging to nascent mental experience. Because it is merely implicit activity in its initial immediacy and structure, it becomes a matter of making itself
explicit and mediate through laborious dialectical progression; yet this requires developmental maturation: mind has much work to do before it becomes a consciously cognizant processential being. Thus, in its prenatal form,
we may only say that mind is unconscious pulsation as lulled apperceptive
experiential process.

From my account, it makes no sense to speak of nascent mind or self
in the beginning as "the summation of sensori-motor aliveness" (Winnicott,
1960, p. 149) or the "center of initiative and a recipient of impressions"
(Kohut, 1977, p. 99) without explaining how selfhood and conscious life are
prepared by unconscious mediatory relations. Psychoanalysts from Freud to
Klein, Winnicott, and Kohut were not able to provide us with a satisfactory
account of self-development from the standpoint of genesis: although the ego
is a progressive developmental accomplishment present at birth only in a
naive form, we must account for how prenatal maturation of the ego prepares
the psyche for later self-transformations and functional tasks. This requires

explicating the dialectical maneuvers that bring consciousness into being in the first place. Because the self-development of the self simply does not pop up as the ego of consciousness, we must first examine the context and contingencies the soul first encounters in its initial immediacy. The term *soul* is used here, as with Hegel, to describe the immediacy of subjectivity as an unconscious state of undifferentiated oneness or unity with its natural corporeality. Thus, unlike Freud, who discusses the soul as the unification of unconscious and conscious life, here the soul is strictly an unconscious, affective embodiment. It does not belong to the sensuousness of consciousness, albeit sensuousness in the form of affective self-certainty is its experiential modality.

It is important at this point to reemphasize that the soul in its immediate unconscious unity, undifferentiated from its sentient nature, is a *lulled* or subdued experiential, apperceptive activity. The term *apperception* is used here to denote the felt sensuousness or self-apprehension of the soul's self-immediacy. In its implicitness or initial experiential form, the soul must undergo an internal evolution that arouses itself to a state of experiential *mediacy*. This is the initial dialectical instantiation of psychic life, a relation the unconscious first has with itself. And this is a process that unfolds from within itself, from within its own interior constitution. This self-relation the soul has with itself is the first transition to giving itself determinate life. Before that, soul is ontologically determined immediacy.

In its transition from implicitness to explicitness, immediacy to mediacy, it seizes on its teleological nature as determinate being. Soul, or what I will call the incipient unconscious ego, undergoes an unrest; moreover, an intensification of its already unrestful nature as pure activity, and generates the initial movement of its own becoming. Hence, unconscious being is already thrown into participation with the process of its own becoming as an unconscious trajectory of determinate mediatory relations. Thus, in the beginning stages of the soul's development, the lulled being of unconscious experience undergoes an internal tension and awakens within its natural immediacy as a sensuous, corporeal embodiment.

This is a gradual architectonic process of unfolding dialectical relations that becomes contextually realized through self-generative expression. These dialectical operations undergird psychic development and are the fundamental dynamic activities of erecting mental structures and order (as continual, interactive processes of interrelated and complementing forces) within the mind. In this lulled, rudimentary form of mind, the organism is a passive activity, asleep (as it were) in its own inwardness. We may reasonably say at this point that mind is largely a subdued flow of activity, pulsation, or calm throb of experience that is relatively simple, lacks complexity and internal cohesion, and is relatively constituted through its physiological contingencies. But unlike Freud's quiescent organism, mind undergoes a profound restlessness or inner rumble of negativity that it experiences from within its coma-like condition as an eruption to *be*. Such restlessness is due to the opposition it encounters from within its own interior—not from externality, yet perhaps it is experienced as an alien presence or presentation of tension similar to Freud's envision of drive. This drive, however, acts as an internal impetus to awaken, to move, to mobilize itself to more concrete experience: in its initial state of unconscious arousal, it takes itself as its own being that is vibrant and sentient.

Here unconscious apperception arouses itself to *be* and to project life into itself as the form of feeling self-certainty. The soul intuits its own presence as such through the affective embodied experience of its immediate self-awareness. This self-awareness, however, is not the self-reflective, directive aspects of self-consciousness belonging to the ego of conscious perception and introspection. Rather, it is a prereflective, nonpropositional form of self-certainty as immediate subjective sentient–affective experience, what I have called *unconscious self-consciousness* (Mills, 2000a). The amorphous self knows itself in its immediacy as unconscious experiential subjectivity.

But why does drive emerge to begin with? What urge or impulse awakens mind from its internal slumber? Here mind is a restless indeterminate immediacy, a simple self-enclosed unconscious unity that pulsates and exists in a state of *disquieted* quiescence. It undergoes upheaval because of certain instinctual, motivational currents pressing for expression as a primordial hunger or longing to experience, to feed, to fill itself, namely, as appetition or *desire*. Here we have something to learn from the idealists:[8] human subjectivity is a desirous enterprise—it yearns, it seeks, it finds. But why do we desire? In other words, what constitutes desire in the first place? Freud finds its source in somatic organizations, and we have good reason to believe that desire is a natural process emanating from the body informed by evolutionary pressures; but this does not adequately address the ontological status of desire, nor does it mean that drive devolves into biology as we have previously shown. Freud (1915a) is unmistakable in telling us that the pressure or force of a drive is its very essence (*Wesen*), hence not simply reducible to its subterranean material-efficient causal determinants. But why does unconscious desire experience such pressure to begin with? What is its *reason* to desire?

Mind desires because it stands in relation to absence or lack. Thus, drive emerges from a primal desire, the desire to fill the lack. In the most primitive phases of psychic constitution, mind is an active stream of desire exerting pressure from within itself as drive, clamoring for satisfaction, what Freud would call pleasure. But unlike Freud, who sees pleasure as tension reduction, mind may be said to always crave, to always desire. While a particular drive or its accompanying derivatives may be sated, desire itself may be said to never formally stop yearning: it is condemned to experience lack. Unlike Lacan (1977), however, who describes desire as "lack of being," and Sartre (1943) who initially views human experience "as lack," here unconscious desire is *being-in-relation-to-lack*.[9]

Within the very process of unconscious genesis, we may observe the overwhelming presence of death. The dialectic is conditioned on the premise of negation and lack, a primacy of the *not*. Nothingness or lack informs the dialectic that we experience as desire. Desire is teleological (purposeful) activity, a craving—at once an urge and an impetus—an infinite striving, a striving to fill the lack. Absence stands in primary relation to presence, including the being or presence of absence; hence this is why desire remains a fundamental being-in-relation-to-lack. While drive gradually becomes more expressive and organized into mental life, the deep reservoir of the unconscious begins to fill as psychic agency simultaneously incubates and transposes itself through its own determinate activity. In its original state, however, being and nothing, life and death, are the same.

THE EGO AND THE ABYSS

Following our dialectical analysis of the coming into being of unconscious agency, we can readily see how this developmental process proceeds from the archaic and unrefined immediacy of our sentient corporeal nature to the standpoint of ego development belonging to the higher activities of cognition: mind awakens from its initial primordial indeterminate immediacy and unfolds into a more robust, determinate progressive organization of psychic life—from the most primitive to the most exalted shapes of human consciousness. But initially mind has its form in the natural immediacy in which it finds itself as nonconscious prereflective, affective, embodied experience. The self-certainty the unconscious soul has of itself in its natural immediacy may be summarized by the following dialectical phases:

- Mind awakens as unconscious apperception due to internal compulsions to experience and reveal itself to itself as sentient, apperceptive corporeal activity,

- The coming into being of unconscious subjectivity undergoes a gradual internal upheaval due to the pressures of desire and drive that it

- Experiences as affectively laden, embodied sensuous self-certainty. This predevelopment of the human being no doubt takes place in the prenatal fetal milieu that is essentially innately predisposed orientations of the organism belonging to and awakening as the privatization of unconscious subjective experience.

We have determined that restlessness due to desire as the experience of lack is the initial point of genesis of felt psychic expression. The psyche at this level takes itself as its initial form, which is none other than the affective self-certainty of its embodied natural immediacy. So far we have used the term *soul* to designate this intermediate process of psychic development, but are we justified in going further? When does unconscious subjectivity become an organized agency to the point we can say there is an I and/

or an It? Is it legitimate to say that as soon as there is any unconscious activity at all this constitutes agency, or must agency derive from a higher developmental state or occasion? Because there is a mediatory transition from restless desire to the urge or drive to experience *itself*, I think we are justified in saying that at this phase in the epigenesis of the unconscious mind we have the rudimentary form of ego, which has as its task to become more aware and develop even further as a subjective being in the world. Because mind mediates its immediate naturality as experiential affectivity, this constitutes a dialectical movement of determinate affirmation of self even though such determination is still profoundly primitive and elementary. This determination of the mind's self-instantiation places ego development prior to birth within its prenatal environment where it prepares for conscious awakening and thereafter. Therefore, the ego is not merely an agency constituted *at* birth, instead it is prepared in the unconscious soul long beforehand.

Schematically, we may trace the initial unfolding of the incipient unconscious ego as it progresses from (1) desire to (2) apperception to (3) sentience, each phase being merely a moment in the constitution of subjective agency through its own determinant dialectical mediation (see Figure 1). We can readily see how this process of modification continues to proliferate in a consecutive sublated dynamic fashion eventually becoming the ego of consciousness embracing and incorporating its newfound experiences and developmental acquisitions.

Up to now, I have emphasized the affective embodied experience the ego has with its own immediacy within its unconscious totality. That is, the ego only knows itself as a feeling sentient being. In fact, it has no content other than its original form of unity within its natural corporeal condition of unconscious sensuousness. This sensuousness, however, is not the sensuousness of

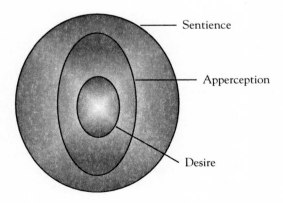

Figure 1. Epigenesis of the unconscious ego.

conscious perception, instead it is the felt inwardizing of experiential immediacy. But as soon as the ego feels itself as an experiential being, it already preforms the mediatory action of *cognizing* its own existence. This shift from waking within its natural immediacy to experiencing itself as a feeling agent constitutes the birth of the psyche. We may refer to this activity as a process of *intuition* that is both a form of sensuousness as well as a form of thought. Here, the rigid bifurcation between emotion and thought must be suspended, for unconscious affective apperception becomes the prototype for thinking which we attribute to conscious subjectivity: thought—reason—is the materialization of desire. In effect, the nascent self intuits its own being by collecting or gathering up the sensuous data it experiences internally, from within its own self-interior, and then posits or thinks itself *in* this state, hence this process is both an affective and cognizing activity. This is not to imply that the self thinks itself into existence as many modern philosophies of the will contend; rather, thinking is initially experiential affectivity as self-certainty. While the higher operations of conscious cognition do not concern us here, we have shown how consciousness is dialectically prepared within unconscious subjective experience. In this way, the unconscious ego imposes its own experiential order on the phenomenology of consciousness that arises in the ego on the actual physical birth of the human infant. However, despite the intensification of the senses that accrue through cognitive development, the resonance of the ego's initial unconscious affective states becomes the touchstone for mind to filter and compare all subsequent experiential encounters. The life of feeling remains an essential aspect of human subjectivity.

The self experiences itself as sensuously embodied thought that eventually becomes further divided, differentiated, organized, and expressed dialectically as the higher shapes of psychic development unfold. I have referred to this generic process of psychic progression as a projective identifictory trajectory of dynamic pattern whereby the self divides itself via internal splitting, then projects its interior into externality as affirmative negation, and then identifies with its disavowed shape which it seizes upon and reabsorbs, hence reincorporating itself back into its transmuted inner constitution (Mills, 2000a). This is a progressive dynamic pattern of unconscious architectonic trajectory that moves far beyond the notion of projective identification first espoused by Klein (1946) and Bion (1962). In fact, this process itself is the ontological force of the dialectic responsible for the evolution of mind. It is from that dim interior of unconscious void where the ego must liberate and elevate itself from its solitary imprisoned existence to the experiential world of consciousness. Yet the embryonic ego first knows itself, not as a conscious subject, but as a prereflective, unconscious self-consciousness; in other words, as inwardizing self-intuition.

The unconscious ego comes into being as an agency that has some crude capacity for dialectical mediatory relations, and in determining the point of such transmogrifications, we can reasonably say there is determinate

teleological expression. The ego's dialectical mediation of its natural immediacy and affective experience of itself as self-certainty becomes the logical
model of psychic progression. It is in this way that the unconscious mind
progresses from the most archaic mental configurations of unconscious impulse or urge to the refined experiences of self-consciousness. But this assessment leaves us with the difficult question of difference between ego and
drive—what Freud dichotomized as the I and the It. Rather than conceive of
the ego and the domain of the drives as two separate entities, I believe it
becomes important to reconceptualize this duality as a monistic process of
psychic differentiation and modification showing how the ego is in fact the
organized embodiment and experience of drive. Because the ego is ontologically
fueled by the dialectic of unconscious desire, and desire is the very force
behind the appearance of drive, the division between the I and the It is
essentially annulled. It is how drive *appears* as ego that we may observe such
differences, while, ontologically speaking, ego and drive are identical.

In relation to Hegel's philosophy, I have relabeled the domain of the
It as an unconscious *abyss* that I think more precisely captures the multiple
processes of unconsciousness that Freud tried to systematically categorize. Yet
while Freud alerts us to his view of the unconscious as consisting of three
divided agencies, with the ego and superego being further split into conscious and unconscious counterparts, I envision the abyss from the standpoint of a monistic developmental unconscious ontology that gives rise to
higher forms of psychic organization that interact with and interpenetrate
the experiential and intersubjective contingencies that it encounters and
assimilates through a cybernetic function of reciprocal dialectical relations.
The abyss is that domain of unconscious mind that the ego emerges out of
and yet continues to fill and engage through its relation to conscious subjective experience. In a word, the abyss is the indispensable psychic foundation
of human subjectivity—the ontological a priori condition for all forms of
consciousness to emerge, materialize, and thrive. This ensures the primacy
of archaic experience, unformulated affect, emotional vicissitudes, and
prelinguistic and/or extralinguistic reverberations despite the equiprimordiality
of language and unconscious process.

The relation of the ego to the abyss becomes one that requires a degree
of differentiation and negation performed by the ego directed toward all
realms of otherness. In effect, what the ego experiences is alienation, especially its own self-alienation or alienating activity as disavowed experience,
which becomes relegated to otherness and split off from its own self-identity.
Such differentiation is an activity the ego performs within itself through
determinate negation—I am *not* It!, but the ego is what the abyss has become from the standpoint of the ego's self-differentiation from its foreignness
and its original natural immediacy. Therefore, the abyss is the materiality of
nature in which the ego emerges out of but is always immersed in: it experiences itself as drive—as a desirous subjective being, which is the formative

organization and expression of unconscious agency that epigenetically becomes the ego of consciousness. It is only in relation to itself that the ego forges a gap between itself and the abyss—which becomes the domain of all that the self refuses to identify as being identical to itself. We can readily see how the Freudian *Es* may be conceptually subsumed within the abyss of the ego, that element of mind *alienus* to the ego's own experiential immediacy.

We have determined that desire as being-in-relation-to-lack is the essence of mind that fuels and sustains the process of the dialectic. Desire becomes the ontological thrust behind the presence and felt experience of drive, itself the urge, pressure, or impulse toward activity; and this process gives rise to the unconscious ego awakening within its own inwardness to discover itself as a sensuous, apperceptive affective self-intuiting being that knows itself in its natural embodied immediacy. This dialectical transition from indeterminate immediacy to determinate mediacy by which the ego takes its own natural form as its initial object constitutes the coming into being of unconscious subjective agency. Despite its crude organization at this phase of its life, it nevertheless points toward the dialectical process of its own becoming as a progressive teleological expression of subjectivity eventually acquiring conscious cognition and the higher faculties of self-conscious rational thought as development sequentially unfolds. These higher planes of development are forged by the sustaining power of the dialectic, a process that takes place first and foremost within the unconscious abyss of its natural immediacy.

The ego materializes out of an abyss in which it itself remains. In this way, the unconscious ego is itself an abyss that must mediate the multiple, overdetermined, and antithetical forces that populate and besiege it. In the ego's determinate activity of mediation, it sets itself in opposition to otherness that it must sublate, and this inevitably means that certain aspects of its interiority (e.g., content, images, impulses, wishes, ideation) must be combated and/or superceded. It is only on the condition that the ego intuits itself that it gives itself life felt as subjective experiential immediacy. When seen from the standpoint of the ego's mature development, the abyss becomes anything that the ego refuses to identity as belonging its own constitution.

Freud (1923) tells us that "the ego is first and foremost a bodily ego" (p. 26) by the simple fact that we are embodied. But he did not fully describe this process: the ego is first and foremost an unconscious embodiment that intuits its Self within the natural immediacy in which it finds itself. Through continual dialectical bifurcation, the ego expands its internal experiential and representational world and thus acquires additional capacities, structures, and attunement through its mediated, conscious relational contingencies and epigenetic achievements. In doing so, the ego forges an even wider and deeper abyss casting all otherness into the liar of self-externalization. Therefore the chasm between the ego and the abyss is one in which the ego creates itself. The ego of consciousness emerges from an unconscious void that it sinks back into at any given moment, thus never truly attaining ontological distinction. The ego first awakens as unconscious subjectivity within the feeling mode of its original being that it experiences as drive, the restless compulsion to experience. This is why ego and drive are not ontologically differentiated; ego is merely the appearance of drive. Drive is embodied natural desire, our original being that goes through endless transformations in the contextualization and enactment of our personal individualities and interpersonally encountered realities. Drive is transporting, and this is what governs the dialectic. The reason why the domain of drive and, more broadly, that of the abyss, seems so foreign to the ego is that from the standpoint of conscious self-differentiation, we our so much more than our mere biologies. We *define* our subjective experiences, and when they come from unintended locations as extraneous temporal encroachments—from the monstrous to the sublime—they are not identified as emanating from within or by one's own determinate will.

Throughout this chapter, I have attempted to show how dialectical psychoanalytic thought explains the coming into being of unconscious subjectivity, thus answering to Freud's adumbrated attempt to explain modification and differentiation of the I from the It. With the current focus on the primacy of emotions in organizing self-experience through intersubjective relations (Aron, 1996; Lichtenberg, 1989; Orange, 1995; Stern, 1997; Stolorow & Atwood, 1992), it is important to emphasize that process psychology explains how affective resonance becomes the locus of unconscious mediatory experience the self first has with itself. This may explain why the life of emotions yields primordial force and direction in forming psychic structure and intersubjective reality, and thus partially answers why certain unconscious emotional experiences predate and resist articulation through linguistic mediums.

NOTES

1. See Freud's *Gesammelte Werke, Chronologisch Geordnet*, 18 Vols. Anna Freud, Edward Bibring, Willi Hoffer, Ernst Kris, and Otto Isakower, in collaboration with Marie Bonaparte (Eds.) (London: 1940–1952; Frankfurt am Main, 1968). All references to Freud's texts will refer to *The Standard Edition of the Complete Psychological Works of Sigmund Freud*, 24 Vols. (1886–1940), Trans. & Gen. Ed. James Strachey in collaboration with Anna Freud, assisted by Alix Strachey and Alan Tyson (London: Hogarth Press, 1966–1995); hereafter followed by the date and page number. I have compared Strachey's translation to the *Gesammelte Werke* and provide my own in places that warrant changes.

2. The noun *Ich* stands in philosophic relation to German idealism, particularly Fichte's (1794) absolute self-positing self. Today it is almost exclusively a Freudian term.

3. A common interpretation of Freud's dialectic is to conclude that there are oppositional forces that are never resolved, hence never canceled, surpassed, or transcended. Instead, it is thought that a multiplicity of opposing processes and contents,

say impulses, wishes, fantasies, and their counterparts, are preserved in deadlocks, thus maintaining the psychic tension that characterizes the psyche. And there is justification for this argument: Freud himself places a great deal emphasis on dualism. But this dualism, as I have argued elsewhere (2002), is the way in which psychic processes appear or unfold phenomenologically, even if such appearances are movements or modifications within unconscious experience as the transmutation of organizational processes that fuel and sustain psychic structure. Freud is a developmental monistic ontologist, and, in this respect, his dialectic is comparable to (albeit not convergent with) Hegel's. As I will point out, Freud's mature theory involves a series of modifications and transmogrifications that are derived from the most primitive unconscious activities to the most exalted self-conscious deliberations, hence psychic organization is a developmental achievement. In the mind, polarity seeks expression, discharge, and resolve. If it does not attain some modicum of compromise, hence negotiated expression, then it can lapse into impasse, therefore a stalemate that can lead to pathology, regression, or fixation at more primitive stages of organization. This is why dream formation, slips of the tongue or pen, significant forgetting, bungled actions, and symptom manifestation are attempts at dialectical syntheses, just as rational discourse and scientific explorations strive for higher (synthetic) levels of comprehension. But these processes are enacted with varying degrees of success and elevation. For example, it can be argued that a repetition compulsion is a failed attempt at achieving a higher stage of transcendence or sublation, which is aimed toward mastery, unification, and wholeness; while sublimation is a more successful and cultivated expression of primordial conflict, such as through art, culture, religion, and social-ethical reform. The mind can never remain "deadlocked" without falling into chaos and despair, and this is why Freud wants to differentiate the abnormal from more adjusted states of mind.

4. This position is in stark contrast to antisubjectivist perspectives popular among many forms of poststructuralism (Lacan, 1977), postmodernism, and linguistic analytic philosophy (Cavell, 1993). These approaches insist that the human subject is subverted by language that structures and orders all experience. I am in agreement with Roger Frie (1997) that while language is a necessary condition of human subjectivity, it is far from being a sufficient condition for capturing all aspects of lived experience. Sole linguistic accounts do not adequately explain how preverbal, extralinguistic, and unformulated unconscious affective experiences resonate within our intrapsychic processes. Furthermore, they assume a developmental reversal, namely, that language precedes thought and cognition rather than acknowledging preverbal forces, unconscious experience, and emotive processes of subjectivity that developmentally give rise to linguistic acquisition and expression. In effect, this claim boasts that meaning does not reside in the mind, rather in language itself. But words don't think, only subjective agents. Despite the historicity of language within one's existing social ontology, the way language is acquired is potentially developmentally different for each child. Furthermore, words may be imbued with functional meaning that resists universal symbols and signifiers, hence ensuring the privatization of internally mediated signification.

5. We must offer a stipulation that while early life predisposes one to neurosis, it does not predetermine a hard-fast developmental sequence: personal maturation is radically molded by context and contingency. Like his concept of drive, which is mobile and transmutational, psychic adaptation requires a certain margin of freedom.

6. In evolutionary biology, as in history and in nature, sex and aggression are necessary conditions for organismic survival and self-preservation. Insofar as species could not continue without natural copulation, so must aggression be harnessed in order to ensure survival. In fact, the whole historical narrative of the human race may be viewed as a "slaughterbench" (Hegel, 1833) in order to advance human civilization, which still requires aggression to enforce law and order (Freud, 1930).

7. In *Contexts of Being*, Stolorow and Atwood (1992) address three realms of the unconscious that they call (1) prereflective—largely culled from Brentano, Sartre, and early phenomenologists, but ultimately dating back to Fichte, (2), dynamic—a recapitulation of Freud, and (3) the unvalidated—from my account, extrapolated from Binswanger and Sullivan (29–36). But the theory and practice of the intersubjective approach are unquestionably focused on the nature of lived *conscious* experience and affective attunement to emotional resonances within the patient through an empathic-introspective stance (a method, attitude, and/or sensibility derived from Kohut, 1971). For example, Stolorow claims, "In place of the Freudian unconscious . . . we envision a multiply contextualized experimental world, an organized totality of lived personal experience, more or less conscious" (Foreword to Buirski & Haglund, 2001, xii). But regardless of current analytic propensities that focus on the understanding and response to conscious rather than unconscious processes, it does not negate the dynamic presence of subjective unconscious activity. Most recently, Timothy J. Zeddies (2000) revisits the notion of the unconscious within relational perspectives emphasizing the intersubjective and dialogically constituted processes that constitute the relational matrix particularly in reference to the patient–analyst relationship.

8. Many Idealist perspectives posit the existence of prereflective, prelinguistic, or nonpropositional self-consciousness. Sartre does this; so do contemporaries such as Manfred Frank (1991) and Dieter Henrich (1966). Such theories derive not only from modern philosophy, but ultimately from a tradition that dates back to neo-Platonism and theosophic-mystical accounts of the soul. In this tradition, the father of German idealism, J. G. Fichte, asserted that the prelinguistic subject originally generates and constitutes its own being; that is, the self freely posits or asserts itself absolutely. In his *Wissenschaftslehre* (1794), Fichte states that "*The self begins by an absolute positing of its own existence*" (99). For Fichte, what ultimately characterizes the ground of human subjectivity is pure "activity as such." Before there is consciousness proper, thought lives underground as an "intellectual intuition" of itself—namely, prereflective, nonrepresentational self-consciousness. This original prereflective self-consciousness is in fact *unconscious*. Such unconscious self-consciousness is the prefamiliarity the self has with itself before achieving conscious self-reflective awareness.

In the Idealist tradition, F. W. J. von Schelling made the unconscious the sine qua non of psychic life. Schelling's revision of Kant's and Fichte's transcendental idealism, together with his own philosophy of identity (*Identitätsphilosophie*) and philosophy of nature (*Naturphilosophie*), led to one of the first systematic conceptualizations of the unconscious. For Schelling (1815), "all consciousness has what is unconscious as ground, and, just in coming to be conscious, this unconscious is posited as past by that which becomes conscious of itself" (150). Freud (1923) echoes this sentiment: "The repressed [past] is the prototype of the unconscious. . . . We can come to know even the Ucs. only by making it conscious" (15, 17). Schelling, like Freud, was deeply engaged with the problem of *Beginning*, that is, original ground

(*Grund*). Hegel (1831c) referred to this primordial ground as a "nocturnal abyss," what he had earlier labeled in the *Phenomenology* (1807) the realm of "*unconscious Spirit*" (278).

In all modern philosophies of the will, an unconscious ground—an *Ungrund*— precedes consciousness. The primacy of the *Ungrund* was first made sensible by the seventeenth century philosopher, mystic, and theosophist, Jacob Boehme, to whom Fichte, Schelling, and Hegel owe much. The *Abyss* (*Abgrund*) or *Ungrund* is the "ground without a ground," a subject who "seeks," "longs," "lusts" and "finds." This conceptualization of unconscious activity bears comparison to a standard neo-Platonic idea: Proclus, Erigenia, and Plotinus conceived of the *Ungrund* as the *ens manifestativum sui*, "the being whose essence is to reveal itself" (see Koyré, 1929; Mills, 1996; von der Luft, 1994; Walsh, 1994; Weeks, 1991).

9. For both Sartre and Lacan, consciousness itself takes the form of *lack*. While Lacan (1977) refers to a "lack of being" throughout his *Écrits*, Sartre (1943) is more specific when he tells us that "human reality . . . exists first as lack. . . . In its coming into existence, human reality grasps itself as an incomplete being" (89). For Sartre, human subjectivity is desirously compelled to fill the lack through projection of a future transcendence, hence a "being-for-itself."

REFERENCES

Aristotle (1962). *Nichomachean Ethics*. Trans. Martin Ostwald. Englewood Cliffs, NJ: Prentice-Hall.

Aron, Lewis. *A Meeting of Minds*. Hillsdale, NJ: Analytic Press, 1996.

Beebe, B., J. Jafee, & F. Lachmann. "A Dyadic Systems View of Communication." In *Relational Perspectives in Psychoanalysis*. Ed. N. Skolnick & S. Warchaw. Hillsdale, NJ: Analytic Press, 1992.

Benjamin, Jessica. "Recognition and Destruction: An Outline of Intersubjectivity." In *Relational Perspectives in Psychoanalysis*. Ed. N. Skolnick & S. Warchaw. Hillsdale, NJ: Analytic Press, 1992.

Bettelheim, Bruno. *Freud and Man's Soul*. New York: Vintage Books, 1982.

Bion, W. R. A Theory of Thinking. In *Melanie Klein Today: Developments in Theory and Practice. Vol. 1: Mainly Theory*. Ed. E. B. Spillius. London: Routledge, 1988.

Bornstein, R. F. The Impending Death of Psychoanalysis. *Psychoanalytic Psychology* 18, no. 1 (2001): 3–20.

Buirski, Peter, & Pamela Haglund. *Making Sense Together: The Intersubjective Approach to Psychotherapy*. Northvale, NJ: Jason Aronson, 2001.

Burbidge, John. "Hegel's Conception of Logic." In *The Cambridge Companion to Hegel*. Ed. F. C. Beiser. New York: Cambridge University Press, 1993.

Cavell, Marcia. *The Psychoanalytic Mind: From Freud to Philosophy*. Cambridge, MA: Harvard University Press, 1993.

Fichte, J. G. *The Science of Knowledge*. Trans. & Eds. P. Heath & J. Lachs. Cambridge: Cambridge University Press, 1794/1993.

Fisher, S. & Greenberg, R. P. *Freud Scientifically Reappraised*. New York: Wiley, 1996.

Frank, Manfred. *Selbstbewesstsein und selbstkenntnis*. Stuttgart: Reclam, 1991.

Freud, Sigmund. *Gesammelte Werke, Chronologisch Geordnet*, 18 Vols. Ed. Anna Freud, Edward Bibring, Willi Hoffer, Ernst Kris, and Otto Isakower, in colloboration with Marie Bonaparte. London: 1940–1952; Frankfurt am Main, 1968.

————. *The Standard Edition of the Complete Psychological Works of Sigmund Freud*, 24 Vols. (1886–1940), Trans. & Gen. Ed. James Strachey in collaboration with Anna Freud, assisted by Alix Strachey and Alan Tyson. London: Hogarth Press, 1966–1995.

————. *Project for a Scientific Psychology. Standard Edition*, Vol. 1, 1895.

————. *The Interpretation of Dreams. Standard Edition*, Vols. 4–5, 1900.

————. *Three Essays on the Theory of Sexuality. Standard Edition*, Vol. 7, 1905a.

————. "Psychical (or Mental) Treatment." *Standard Edition*, Vol. 7, 1905b.

————. *On the History of the Psycho-Analytic Movement. Standard Edition*, Vol. 14, 1914.

————. "On Narcissism: An Introduction." *Standard Edition*, Vol. 14, 1914.

————. "Instincts and Their Vicissitudes." *Standard Edition*, Vol. 14, 1915a.

————. "Repression." *Standard Edition*, Vol. 14, 1915b.

————. *Introductory Lectures on Psycho-Analysis. Standard Edition*, Vols. 15–16, 1916–1917 [1915–1917].

————. *Beyond the Pleasure Principle. Standard Edition*, Vol. 18, 1920.

————. *Group Psychology and the Analysis of the Ego. Standard Edition*, Vol. 18, 1921.

————. *The Ego and the Id. Standard Edition*, Vol. 19, 1923.

————. "The Resistances to Psycho-Analysis." *Standard Edition*, Vol. 19, 1925a [1924].

————. "Negation." *Standard Edition*, Vol. 19, 1925b.

————. *Inhibitions, Symptoms and Anxiety. Standard Edition*, Vol. 20, 1926.

————. *Future of an Illusion. Standard Edition*, Vol. 21, 1927.

————. *Civilization and its Discontents. Standard Edition*, Vol. 21, 1930.

————. *New Introductory Lectures on Psycho-Analysis. Standard Edition*, Vol. 22, 1933 [1932].

————. *An Outline of Psycho-Analysis. Standard Edition*, Vol. 23, 1940 [1938].

Frie, Roger. *Subjectivity and Intersubjectivity in Modern Philosophy and Psychoanalysis.* Lanham, MD: Rowman & Littlefield, 1997.

————. Psychoanalysis and the Linguistic Turn. *Contemporary Psychoanalysis* 35 (1999): 673–697.

Gedo, J. *The Languages of Psychoanalysis.* Hillsdale, NJ: Analytic Press, 1996.

Greenberg, J. & Mitchell, Stephen. *Theories of Object Relations.* Cambridge: Harvard University Press, 1983.

Grünbaum, Adolf. *The Foundations of Psychoanalysis.* Berkeley: University of California Press, 1984.

Hanly, Charles. *The Problem of Truth in Applied Psychoanalysis.* New York: Guilford Press, 1992.

Hegel, G. F. W., *Phenomenology of Spirit.* Trans. A. V. Miller. Oxford: Oxford University Press, 1807/1977.

————. *Science of Logic.* Trans. A. V. Miller. London: George Allen & Unwin, 1812/1831/1969.

————. *The Encyclopaedia Logic*, Vol.1 of the *Encyclopaedia of the Philosophical Sciences.* Trans. T. F. Geraets, W. A. Suchting, and H. S. Harris. Indianapolis: Hackett Publishing Company, 1817a/1827/1830/1991.

————. *Philosophy of Nature.* Vol. 2 of the *Encyclopaedia of the Philosophical Sciences.* Trans. A. V. Miller. Oxford: Clarendon Press, 1817b/1827/1830/1970.

————. *Hegel's Philosophie des subjektiven Geistes / Hegel's Philosophy of Subjective Spirit*, Vol. 1: Introductions, Vol. 2: Anthropology, Vol. 3: Phenomenology and Psychology. Ed. M. J. Petry. Dordrecht, Holland: D. Reidel Publishing Company, 1817c/1827/1830/1978.

———. *Introduction to the Lectures on the History of Philosophy*. Trans. T. M. Knox and A. V. Miller. Oxford: Clarendon Press, 1833/1985.

Heidegger, Martin. *Being and Time*. San Francisco: Harper Collins, 1927.

Henrich, Dieter. Fichte's original insight. Trans. D. R. Lachterman. In *Contemporary German Philosophy*. Vol. 1. Ed. D. E. Christenson. University Park: Penn State Press, 1982.

Kant, I. *Critique of Pure Reason*. Trans. N. K. Smith. New York: St. Martin's, 1781/ 1965.

Klein, Melanie. "Notes on Some Schizoid Mechanisms." *International Journal of Psychoanalysis*. 27 (1946): 99–110.

Kohut, Heinz. *The Analysis of the Self*. New York: International Universities Press, 1971.

———. *The Restoration of the Self*. New York: International Universities Press, 1977.

———. *How Does Analysis Cure?* Ed. A. Goldberg & P. Stepansky. Chicago: University of Chicago Press, 1984.

Koyré, Alexandre. *La philosophie de Jacob Boehme*. New York: Franklin, 1968/1979.

Lacan, J. *Écrits: A Selection*. Trans. Alan Sheridan. New York: Norton, 1977.

Laplanche, J. *Life and Death in Psychoanalysis*. Baltimore: Johns Hopkins, 1970.

Lear, Jonathan. *Love and Its Place in Nature: A Philosophical Interpretation of Freudian Psychoanalysis*. New York: Noonday Press, 1990.

Lichtenberg, Joseph. *Psychoanalysis and Motivation*. Hillsdale, NJ: Analytic Press, 1989.

Mahler, M. S., Pine, F., and Bergman, A. *The Psychological Birth of the Human Infant*. New York: Basic Books, 1975.

Meissner, W. W. "The Self as Structural." *Psychoanalysis and Contemporary Thought* 23, no. 3 (2000): 373–416.

Mills, Jon. "Hegel on the Unconscious Abyss: Implications for Psychoanalysis." *The Owl of Minerva* 28, no. 1 (1996): 59–75.

———. "Hegel on Projective Identification: Implications for Klein, Bion, and Beyond." *The Psychoanalytic Review* 87, no. 6 (2000a): 841–874.

———. "Dialectical Psychoanalysis: Toward Process Psychology." *Psychoanalysis and Contemporary Thought* 23, no. 3 (2000b): 20–54.

———. *The Unconscious Abyss: Hegel's Anticipation of Psychoanalysis*. Albany: State University of New York Press, 2002.

Mitchell, Stephen A. *Relational Concepts in Psychoanalysis: An Integration*. Cambridge, MA: Harvard University Press, 1988.

Ogden, Thomas H. *The Matrix of the Mind*. Northvale, NJ: Aronson, 1986.

Orange, Donna M. *Emotional Understanding*. New York: Guilford Press, 1995.

Orange, Donna M., George Atwood, and Robert D. Stolorow. *Working Intersubjectively: Contextualism in Psychoanalytic Practice*. Hillsdale, NJ: Analytic Press, 1997.

Plato. *The Collected Dialogues of Plato*. Ed. Edith Hamilton & Huntington Cairns. Princeton: Princeton University Press, 1961.

Reisner, Steven. "Eros Reclaimed: Recovering Freud's Relational Theory." *Relational Perspectives in Psychoanalysis*. Ed. N. J. Skolnick & S. C. Warshaw. Hillsdale, NJ: Analytic Press, 1992, pp. 281–312.

Sartre, J. P. *Being and Nothingness*. Trans. H. E. Barnes. New York: Washington Square Press, 1943/1956.

Schelling, F. G. J. (1811–1815). *Ages of the World.* Trans. F. de Wolfe Bolman. New York: AMS Press, 1967.

Stern, Daniel. *The Interpersonal World of the Infant.* New York: Basic Books, 1985.

————. *Unformulated Experience: From Dissociation to Imagination in Psychoanalysis.* Hillsdale, NJ: Analytic Press, 1997.

Stolorow, Robert & George Atwood. *Contexts of Being: The Intersubjective Foundations of Psychological Life.* Hillsdale, NJ: Analytic Press, 1992.

Stolorow, Robert, B. Brandchaft, & George Atwood. *Psychoanalytic Treatment: An Intersubjective Approach.* Hillsdale, NJ: Analytic Press, 1987.

Sulloway, Frank. *Freud: Biologist of the Mind.* Cambridge, MA: Harvard University Press, 1979/1992.

von der Luft, Eric. Comment. In *History and System: Hegel's Philosophy of History.* Ed. R. L. Perkins. Albany: State University of New York Press, 1994.

Walsh, David. The Historical Dialectic of Spirit: Jacob Boehme's Influence on Hegel. In *History and System: Hegel's Philosophy of History.* Ed. R. L. Perkins. Albany: State University of New York Press, 1994.

Weeks, Andrew. *Boehme: An Intellectual Biography of the Seventeenth-Century Philosopher and Mystic.* Albany: State University of New York Press, 1991.

Whitehead, Alfred North. *Science and the Modern World.* New York: Free Press, 1925.

Winnicott, W. D. Ego Distortion in Terms of the True and False Self. In *D. W. Winnicott, Collected Papers.* London: Tavistock, 1958.

Zeddies, Timothy J. "Within, Outside, and In Between: The Relational Unconscious." *Psychoanalytic Psychology* 17, no. 3 (2000): 467–487.

EIGHT

TEMPORALITY AND THE THERAPEUTIC SUBJECT: THE PHENOMENOLOGY OF TRANSFERENCE, REMEMBERING, AND WORKING-THROUGH

<hr>

Maria Talero

BY FOCUSING PRIMARILY on Freud's description of the history of psycho-analytic practice in his essay "Remembering, Repeating and Working-Through," I will argue that the progress of psychoanalysis is precisely its progress to a phenomenological conception of lived time. I will begin with a brief description of the relation between past and present in Freud's conceptions of transference and hysterical amnesia and then turn to a longer study of "Remembering, Repeating and Working-Through," supported by a close reading of relevant material in several of Freud's other writings, to understand the way the practice of therapy engages the relation of past and present. Drawing on Merleau-Ponty, I will conclude that such therapy is the very form of human freedom.

TRANSFERENCE: THE PRESENT INVOKES THE PAST

The term *transference* refers to the way that a patient undergoing psycho-analysis comes to develop a powerful, often erotic, attachment to the analyst as part of the normal course of therapy. This erotic attachment bears the

stamp of the patient's individual 'style' of loving, that characteristic pattern
of setting up certain aims and conditions in one's love relationships that
each of us develops in early childhood, and that forms a kind of "stereotype"
that is reproduced and repeated each time a new person awakens erotic
expectations in us.[1] Just as in any other significant love relationship, the
erotic feeling for the analyst, when it emerges, is woven into this characteristic pattern, and thus it draws on the erotic or libidinal energies originally
directed toward our earliest caretakers.[2] The transference places at the analyst's
disposal all the powerful affectionate feelings that, as a child, the patient
once felt for his caretakers: the patient develops the aim of "pleasing the
psychoanalyst and winning [her] applause and love";[3] he is motivated in the
therapy and produces remarkable changes in his situation, all in order to
please the analyst as he once wanted to please his mother and father. But
also invoked in the transference are the patient's inevitable hostile or aggressive feelings toward his parents, and these too make their way into the
patient's behavior toward the analyst.[4] The analytical situation effectively
becomes a stage on which some of the most important parts of the patient's
past are reenacted. Freud says that "the patient produces before us with
plastic clarity an important part of his life story, of which he would otherwise
probably given us only an insufficient account. He acts it before us, as it
were, instead of reporting it to us."[5]

If we consider the respective roles of the psychological past and present
in the phenomenon of transference, we find a distinctive relationship at
work. It is the patient's present situation that has in effect 'summoned' the
past to come forward. The special context created by the analytic situation,
a context enacted in 'the here and now' of the patient's present life, is
somehow able to exercise a distinctive, almost 'hypnotic' magnetism that
leads the patient to begin repeating the past,[6] and to start putting on display
the stereotypical responses and archaic forms of his particular way of being
in love. Something about this present situation is so compelling as to influence
the patient's past so as to make it come forward and reenact itself.

The present, then, has a kind of power over the past; it can summon
it into being, or reanimate it, as the phenomenon of transference no less
than ordinary experiences of falling in love so powerfully show us. We will
say that in the phenomenon of transference what we see is the power of the
present to embody the past, to reproduce it and give it a "plastic" form, not
as a memory but as an actual relationship in the patient's present life.

HYSTERICAL AMNESIA: THE PAST REVOKES THE PRESENT

Let us compare the relationship of past and present as it occurs in a particular
form of neurosis, the one with which Freud's researches first began. In hysteria,
the patient displays bodily symptoms that have as their origin a wishful impulse that has arisen in a context in which it is unacceptable, either because

it is in conflict with the patient's other wishes or because it is at odds with ethical or aesthetic standards of his personality.[7] This painful conflict is relieved by the "conversion" of the psychological impulse into a bodily symptom.[8] The body, in other words, has become the vehicle of expression for a conflict that is no longer *remembered* as such, but has been pushed out of consciousness and 'forgotten,' only to be reproduced in somatic form. So Freud says: "There had been a short conflict, and the [result] of this internal struggle was that the idea which had appeared before consciousness as the vehicle of this irreconcilable wish fell a victim to repression, was pushed out of consciousness with all its attached memories, and was forgotten."[9]

A cloud of amnesia settles on the original circumstances in which the wish arose, a "forgetting" that is the correlate of the bodily "remembering" that is the hysterical symptom. The patient no longer explicitly remembers the situation that presented the traumatic conflict, but rather 'remembers' it by reproducing it in a bodily manner: the conflict and its attendant memories have become repressed. But what is crucial here is that this repression takes place through two concomitant processes, two psychological currents that cooperate in bringing about the "forgetting." Freud calls these two currents *primary* and *secondary* repression.[10] Hysterical amnesia, or the selective forgetting of certain particular experiences in the patient's past, is only possible on the basis of a more original repression *that makes possible that very selectivity*. In other words, the disappearance of events from my conscious awareness and memory is not simply something that can just 'happen.' The amnesia is selective, and erases particular events and circumstances 'attached' to the original impulse—specific aspects of the situation in which it first arose.[11] Something is working to carve out an 'area' for the amnesia to operate in, a particular arena of sensitivity to be abolished; after all, the amnesia does not spill out into every area of the patient's life, and the traumatic event, even though repressed, retains its historical features. But—Freud argues—this could only happen if there were already some meaningful core of repressed significance, more original and more volatile, in place already. The repression that we recognize in the hysterical patient, that selective "forgetting" of certain traumatic wishes and the circumstances surrounding them, and the accompanying conversion of these into bodily symptoms, is a *secondary* stage of repression that is only possible on the basis of an earlier "forgetting," a primary repression of psychological trauma that first lays down the 'coordinates,' so to speak, for what will count as traumatic in later life. Hysterical amnesia is dependent on infantile amnesia.[12] Freud says:

> Hysterical amnesia, which occurs at the bidding of repression, is only explicable by the fact that the subject is already in possession of a store of memory-traces which have been withdrawn from conscious disposal, and which are now, by an associative link, attracting

to themselves the material which the forces of repression are engaged in repelling from consciousness.[13]

The repression of the apparently 'forgotten' memories is premised on the association between an earlier repression of much older memories[14] and the later circumstances and features of the situation that give rise to the hysterical symptom. So by means of this "associative link" the repressed memory-traces of very old events and situations occurring in early childhood pull sections of the present out of the reach of consciousness, and these too become repressed. It is as if a sector of the person's present has been erased from the past. What Freud is asserting, then, is that the repression can only be carried out if something in the patient's already established history of repression demands it.[15] It is as if the memories are pulled into the 'waiting arms' of already repressed material. In hysterical amnesia, the past alters the present.

THERAPY

What we have seen in our examination of transference and hysterical amnesia is that the relationship of the past to the present in psychological illness is one of *reciprocal influence*, or mutual reinterpretation. But to test this thesis, we must turn to the place in Freud's thought where the question of precisely *how* the past is related to the present is most vitally at stake, namely, in his account of the actual practice of therapy.

In speaking of the "phenomenon" of therapy, we mean by this the endeavor of taking hold of and beneficially transforming the patient's relationship to his own past within a therapeutic context—an endeavor that is commonly recognized to be possible and that continues to be a practical goal for many people across a broad spectrum of therapeutic traditions. For Freud, the very fact that therapy is possible is what shows us, in the most practical terms, how present and past are related in psychological life.[16] What we will now see is that for Freud, the possibility of therapy depends on acknowledging the inseparability and mutual influence of past and present. The successful *practice* of therapy actually depends on getting the basic *theory* of temporality right, for it is only if one is able to understand how past and present are in fact woven together for the patient that one can address this interweaving in such a way as to bring about a therapeutic cure. It is in Freud's practice, curiously enough, that we find indications of an *implicit* theoretical recognition of the lived relationship to time that gives meaning to normal psychological life and helps explain the strange contours of psychological illness.

PSYCHOANALYSIS AS REMEMBERING

Freud begins his 1914 essay "Remembering, Repeating and Working-Through" by reviewing the phases in the development of psychoanalytic technique.

The first phase he describes is the phase of "catharsis," in which the patient was to recover his memories by means of hypnosis: "In these hypnotic treatments the process of remembering took a very simple form. The patient put himself into an earlier situation, which he seemed never to confuse with the present one, and gave an account of the mental processes belonging to it."[17] At this stage, the primary goal of analysis seemed to be a kind of return to and retrieval of the 'contents' of a preserved past. By "making the patient revert to the psychic state in which the symptom had appeared for the first time,"[18] the analyst gains a kind of privileged perspective over the troubling contents of the hysterical patient's memories; however, and more important, the patient undergoes a cathartic transformation in which these troubling contents are 'released':

> In this state, there came up in the hypnotized patient's mind memories, thoughts and impulses which had previously dropped out of consciousness, and, as soon as he had related these to the physician, accompanying this expression with intense emotion, the symptom was overcome and its return done away with.[19]

The traumatic past is cathartically 'excised,' so to speak, from the patient's unconscious without even requiring the latter's self-conscious participation in this process.

There is in fact a certain theoretical model of how past and present are related that is implicitly at work here. However, motivated by preeminently practical considerations,[20] Freud gradually moves away from and ultimately renounces up this approach to therapy.[21] Among the reasons he gives, two in particular are of interest. First of all, he says, the process of "retrieval" of past contents is complicated by the fact that most of the time, the patient's recollection, under hypnosis, of the original traumatic circumstances revealed not a single event, but rather a series of experiences leading much farther backward in time;[22] thus, instead of catching hold of an originary past event, hypnosis begins to unfold a complicated series of events, all intertwined and associated with each other, leading to the earliest recesses of childhood. Second, and most important for our purposes, is Freud's conviction that the therapeutic results of hypnosis are necessarily short-lived because they entirely bypass the *resistances*, or unconscious mental forces that are actively bringing about the repression.[23] In other words, the process of hypnosis does not engage with the active, *present-day* dimension of the traumatic past—the way that, through his symptoms, "the patient clings to his disease and thus even fights against his own recovery."[24] This present-day significance of symptoms is called by Freud the "gain from illness," and we will return to examine its significance later.

After hypnosis was given up as a therapeutic technique, the aim continued to be to get the patient to remember, but now by interpreting his or her free associations.[25] The method had changed, but the goal remained the same: to bring the unconscious past into the present where its troubling contents could finally be laid to rest. But this is a longer route to the goal, one that approaches the past only gingerly, through the present-day associations of the patient in the patient's normal, waking state. Also, the privileged standpoint of the analyst is partially relinquished. The process of examining the patient's free-associations is a process of *interpretation*, and Freud recognizes in it a kind of "division of labor" that requires the patient's active cooperation and willing participation.[26] The patient becomes party to the interpretation and piecing together of the long series of events and situations that gave rise to his or her symptoms.

But what is significant is that this is not, for Freud, where psychoanalysis ultimately ended up. The final stage of psychoanalysis, which he calls "working-through" and which is Freud's subject in the rest of the paper, is distinguished from the others mainly by having relinquished the goal of direct therapeutic access to the past. Instead of trying to get the patient to remember particular repressed portions of the past—events, facts, situations— the analyst "now contents [herself] with studying whatever is present for the time being on the surface of the patient's mind."[27] A path from the psychological present toward the past will now be built in a fundamentally different way. Ultimately the goal is the same: to get the patient to remember— nonetheless, the *route* to remembering is very different, as we will now see, both in terms of practice and in terms of theory. It is the areas of 'resistance' that signal repressions, and no longer the particular traumatic events of the past, which are now the primary targets of the analytic work.[28] What this means is that the emphasis has shifted from the illness as a phenomenon of the past to the illness as a present-day force.

Psychoanalysis proper, according to Freud in this essay, involves all three components, remembering, repeating, and working-through. What I will do now is to look at each of these in turn to see how they implicitly construe the relations of past and present: however I will both follow Freud's own explanations and depart from them a little. In the names he gives to the three essential elements of psychoanalysis, I think we can find three different ways of conceiving the relationship of past and present. That is, remembering, repeating, and working-through, as much as they are practical methods of psychoanalysis, are equally theoretical conceptions of how past and present are related in psychological life. That Freud sees all three as necessary, I want to show, is evidence that at the heart of his conception of therapy is a grasp of the phenomenological conception of lived time.

REMEMBERING AND REPEATING

What is most striking about the form psychoanalysis ends up taking compared to its beginning stages in hypnosis and free association is that instead of trying to go directly to remembering, the process begins with almost the direct opposite of remembering. Instead of remembering, the patient begins by *repeating*. As Freud says: "the patient does not *remember* anything of what he has forgotten and repressed, but *acts* it out. He reproduces it not as a memory but as an action; he *repeats* it, without, of course, knowing that he is repeating it."[29]

What is the difference between remembering and repeating? The ability to remember is the ability to stand at a distance from our own past and to look 'back' at it. Implied here is the separateness of past and present. To remember is to remember what is past, and to know that it is not the same as what is present: it is to know the difference between then and now. The implicit model here is one of two distinct and separate zones of a person's life—even two distinct places, as, for example, when we speak of remembering as "revisiting" the past. To remember implies the ability to keep past and present separate. But for one who *repeats* instead of remembering, there is no longer any straightforward distinction between past and present. Such a person lives his or her past as if it *were* the present. So, for example, Freud says:

> For instance, the patient does not say that he remembers that he used to be defiant and critical towards his parent's authority; instead, he behaves in that way to the doctor. He does not remember how he came to a helpless and hopeless deadlock in his infantile sexual researches; but he produces a mass of confused dreams and associations, complains that he cannot succeed in anything and asserts that he is fated never to carry through what he undertakes.[30]

We are reminded of the way that the hysterical symptom 'reproduces' the past almost blindly, outside of the patient's own recognition. The most basic trajectory of repressed, traumatic memories is *toward the present*: they actively seek a kind of embodiment in the patient's present life through the "compulsion to repeat."[31] In general: "The unconscious feelings strive to avoid the recognition which the cure demands; they seek instead for reproduction, with all the power of hallucination and the inappreciation of time characteristic of the unconscious."[32] In the face of this refusal to remember, the therapist does not bring forward the 'contents' of the past as if bringing them out of a container and asking the patient to recognize them. Rather, she works to build a context in which transference will take hold, and then turns to the patient's behavior to witness the direct transcription of the past into the present in the form of compulsive behavior. For to repeat, is, in a way, precisely not to remember; it is to treat the past and the present as if they were the same thing (and, in so doing, to efface the possibility of inquiring into their relationship). The one who is compelled to repeat cannot remember, and thus cannot take up any real perspective on his past. When a person compulsively repeats, it is as if she has lost her memory—or lost the ability to stand at a distance from, and thus in relationship to, her past. Thus, to remember is precisely not to repeat, and to repeat is precisely not to remember.

Psychoanalysis thus found itself forced, under the vital necessity of following the path that proved itself to be most *therapeutically* efficacious, to revise its goal of proceeding directly toward remembering. It had to consent to begin where one might most despair of the possibility of remembering: in the very depths of repetition, in all its bleakness. For the past that is summoned up by the transference sweeps into the patient's present with enveloping force, not merely restricted to the analytic relationship but rather charging the whole of his life with its psychologically troubled meaning.[33] Thus Freud says:

> We must be prepared to find, therefore, that the patient yields to the compulsion to repeat . . . not only in his personal attitude towards his doctor but also in every other activity and relationship which may occupy his life at the time—if, for instance, he falls in love or undertakes a task or starts an enterprise during the treatment.[34]

The patient models or transcribes the past directly into the present—not as clearly demarcated from it but rather as fused with it in its very significance. The compulsion to repeat takes up the fabric of the present and *seamlessly* integrates it with that of the past.

What I want to argue, then, is that this is only possible if the relationship to time in normal psychological life is of a certain character. I want to claim that Freud's description of therapy throws into relief a fundamental aspect of our human relationship to time: that we are always engaged in a process of living the past as present, and the present as past. Past and present significances are *generated out of each other*. The psychological past and the psychological present are always, for us, in a state of mutual reinterpretation.

Precisely because the patient's fundamental relationship to time is one in which past and present are fused in a reciprocally determining unity, his *therapeutic* relationship to time must take a certain form. Psychoanalysis cannot simply be the effort to help the patient access his past and bring it forward for his and the analyst's scientific perusal. For it is not a strictly demarcated past that the patient is reproducing, but rather what we might call a 'past-present,' a single continuity of significance. The two psychological dimensions must be treated as a unity. In recognition of this, Freud says: "We have . . . made it clear to ourselves that the patient's state of being ill cannot cease with the beginning of analysis, and that we must treat his illness, not as an event of the past, but as a present-day force."[35]

The psychoanalyst can no longer make her theoretical stand on the clear ground of the patient's present and analyze past events that are never confused with that present. The analysis must take its start from this new theoretical unit, the 'past-present,' and contend with the problem of *distin-

guishing past and present significances in it. The "work" of the therapy can now be likened, according to Freud, to the work of a sculptor, who proceeds, unlike the painter, by 'the method of taking away' rather than 'the method of adding on.'[36] In its earlier forms, psychoanalysis tried to proceed as if by 'adding on' interpretations over past contents, repainting them, so to speak, with a different meaning. Now something fundamentally different must happen. Like sculptors, the patient and the analyst must work together to take away the obstacles to remembering—the resistances that maintain past and present in a state of repetitive, unrecognized fusion, as opposed to a *recognized* unity—and to bring out a fundamentally new meaning from the memories of the past.[37] Remembering must be an achieved result brought about through an understanding of, and cooperative participation in, the patient's lived relationship to time. This, I am claiming, is the real weight of Freud's transformed conception of psychoanalysis, and also the reason why psychoanalytic process must begin now with a long, difficult process of repeating instead of trying to directly bring about remembering. The name Freud gives to this process is, appropriately, working-through.

THERAPY AS WORKING-THROUGH

What I would like to explain now is the way that I see in his description of working-through something very like a phenomenological conception of temporality, compatible with the one that we find in Merleau-Ponty's *Phenomenology of Perception*. For Merleau-Ponty, we enjoy an opening onto 'a present' only because we have a determinate past that accompanies us at all times, in the form of our embodiment. Our bodies, with their deep-seated interpretive habits ranging from language to sexuality, are the very presence of our past in our present. It is only *because* we have such bodies—bodies with the past soaked into them—that we are able to eat, speak, play basketball, or fall in love in the here and now. Without such habit-bodies to guide us we would never even be able to recognize our world: all experience takes shape out of the 'sculptor's material' of the sedimented past that is our embodiment.

For Merleau-Ponty, the past is then in a certain sense inseparable from the present. Our determinate past just *is* our freedom to act in the present: the interpretive habits that we have accumulated give us, in one and the same body, our powers as well as our limitations. And yet this does not mean that our present is fully determined: the structures of the past embodied in habit are precisely indeterminate to the extent to which they are still open to transformation. We are still responsible for our freedom, for Merleau-Ponty, precisely because of the way that the past and present are premised on each other in an ongoing, dynamic process of mutual reinterpretation. Our past is our determinacy: the solidified world of stable structures deployed by our body with its habits. But our present is our freedom, for it harbors the possibility of recognizing that our present is preparing a future, that the ground we lay now is a past-to-be that will nourish a present-not-yet-born. This is the move to recognizing the very structure of our temporality, a recognition that is inseparable from the responsibility to guide and transform this dynamic temporal process that is our life.[38]

It is when you give full weight to your past, and witness its very presence here with you today, that you understand that you are preparing a past for yourself with your every action and decision. When Freud speaks of therapy, he is speaking about this very same process of guiding and transforming the temporal process by which meaning emerges.

To strive to transform the meaning of the past through therapy, you must recognize that psychological *freedom* will come through no other route than through psychological *determinacy*. This is why the determinate features of our psychological past need to be lived as present-day forces, if they are to be transformed—this is why remembering must first go by way of repeating. *The new meanings do not get built anywhere else but in the very structures of the old meanings.* It is for this reason that the phenomenon of transference plays such a central and all-important role in psychoanalysis as Freud ultimately understands it. It is in the transference that the process of working-through takes place, and it is to the peculiarities of this phenomenon that we will now turn.

What is perhaps most remarkable about the part that transference plays in the therapy is its tremendous *volatility*: it is one of the most powerful forces facilitating the analysis and is simultaneously the motivation for the most active attempts on the part of the patient to undermine it. Freud draws vivid military analogies that liken transference to house-to-house fighting in a bitter armed conflict between opposing forces,[39] and yet he also argues for its validity as genuine love, not merely as an illusion of illness.[40] The ambivalent energy of transference only increases in strength as the analysis progresses, gradually drawing everything into it as into a vortex. As each pathogenic complex is approached—as the analysis draws nearer to disclosing it—the resistances around it increase in intensity and fasten on the analytic situation itself as the best means of concealment. Thus, Freud says, "These incidents all converge towards a situation in which eventually all conflicts must be fought out on the field of transference."[41] In other words, the past can only be solicited through its present-day significance.

The analysis must recognize that the illness is already deeply interwoven with the concerns and circumstances of the present. Each symptom is actually *integrated* with reality and not simply ignorant of it, as it might first appear to the casual observer who sees only in the sufferer of psychological illness only a victim of the past, trapped in a compulsion to repeat long-gone events. Each symptom actually embodies a "compromise" between past and present realities, one that "must offer some advantage [and] admit of some useful application, or else it would meet with the same fate as the original instinctual impulse itself which has been fended off."[42]

This "gain from illness" (which we visited earlier) must be transformed into a phenomenon of the transference itself. So Freud says:

> Provided only that the patient shows compliance enough to respect the necessary conditions of the analysis, we regularly succeed in giving all the symptoms of the illness a new transference-meaning. . . . The new condition has taken over all the features of the illness; but it represents an artificial illness which is at every point accessible to our intervention. It is a piece of real experience, but one which has been made possible by especially favorable conditions, and it is of a provisional nature.[43]

It is for this reason that the transference is the most central phenomenon in the development of the analysis: because it is in the transference that the patient experiences his or her illness as a possible source of new meaning. But for this to happen, it must really be a present-day phenomenon. The patient must stand to gain from this new situation as a genuine relationship of concern to his present life. It must matter to him vitally and so draw on his most powerful resources for love and hate, springing from his earliest childhood experiences and memories.

In other words, the recognition that the past is not a closed repository of meaning must be lived through by the patient, in his powerful, ambivalent love for the therapist, as a real experience. The patient is only able to truly remember—that is, to distinguish his past determinacy from his present freedom—when he witnesses the extent to which his freedom is being dictated and curtailed by his past. But this is not a theoretical insight or an intellectual recognition formulated in conceptual terms: it is, first and foremost, a *living relationship*, a *situation*, a *new meaning* that has emerged like a work of art from the material of the past. The therapist's job is to help the patient remember: and this means to *strengthen* and *reembody* the past—to allow the patient to feel the weight of the past as *fused* with the present by repeating, and then to feel the distinctness of the past and the present that comes from recognizing the possibility of transformation that lies within the very determinacy of this reembodied past. Freud describes this as the experience that allows the patient to become 'convinced':

> Only when the resistance is at its height [in the transference] can the analyst, working in common with [her] patient, discover the repressed instinctual impulses which are feeding the resistance; and only by living through them in this way will the patient be convinced of their existence and their power.[44] . . . It is undeniable that the subjugation of the transference-manifestations provides the greatest difficulties for the psychoanalyst; but it must not be forgotten that they, and they only, render the invaluable service of making

the patient's buried and forgotten love-emotions actual and manifest: for in the last resort no one can be slain *in absentia* or *in effigie*.[45]

Only now can we truly say the patient is remembering in the fullest sense.
This *genuine* remembering, as opposed to the 'remembering' of hypnosis, is
what Freud means by the process of working-through: it is the process of
adopting a stance toward your own temporality that no longer denies that
the past is *here*, and that nonetheless it is changing at every moment into a
new past-yet-to-be that can be taken hold of and transformed. To quote
Freud again: "[the patient's] illness itself must no longer seem to him con-
temptible, but must become an enemy worthy of his mettle, a piece of his
personality, kept up by good motives, out of which things of value for his
future life have to be derived."[46]

CONCLUSION: THE CURE

We can now see how the very possibility of therapy is dependent on what
model is used to conceive the relationship of past and present. For the model
that is built on remembering, the traumatic past must be eradicated and
replaced with a more 'innocuous' past, one better integrated with the present.
Such a conception aims to 'clean house,' in a sense, and get rid of all the
memories which have a pathological effect on the person's present by transforming them somehow into harmless ones. (Like the difference between
experiencing the past as a stalker, someone who phones you in the middle
of the night and follows you around and sends you threats, and experiencing
the past as a china figurine or souvenir plate in a glass cabinet in the living
room). This stance by itself will never be therapeutic precisely because it
denies the lived continuity of past and present; the way that symptoms are
expressions not only of earlier trauma but also of an active compromise with
present-day circumstances. If the past could be transformed simply *as past*,
then the techniques of hypnosis that inform the patient about the 'contents'
of his repressed memories would have sufficed to transform them, or in Freud's
language, "one would suppose it would be enough to treat them as parts of
the id and to bring them into relation with the rest of the ego by making
them conscious."[47]

The model that is based on repeating, on the other hand, is a stance
of denial and refusal. Taken on its own, such a stance will only produce
further entrenchment, for what it denies is precisely the openness of past and
present to *redefinition* through each other. This stance ignores the essential
indeterminacy and plasticity of both sectors (the way that they are always
involved in a reciprocal interplay with each other, the present invoking the
past and the past revoking the present) and lives instead in a kind of ongoing
practical assertion that past and present are fused, that the past inexorably
compels and determines the present to take a certain shape. Freud's own

conception cannot simply be either of these: it must be both at the same time. If, for Freud, successful therapy requires a process of working-through in contradistinction from just repeating or remembering, this really means that his notion of a cure is simply a variant of a more basic process of working-through that we are always involved in as embodied human beings. The patient's stance in the therapy—his or her lived recognition of the interpenetration of the past and the present—is an attitude of practical engagement that carries in it an implicit understanding of the relationship between past and present in which neither dimension is denied for the sake of the other. This chapter has aimed to show that the success of this stance is vitally dependent on factors pertaining to this practical understanding, such as the interplay between primary and secondary repression, the 'gain from illness,' the resistances and the transference; and yet the theoretical recognition for this understanding has remained only implicit in Freud's work. Freud's practical methods, however, reveal the importance of not blinding oneself, whether one is the patient or the analyst, to the power of the past to guide our interpretations of the present, and to the power of the present to rewrite the past. The "cure" only comes with the lived, practical understanding of lived time, taken up by the patient herself in and through the circumstances of her situation. It is the patient, confronted with the concrete circumstances of her history and the need to take them up in a dynamically transformative manner, who enacts the reciprocal interpenetration of past and present implicit in Freud's own theoretical constructions and explicit in the phenomenological conception of lived time.

But this is the stance of freedom as well as therapy: a stance that *lives* in the past and the present as mutually interpenetrating, and, in so doing, unfolds an authentic future out of this interpenetration. What psychoanalysis implicitly recognizes is the possibility of the freely lived future that emerges out of our embodied relationship to time: it is this recognition that we are really seeing at work in Freud's changing conception of therapy. If for Freud, in a very practical sense, the true therapeutic activity is one that is carried out in the very thick of a person's existential situation, this suggests that there is less of a divide between the therapeutic context and the context of everyday life than we commonly take there to be. If therapy takes place by 'working-through' the past as a living force within the present, then by recognizing the character of our own relationship to time, we may better adopt a therapeutic and liberating stance toward it. Our experience *itself* as a process of 'working-through' can be taken up in various ways, some of which deny this and some of which cooperate in it. That therapy is possible—that the meanings of the world of profound psychological illness can be changed—suggests that it is more generally possible to join in this process of 'working-through.' We can become active participants in the work of bringing this reciprocally determined meaning to expression, like the sculptor bringing the work of art out of the marble. The therapeutic cure is effected by responsible attention to the way that the past and the present will continue to work through each other, with the goal of transforming this relationship not by replacing it but by cooperating with it. Our task is not to free ourselves from the past but to be free within the past that embodies us.

NOTES

1. "The Dynamics of Transference." In *Therapy and Technique* (New York: Macmillan, 1912/1963), 105.

2. Ibid., 107.

3. *Outline of Psychoanalysis* (New York: Norton, 1940/1969), 32

4. Ibid., 32–33.

5. *Outline of Psychoanalysis*, 32.

6. Freud compares hypnotism to falling in love in *Group Psychology and Analysis of the Ego* (New York: Bantam, 1921/1960), ch. VIII.

7. "Five Lectures on Psychoanalysis," Second Lecture, in *The Standard Edition of the Complete Psychological Works of Sigmund Freud* (London: Hogarth, 1909/1978) Vol. XI, 24.

8. Ibid., 18.

9. Ibid., 24.

10. "Repression" in *A General Selection from the Works of Sigmund Freud* (New York: Liveright, 1915/1957), 89.

11. Ibid., 89–90: "Repression acts, therefore, in a *highly specific* manner in each instance; every single derivative of the repressed may have its peculiar fate."

12. *Three Essays on the Theory of Sexuality* (New York: HarperCollins, 1905/ 1962), 41–42. Henceforth abbreviated as TES.

13. Ibid.

14. Ibid., 41.

15. "The second phase of repression, repression proper, concerns mental derivatives of the repressed instinct-presentation, or such trains of thought as, originating elsewhere, have come into associative connection with it. On account of this association, these ideas experience the same fate as that which underwent primal repression. Repression proper, therefore, is actually an after-expulsion. . . . Probably the tendency to repression would fail of its purpose if . . . there were not something previously repressed ready to assimilate that which is rejected from consciousness." ("Repression," 90).

16. For an example of an explicit statement of this primarily practical orientation, see "Five Lectures," Second Lecture, in SE, Vol. XI, 23: "Starting out from the mechanism of cure, it now became possible to construct quite definite ideas of the origin of the illness."

17. "Remembering, Repeating and Working-Through" in *Therapy and Technique*, 147. Henceforth abbreviated as RRW.

18. "Freud's Psychoanalytic Method" (author Sigmund Freud; article written in the third person) in *Therapy and Technique*, 1904, 55.

19. Ibid, 55–56.

20. "Five Lectures on Psychoanalysis," Second Lecture, in *Standard Edition*, Vol. XI, 22.

21. Ibid., 56.

22. *On the History of the Psychoanalytic Movement* (New York: Norton, 1914/1966), 10.

23. "On Psychotherapy" in *Therapy and Technique*, 1904, 67. (See also "Freud's Psychoanalytic Method" in *Therapy and Technique*, 59).

24. Ibid., 67.

25. RRW, 157.

26. Ibid., 158.

27. Ibid.

28. Ibid.

29. Ibid., 150.

30. Ibid.

31. *Beyond the Pleasure Principle* (New York: Bantam, 1920/1963), 38–40.

32. "Dynamics of the Transference," in *Therapy and Technique*, 1912, 114.

33. RRW, 161.

34. Ibid.

35. RRW, 151.

36. "On Psychotherapy," in *Therapy and Technique*, 66.

37. Ibid., 67: "Analytic therapy . . . does not seek to add or to introduce anything new, but to take away something, to bring out something; and to this end concerns itself with the genesis of the morbid symptoms and the psychical context of the pathogenic idea which it seeks to remove."

38. I am drawing primarily on Merleau-Ponty's *Phenomenology of Perception* (Trans. Colin Smith, London: Routledge and Kegan Paul, 1962), particularly the chapter entitled "The Body as Object and Mechanistic Physiology" (see in particular 82–87) on the notion of the habit-body; I am also drawing from the chapter entitled "The Spatiality of One's Own Body and Motility, " in particular 137–147.

39. "Dynamics of the Transference," in *Therapy and Technique*, 110.

40. "Observations on Transference Love," *Therapy and Technique*, 1915, 176.

41. "Dynamics of the Transference," in *Therapy and Technique*, 111.

42. *On the History of the Psychoanalytic Movement*, 53.

43. RRW, 154.

44. RRW, 165.

45. "Dynamics of the Transference," 114.

46. RRW, 163.

47. "Analysis Terminable and Interminable," in *Therapy and Technique,* 1937, 258.

NINE

FREUD AND KIERKEGAARD ON GENOCIDE AND THE DEATH DRIVE

Bruce Wilshire

BY "GENOCIDE" I mean any systematic persecution of members of a group just because they are members of that group. I mean all members: men, women, children, even fetuses. The term is broad enough to include not only removal from the face of the earth, but also forced removal from their home territory. I use the term in the broad sense employed in the UN resolution 260 (III), 1948: "The intent to destroy, in whole or in part, a national, ethnical, racial or religious group, as such." For example, "Causing serious bodily or mental harm to members of the group."

As I will develop these themes, the "mental" aspect is peculiarly salient: the genocided group's mode of experiencing the world is to be destroyed, or it is to be thrown out of action in some way and invalidated. That alien mode of experiencing is to be prevented from disrupting or infecting the home group's mode, its world-experienced.

Genocide is a form of warfare, but it must be distinguished from war in the usual sense. From the standpoint of war, the reason usually given for the aggression is national security. In the case of genocidal aggression that reason may be given also, but it is at best a pretext or a rationalization. For example, the Nazis' genocide of the gypsies could not, with a straight face, be laid to their threat to German national security. They disgusted, and I think frightened, the Nazi leaders. They threatened that group's security, but now security on a deeply psychical level, what political scientists and historians tend not to talk about. The Nazis experienced the gypsies as irregular, disorderly, dirty. They threatened to disrupt the Nazis' treasured sense of control, orderliness, cleanliness—indeed, of civilization and truly human life.

It is not outrageous to suggest psychoanalytical explanations for trying to grasp the Nazis' actions. For a prime example, anal obsessiveness: the dread of untoward and uncontrolled anal expulsion and soiling. Then the reaction formation to this: anal retentiveness—"hoarding the treasure"—and perhaps oral biting. Enter Freud.

I

Freud is a major thinker whose full stature was not reached until he approached old age and broached the idea of the death drive. As essential as his early work on psychosexual development and the pleasure principle was, it is only part of the picture. (What is truly a fault in his scheme, I believe— his androcentrism and overemphasis on the phallus—cannot disqualify a major thinker.)

Freud's work on the death drive first appears full scale in *Beyond the Pleasure Principle* and *Civilization and Its Discontents*. These books appeared in his sixties and seventies. At least equally important, they appeared after World War I. The atrocities, agonies, and absurdities of that conflict prompted major thinkers to radically new attempts to see things whole, to glue back together, if only in thought, a world-experienced that had flown to pieces. Freud's late work is a part of this effort.

Let's tarry a bit on this point. Greatness is as much a matter of accident and opportunity as it is of native genius and destiny. As nonhuman animals must cognitively map their territory, so must we on a much larger scale. For us, the great questions know no bounds. For example: What time is it for the human race? Where are we? Where do we come from? and Where are we going?

Major thinkers stood stunned by the war, these questions thrown into their faces. How could this have happened? Henry James, the American novelist and dramatist, achieved and relished his fame in the Edwardian age, roughly 1890–1910. He actually moved to Edwardian Britain, an environment that would directly feed his fascination with upper-class elegance: those privileged persons' urbane self-congratulation, assumed control, self-indulgence, foibles. Henry's elder brother, William, did not live to see the advent of the horror of 1914–1918. Henry did, and looking back over the Edwardian age wrote something to this effect: To think that all the while all *that* was tending toward *this*! The world had turned over and shown a grotesque underbelly.

Just a few moments to sketch the postwar time (as a book has it, *Freud and His Time*). The greatest philosophical thought of the century was squeezed into eruptive presence, into parturition, in the dozen or so years following World War I. Quickly: Dewey's *Human Nature and Conduct* and *Experience and Nature*; Heidegger's *Being and Time*; Whitehead's *Process and Reality*;

Hocking's *The Self: Its Body and Freedom*; and Wittgenstein's manifold groping and probing work, much of it unpublished at the time. (Following his experience in the trenches he could no longer believe that a logical prettying up of language could do the job of locating us: "atomic and molecular propositions mirroring atomic and molecular states of affairs," etc.) And we shouldn't leave out Ernest Hemingway, the great writer, often criticized for lacking a "social consciousness." But he was conscious of exactly the most fundamental question: Would society survive its bacchanalian orgy of death?

Part of Freud's power and charm are his moments of candid self-revelation. He writes that he can't understand how he and his movement of thought—so probing, so clear-eyed, and relentless it seemed—could have all along missed the true dimensions of human aggression, and, in general, the actual complexities and perversities of human motivation.[1]

No book was ever better titled: *Beyond the Pleasure Principle*. Yes, he (and Karl Abraham, for example) had seen the pleasure an infant derives from witholding evacuation of the bowels until the parent or caregiver offers a greater reward. Yes, he (and many of his followers) had seen the power plays and games that often go on between therapist and patient; and the strange forms that love, eros, and libidinal pleasure take in interactions of veiled dominance and submission.

But Freud saw that none of this, singly or together, could account for the monstrous aggression of the first World War. For that war to have been commenced and then continued so long, the participants must have *enjoyed* it somehow. Yes, of course, he had long talked about the perverse joys of sadism, enjoying others' suffering. But how could people with an ounce of reason have so persisted in this war when they themselves were enduring such suffering, wretchedness, misery? How?

Freud's proposed explanatory hypothesis inaugurates a radical shift in his views, one that opens the door to a reconceptualizing of the human condition, or what used to be called our place in the universe. He suggests a *primal* masochism.[2] That is, an infliction of suffering on ourselves because we implicitly believe that we deserve it, and so derive pleasure from "doing right." What appears as sadism may very well be primal masochism deflected onto the alien group, the *others*. We let them suffer for us. To confront a primal masochism is to look the insidious and complex death drive right in the face.

When we set up a whole group to suffer for us, we are genocidal. Vicarious suffering—a neat trick. Freud's psychodynamic conceptions allow us to make sense of this. We can both identify ourselves with another group and repudiate the identification.

Now, the most basic concepts and issues are at stake here. Issues of identity are always the most conceptually difficult. For we are inherently socializable organisms. So we must mean both personal or individual identity, on the one hand, and on the other, the collective or corporate identity—the

group's. The interplay of personal and corporate identity is intricate and vex-
ing. (Freud repeatedly stresses the difficulties in plumbing the ways in which
an individual organism identifies with others, others singly and in groups.) An
individual organism introjects the home group's standards, and does so beyond
its abilities to consciously acknowledge the extent of the introjection.

This is directly germane to the question of genocide: human organisms
will incorporate their group's terror in times when the group fears that its
mode of knowing and experiencing the world is not the only way. It is
threatened by an alien group's different mode. For, group members think,
there can be only one world. Moreover, to be a meaningful world, it must be
a world that is experienced or experienceable. And how could any mode of
experiencing except ours be the true or correct way? Our mode is the only
way we know! If the home group cannot bear its insecurity and terror, it may
very well set up the other group to suffer for it, even to the point of exter-
minating it: fear and guilt, displaced primal masochism—genocide.

In his *Group Psychology and the Analysis of the Ego*, Freud builds on
other psychologists' work, for example, Le Bon's and McDougall's. But he
believes they inadequately recognize the role of the leader in the dynamics
of the group. Why at times do members of a group cling so desperately
together that they are willing to exterminate another group? Freud helps us
understand the complexities. The leader is the head of the corporate organism: all eyes are on the leader. He—typically it is a male—is perceived to
love them. They can be bonded in love for each other because they all share
the leader's love. (For example, St. Paul repeatedly exhorts Christians to love
one another because Christ first loved them.) If an alien group threatens the
corporate body and its head, this threatens the cohesion, the very identity
and survival, of the whole group.

Freud believes that our rootedness in primal dependence on authorities
in the family is never totally lost. Children are deeply egocentric and tend
to blame themselves when something goes wrong in the family. If the group
wobbles, children fear they will be held responsible for disobeying—or letting down—the head. In the case of calamity, "we deserve the ultimate
punishment, death." (In the Christian scenario, we have all deserved death,
and only the death of God-as-human, Jesus Christ, can atone for our sin.)
Now, if we can only deflect this guilt onto the alien group that threatens us!?

For Freud, the voice of conscience—the superego—is the voice of early
authorities long ago introjected, that source mainly forgotten (he particularly
stresses the father-authority). Nothing is easier to excite than the guilt we
feel over acts that we feel ought to be punished. So we tend to punish
ourselves and feel the pleasure of "setting matters straight." But pleasure is
immensely complex here, and when the ambivalence of pleasure and pain,
and pleasure and guilt, is intolerable, we may let the other group suffer for
us. All in all, Freud believes that it is very difficult for civilized human beings
simply to be happy.

But, again, how is it that other groups can suffer for us? Aren't we aware that we are ourselves and they are *other*? But Freud had long known of the limits of our awareness, and of how the strength and scope of awareness fluctuates radically from situation to situation and from time to time. In relatively calm, self-reflective moments, we make distinctions that we simply can't and won't make in frenzied moments of tension. In certain moments we identify blindly with our home group: most of us are little more than appendages of the corporate body.

And the smearing of identity goes farther than this. For if, I believe, the corporate individual's identity begins to crumble, it will recognize another group as other *only to the extent* of letting it do our suffering for us. Primal masochism is deflected onto those others. Genocide.

There is something dream-like about certain moments of what we call our waking life. Thinkers and writers have dwelt on this: Thomas Wolfe, Cervantes, Calderone, Shakespeare, and many others. But it is Freud who most convincingly puts his finger on the processes of "the dream-work" in actual, literal dreaming—processes that, I think, spread and ooze into what we call our waking life. He first puts his finger on these in some of his earliest mature studies on the interpretation of dreams.

Take the process of what he calls "condensation." Condensation is a product of many overdetermined wishes, conflicts, and their derivatives merged into single "contents" or combinations thereof. That is, things that a third-person observer—or dreamers themselves when lucidly awake—would distinguish are conflated in the dream. Why?—To express certain matters that are frightening or disgusting, given our superego and social conditioning, but without owning up to precisely what is being expressed. That is, to express something in a form that disguises it from oneself. Relief from guilt is achieved through the self-censoring of expression that he calls condensation.

Condensation, I believe, is going on frequently in what we call our "fully waking life." Condensation of matters that we would distinguish if, say, we were asked to do so by somebody else. But usually there is no Socrates present to ask us the pointed and timely question and to rouse us from our prereflective lethargy and trance. Individuals, experiencing and experienced, get smeared with individuals, and groups with groups.

Much of the plausibility of thinking that this smearing of distinctions goes on in "fully waking life" derives from another of Freud's early investigations, *The Psychopathology of Everyday Life*. Here he analyzes and exposes what most people call "accidents." Many slips of the tongue, or slips of the dishes, which we commonly chalk up to accidents, Freud exposes as the fruits of motivations, desires, and aversions that we passionately resist acknowledging.

When these early insights of Freud's are augmented with his late insight into primal masochism and the will to death and destruction, we have gone a long way to thinking the "unthinkable," genocide. Blurry and aberrant identifyings and distinguishings are going on in the twilight. These are not unmotivated, are not without thought, but the thought is wild and irresponsible, feverish and terrified. The big-brained human organism panics, acts wildly and madly. "We deserve to die," it is dimly but agonizingly felt. "Let them do our dying for us!" As condensation is a symptom of unbearably clogged and conflicted desires and fears, so is genocide. Suffering and destruction are self-inflicted only on the condition that we find a circuitous route to destruction. Genocide can be viewed as one such circuitous route.

II

Genocide can occur if an already threatened and self-deflated group's whole experienced and experienceable world is threatened by another group's way of experiencing the world. The genocidal group's experienced world falls away from under the members' feet. There is a psychical earthquake. This means dissolution and death unless the other group can be exterminated or radically weakened.

A central point to my argument: we always fall far short of knowing or even imagining all that impinges on, supports, or in any way influences our lives. Nevertheless, a necessary condition for sanity is that we make sense, to some extent, of the world that holds us. We make sense of things; they are meaningful to us, in terms of how we take them to be experienceable by us. For example, an apple is experienced to be a distinctly different thing from a knife, because one is to be cut, while the other is to do the cutting; one is to be eaten, the other is not, and so on. A condition necessary for sanity is that we make sense of the world around us, and we can do this only in terms of its experienceability. As I said, surely there can be only one world, and what could it be but the world-experienced-and-experienceable-by-us? Since our mode of making meaning is involved, how could we even imagine anything else? Particularly when our home group is shaky for any reason, the other group's mode of experiencing their world-experienced must be wrong, must be defective and subhuman. At all costs, it must be prevented from infecting our mode of experiencing, our world-experienced.

Now, the home group may feel worthy of death, may tacitly desire it, but such death, after all, would be untimely: the group also is impelled by the instinct to survive in the world, to live. It cannot wholly lose the sense of its own identity. The trick is turned if primal masochism is deflected onto the other group. Seen in the smearing of twilight they are not clearly not us! And *every* one of *them*—man, woman, child, fetus—must be exterminated. For every one of them carries the disease of another way of experiencing the world, another world-experienced. And there can only be one world—ours! Much the same way that every germ of an infectious disease must be exterminated. Every germ, no matter how small and inconsequential it may appear, can multiply by contagion and fill a vast organism.

III

At this point we can see a very revealing partial convergence of Søren Kierkegaard's views, particularly expressed in *The Concept of Dread*, and that of Freud's. Here Kierkegaard is centrally concerned with the role of possibility in human experience. We have just pointed out that we must make some sense of the world, and we can do so only in terms of how we take it to be experienceable by us. Experience*able*—possibility. I will later use this point to augment what Freud has to tell us. But let us dwell for a few moments on the convergence of the two. Though partial, it is still very important.

Both psychologists come face to face with the experience of guilt. Just what is it about us animals-who-are-human that makes this experience possible and indeed necessary? St. Paul asserted that we are created halfway between the brutes and the angels. That's a start! It's easiest to run to one side or the other of the dichotomy and to perch there. But we are weirdly intermixed. The action is somewhere "in the middle," though we can't say what "the middle" means precisely in the context of our problematical identity.

In *The Concept of Dread* Kierkegaard tries to explain (to the limits of rationality, he says) how guilt arises primally in human beings. It is tempting, he observes, to think simplistically, dualistically: we are special animals because something spiritual has somehow been injected into our animality. But this is misleading. The crucial terms "spirit," "animal," "injected" are nothing more than reified abstractions. We only play with words—words hypostatized. Our spirituality does distinguish us from other animals, he believes. But for either of the terms—*animal, spiritual*—to get a purchase on our reality, our "soulish" life must mediate them. This is our sentiency as animals. Except, that in mediating the animal and the spiritual our soulish life is itself something different from an animal's! All our terms wobble, but we must persist in struggling to understand ourselves.

For Kierkegaard, innocence is ignorance. But we cannot help wanting to know. So we imagine an unencompassable array of possible ways for things to be and for events to happen. In our ignorance, some of these must actually be unknown, we sense, so some of them must be dangerous, we suppose—dreadful. We are simultaneously attracted and repelled by them— "sweet dread" perhaps.

Some background: as the dualism dividing animal and spiritual is simplistic and misleading, so is that dividing sleeping and waking, Kierkegaard sees. In sleeping, otherness or difference is smeared or annulled (herewith anticipating Freud's notion of "condensation"). In wakefulness otherness or difference is affirmed. But much of our lives is spent in the limbo state Kierkegaard calls dreaming. This has a special sense, something like daydreaming (compare Freud's notions of unconscious intentions in the psychopathology of everyday life replete with its "accidents"). In dreaming, Kierkegaard affirms, otherness or difference is "a nothing vaguely hinted at."

The payoff: in our inevitable formulation of possibilities for things to be, some of them, inexorably, must be dangerous or lethal, we feel. But in dreaming we don't differentiate our formulation of them as possibilities from an actual indulging in them. We, the "rational animal," swoon, Kierkegaard says, and "we arise guilty." It's not that we are not free, but for us human animals, freedom is inevitably trammeled. We arise befuddled and guilty.

Genocide is a weakness in the human condition per se. It is a dreadful possibility for any human group under certain conditions. Nothing is easier and slipperier than projecting primal guilt onto those *others*, to let them die for us. It is tempting to speak of "the excitement of evil." But it's a premature answer that blocks the road of further inquiry into a deeper level of human being. Drawing on the funded folk wisdom of *Genesis*, Kierkegaard points out that God prohibits eating the fruit of *that* tree, the one *we* readers of the Bible know as "the tree of the knowledge of good and evil." But the primal agents themselves, Adam and Eve, have not yet eaten of it, so they don't know that it is evil to eat it. They just sense, vaguely but fundamentally, that it is dangerous, out of bounds, too much, forbidden.

With marvelous insight, Kierkegaard points out that there is "physiognomic communication." It is ineluctably bodily communication, and we are ineluctably bodies. It is primally communicated in a tone of voice, say—a tone of warning, of foreboding, of danger. It is, he says, something that a nonhuman animal can understand very well! Except that when it is communicated to humans it has spiritual ramifications, possibilities, and dangers that it apparently does not have for the other animals. Do other animals, predators, kill all the members of the prey group, and do it, in some sense, intentionally? That would be maladaptive, as evolutionary biology would affirm. But we human organisms do not repose comfortably within the biological realm alone. We are caught up in the spiritual as well, the domain of trammeled freedom. That is, the domain in which possibilities are wildly projected, and in which guilt arises out of a "nothing vaguely hinted at." This is a guilt all too easily unloaded onto others.

Religion is the primal way that humans try to make sense of the world. And we must try. So another group's religious mode of experiencing the world may be terrifically disturbing to the home group. Kierkegaard was a Christian, and avidly practiced it. But at least as avidly, he attacked the way Christianity had been institutionalized through history in its official groups.[4]

IV

That there is a death drive, as Freud asserted, is, I think, importantly true. However, I believe I depart somewhat from him in construing just what it means and what it presupposes; therefore also in what it means for the phenomenon of genocide. In short, I depart from Freud in the construal of human cognition and spirituality, and in the fundamental human reality of world-known, world-perceived, world experienceable by us. This is a key for grasping genocide: a shaky home group cannot clearly distinguish its world-experienced from an alien group's. But the two worlds-experienced are incompatible. A psychical earthquake is triggered. The possibility of annihilation yawns before us.

In a moment I will say more about my philosophical differences from Freud. I react against his (somewhat sophisticated) version of nineteenth-century positivist science—his incompletely questioned "scientific detachment," and his view of "external objects." But first I must try to squeeze more out of his profundity.

Freud came to see in our own age, and in a modern way, what ancient peoples had prized as wisdom: particularly that there is a death drive, a need to return to the organic and inorganic bases of our existence. This return arouses its own kind of pleasure *if* launched at the right time and in the appropriate way. (Aristotle articulated that there are as many kinds of pleasure as there are kinds of basic activities engaged in with a modicum of success.) This divides Freud from monodimensional notions of pleasure endemic to modernist psycho/physical splits of the self, and to the treatment of the body exclusively as an object. This form of modernism culminated in James Mill's moronic idea, "Pushpin (a simple pleasurable game) is as good as poetry."

I think that two forms of the death drive should be distinguished. The first we can call the thoroughly healthy sense. In fact, an essential for any culture to be adjudged healthy, I think, is that it prepares its members for meaningful, timely, even pleasurable death. (For example, Bruce Chatwin in *The Song Lines* writes of old aboriginal men in their dying grounds happily awaiting return to their origins.) As I mentioned, Freud thought we have a deep urge to return to the earth that birthed us, ultimately to the inorganic matrix of all things and to the death that this return entails. It is right and good that we live and die. Without the life cycle successfully completed, we have not fully lived.

It is the key to this ultimate right action that we nearly rite-less moderns so sorely lack. The phony myth and quasi-ritual of maintaining everlasting youth grinds us down to nothing in the end. Almost completely lacking are myths and rituals of individuals' regeneration intimately coordinated with and empowered by the regenerative cycles of Earth—birth, growing, declining, dying, and rebirth of something else, something kindred. So nearly completely lacking are these life rites that most people are only vaguely ill at ease, off-center, knowing that something is missing, but not knowing what. I think Freud's deep interest in totems and prehistoric ritual objects signals his awareness of this healthy form of the death drive.

The other sense of the drive is what for brevity's sake we'll call the unhealthy. It stems from the inevitability of guilt and—related to the just above—inadequate ways to ritualistically deal with, and atone for, guilt. Guilt in some form and on some occasions is inevitable for us humans, for inevitably we sometimes fall short of standards set by authority figures. At times, guilt becomes insufferable, panic-causing. We "ought to die," we feel, but "we are too young to die." So we project the guilt felt primally, masochistically onto those others. Let them die for us. All of them. For in states of emotional frenzy and insecurity—in what Kierkegaard calls a version of dreaming—those others aren't clearly distinguished from ourselves anyway.

For 99% of *genus homo's* presence on earth, we were hunter-gatherers, aboriginals, people of the paleolithic. Through hundreds of thousands of years of prehuman and human adaptation to environments, we took shape, our very nervous systems, muscles, brains, and genes developed. Coeval with this were ritualistically imprinted and perpetually reimprinted ways of surviving and flourishing—the funded wisdom of the human race. Freud and Kierkegaard are right to retrieve items of this mythically encapsulated wisdom to help us find our way today: we the brilliant, conceited, wayward, rootless, disequilibrated. Trying to capture the modern mishmash, I could extend the list of adjectives.

In large part because of the brilliant scientific achievement of dating objects through the carbon-14 ingrained in them, we have a pretty good idea of just how ancient human life is. The Athenian Greeks lived just yesterday. Along with earlier Neolithic people, they signal the tragic rupture of our ancient being-in-Nature. The question is bruited in their work: how can any death be timely and consummatory?

Freud was admiringly aware of another lover of antiquities, Friedrich Nietzsche. Probably he knew that philologist's and philosopher's first great book, *The Birth of Tragedy from the Spirit of Music*. Nietzsche digs behind the tragic theater of the Athenian city-state to an antecedent level: an archaic rite in which satyr figures—hairy goat men—sang and danced the story of the ritual dismemberment of Dionysus. This god was torn to pieces by chothonic figures, the earth maidens, Maenads.[5]

The god's cries are not those of simple pain nor of simple pleasure. They are cries of ecstatic pain and pleasure; for being torn to pieces he is returning to the elements that compose him and out of which he was birthed. There are simple pains: one steps on a nail unexpectedly, for example. There are simple pleasures: say orgasm for orgasm's sake, or a chocolate bon-bon dissolving in the mouth. But we are talking here of complex pain and pleasure, that roiling combination that marks and consummates our strange place and status in the world. Tragically for us moderns, we want to live and grow, but we also want to die and return to our sources. We don't know how to integrate it all. So most of us live an impoverished life of simple pains, simple pleasures, coupled with the vague uneasiness that something is missing. How do we find a timely and healthy and even pleasurable death? For assuredly we will die.

V

Freud was born in 1856. His medical training fell into the grooves of nineteenth-century positivistic, physiological, and mechanistic or deterministic science. It is a mark of his genius and character that this could not contain him. A further tearing of bonds occurred on the threshold of his old age following World War I. More and more he saw that the human organism is not just a pleasure-generating or a pain-avoiding machine. We are tragic figures trying to understand ourselves and find our way in the vast entangled world. Or, we are tragic and pathetic figures trying not to understand ourselves, for appalled by possibilities dimly sensed, we try to keep stumbling ahead stupefied. Freud was developing an engrossing worldview; he was achieving the status of philosopher.

But even in his earlier maturity, fairly late in his development, he retained a clear residuum of positivistic science. For example, he speaks of libido, or life force, sexual in the generic sense: expansive, productive, reproductive, pulsing in potential and power. He assumes a hydraulic model for libido's movement. Due to superego constraints, it may be blocked from gushing forth on the pre-personal level of "primary process," or "glad animal movements" (recall Wordsworth). Then it will be forced to a "higher" level of manifestation and outlet. Say, in the arts or the sciences or in philanthropic work. Or, again, drawing on another metaphor from the nineteenth-century physical sciences, it will be "sublimated" (literally, the transition from a solid immediately into a gas).[6].

This "bottom up" type of explanation does not vanish, but rather recedes from center stage following Freud's espousal of the death drive, and his probing "beyond the pleasure principle." We are seen more and more as whole, complex, interpreting organisms in the world. Easily screwed up, yes—fixated, obsessed—but not just machines. Freud's own life testified to the liberating power of knowledge, insight, decision.

Freud's contributions to a theory of genocide are great. And yet—unless I am badly mistaken—they are insufficient. There is always a semi-hidden residuum of nineteenth-century materialism in his thought to the end.

For a prime example, he speaks of "external objects" in contrast to objects "in the mind," apparently (see Group Psychology, p. 48). If by "external objects" is just meant that there are all kinds of things that exist whether any beings have any idea that they do, or whether thinking beings exist at all, then no damage is done. But Freud's unqualified use of "external" tends to deflect attention from a matter crucial to grasping genocide. Just how are things experienced and experienceable as "external"? What does "external" mean to people, and how does it come to mean this? For it is just another group's different way of experiencing the world, of forming a world-experienced, that so profoundly threatens an already shaky home group. It is this that may prompt the home group to genocidal mayhem.

We see in Freud a kind of detachment of thinker from what is thought about—or of observer from the observed—that the thinker assumes is essential to real knowledge, science. But I don't believe this detachment is completely thought through philosophically. Granted, Freud is certainly not a behaviorist. He is not ignoring that his subjects, his patients, are thinking. His very genius consists in coaxing into the open subjects' troubled thoughts and feelings. And perhaps—for all I know—his very detachment is essential for the process of disclosure to occur! And, obviously, he is not denying that he, Freud, is thinking.

But I believe that to really understand genocide, we must go further. We must, so to speak, think further into our thinking: live and think inside it as it is occurring in our own persons, as it is spreading into a horizon of possibilities for things to be, into what we take them to be experienceable-as. That is, think our thinking as thinkers involved immediately *and* projectively in the world around and through us. For what I have called the psychical earthquake for genociders happens when they dread that the one and only world they know, the one they have learned to live in, is being polluted, torn up, destroyed by the alien group's mode of experiencing, thinking, perceiving. That is, the world-known, the world-perceived and experienced, falls away under people's feet. Our sanity depends on most of our thoughts and perceptions being confirmed by the home group's ways of thinking and experiencing. If this confirmation is shaken, we endure a spasm, a kind of panic of incipient insanity. For, on a gut level, the world known and experienced *is* humans' world, *is the* world. Those others' world-experienced must be a *subhuman world*, and it cannot be the *real*, the *true* world. Exterminate it, and, of course, them! For without them experiencing things, that illusory, counterfeit world cannot exist.

To use a dangerously ambiguous and vague term, I am as much a "materialist" as Freud is. I think that what we immediately sense (I don't say perceive) are electrochemical events in our own brains. But our brains only function as organs in our mimetically engulfed bodies. That is, in bodies resonating mimetically within patterns of behavior laid down in manifold and relentless ways by the culture. It is our world-experienced and perceived that is essential to us (but not only that), and when disturbed by an alien group's patterns of doing and knowing may prompt genocidal extermination of that group. We must try to grasp how complex and life sustaining our settled modes of experiencing and knowing are. Even if they are "life lies," as Nietzsche put it.[7]

I retain both Freud's and Kierkegaard's insights. The genocidal group is insecure, self-deflated, frightened, and guilt-burdened. Genocidal aggression is deflected masochism. We ought to die. But we want to live also, and "we are too young to die"! Let them die for us.

And as I said, we dread all this. In the insanity of genocide, the pulls of possibility running wild, we are simultaneously attracted and repelled by what is beginning to happen, and is happening. The distinction between *them* and us is "a nothing vaguely hinted at," as Kierkegaard saw. Possibility is a nothing that is a strange something. We are sufficiently aware of them as other to kill them, not us. And yet in killing them we also "do what is right," we kill ourselves. Possibility is immensely confusing because it is simultaneously attracting and repelling. It explodes in very definite actuality, the extermination of whole groups of once living human beings.

All this is appalling, of course. It easily boggles the mind. We are at the very limits of mind—both in our thinking and in what is thought-about. But how else can we explain what desperately needs to be explained, insane eruptions of genocide in our very own "enlightened" centuries? We must try to stop these criminal acts. But we haven't a good chance of doing this if we can't understand what causes them.

VI

I can not hope to convey in this short chapter all the reasoning and evidence that informs my book, *Get 'Em All—Kill 'Em: A Study of Genocide*. But I hope to have conveyed enough to persuade the reader that only the most radical and far-reaching hypotheses can begin to explain the peculiar insanity of genocide, what distinguishes it from war in the ordinary sense: That every member of the victimized group must be killed, or at least huddled out of sight, banished, disqualified, forever quarantined. The reason, again and finally, is that every member—even a fetus—carries the bacillus of an infected and infecting world-experienced and experienceable, a world-perceived-and imagineable, a world-thought.

Here I can only suggest a line of investigation that informs my book. It was prompted initially by the manifest anality of at least two leaders of genocides, Pol Pot and Adolf Hitler. Freud's work on anality (in cooperation with Karl Abraham) throws light on the connection of anality and genocide. The home group or corporate body is beleaguered by an alien group. The home group attempts to wall itself up within itself, to "hoard its treasure." A parallelism between the anal-retentive stage in the development of both individual and corporate bodies is suggested. Then the genocidal acts themselves can be compared to the anal-expulsive stage: poisons are dropped on the alien group. Anality gives us a key to the desperate attempts to control and master things exhibited in the regressive phenomenon of genocide.

To unpack this a bit more: in my larger work, I trace at length a parallelism between the individual's body and the corporate individual's. This includes a parallelism of values of the levels of the bodies. The head of both directs what falls beneath it and is of greatest value. The arms execute the heads' directions and are of greater value than the pedal and eliminative functions that get directed, and so on. The body thus ordered orders the world-experienced, perceived, and known. To disorder the bodies—individual and corporate—is to disorder the world-perceived and known by them. This occurs most directly and disturbingly when the lower eliminative functions somehow mix, or threaten to mix, with the heads' higher rational and ordering functions. When these are disordered for any reason, it's as if the world-experienced threatens to give way, go out of control, and disintegrate in a tide of diarrhea. A cause must be found. It is located *in that shit*, the other group, the infecting aliens.

Hitler, for example, played endless variations on this theme. When he ranted that Jewish bankers—their hands filthy with money, with lucre—were taking food out of the mouths of good Germans, he was not saying that they were simply depriving Germans of nutriments. He was saying they were putting excrement in the noble faces and mouths of the Germans—that they were perpetrating the ultimate pollution of the corporate body, the *Volkskorper*. This was enough to trigger many "ordinary Germans," even those not hugely anti-Semitic, into genocidal frenzy.

Let this bit of analysis suggest in closing the enduring fertility of Sigmund Freud's thought, as well as the continuing need to investigate the intricate identities of us selves who are enculturated bodies.

NOTES

1. Freud. *Civilization and Its Discontents*. Trans. J. Strachey (New York: W. W. Norton, 1961 [1930]), 67.

2. Freud. *Beyond the Pleasure Principle*. Trans. J. Strachey (New York: Liveright, 1961 [1920]), 49.

3. Freud. *Group Psychology and the Analysis of the Ego*. Trans. J. Strachey (New York: W. W. Norton, 1959 [1921]).

4. All of Kierkegaard's major works have been translated from the Danish and are readily available. See one of his last great works, *Attack on Christendom*.

5. Nietzsche is discussed in my *Role Playing and Identity: The Limits of Theatre as Metaphor* (Bloomington and Indianapolis: Indiana University Press, 1991 [1982]). Also see "Ways of Knowing," in my *The Primal Roots of American Philosophy: Pragmatism, Phenomenology, and Native American Thought* (University Park: Penn State University Press, 2000).

6. It should be noted that in explaining the fate of the drives (*Instincts and their Vicissitudes*, 1915), Freud maintains that a drive is a malleable and flexible dynamic process—not a fixed mechanism. Hence sublimation, as well as the other ego defenses, are teleological products or choices derived from earlier primitive organizations. (I thank Jon Mills for these qualifying remarks. I also thank Edward Casey for his suggestions throughout.)

7. Consider also Eugene O'Neill's characters in *The Iceman Cometh*, their life-essential "pipedreams."

TEN

THE UNCONSCIOUS LIFE OF RACE: FREUDIAN RESOURCES FOR CRITICAL RACE THEORY

SHANNON SULLIVAN

I RECENTLY ENCOUNTERED a situation involving race in which a Freudian analysis was virtually impossible to avoid. After I presented a paper on racism and the Roma (often called "Gypsies" in English) at an international conference in Slovakia, a Czech member of the audience proceeded to ask critical but friendly questions about my analysis.[1] When doing so, he repeatedly referred to the Roma as "Jews" without hearing his slip of the tongue. After a second reference to the "Jews" in a comment that clearly concerned the Roma, a few members of the audience interrupted him to correct him, and he, embarrassed, said that yes, of course, he meant the Roma. We all laughed away our discomfort and he proceeded with his comment.[2] As he did so, he referred to the Roma as "Jews" for a third time without hearing what he said. The rest of us were so surprised by this that we said nothing, and I answered his question assuming (correctly) that the group he referred to was the Roma. He was followed by another Czech member of the audience who asked critically friendly questions about my paper. In the course of doing so, he too referred to the Roma as the "Jews" twice without hearing his slip of the tongue. The audience and I did not correct him since, by that time, such correction felt pointless. After five occurrences, the substitution of "Jew" for "Gypsy" seemed to have roots too deep and too hearty for a quick conscious correction to eliminate.

Although sexuality, not race, tends to be central to Freud's work, Freud's analysis of the unconscious can be extremely helpful in understanding my conference experience. I find it implausible that my European colleagues' slips of the tongue were insignificant mistakes. More probable is that there were reasons for their slips of which they were not consciously aware.[3] It is as if, in each case, the speaker's unconscious "played a trick on him by betraying his real intentions," and an idea that he wished to keep in his unconscious pushed its way out by means of a verbal mistake (PEL, pp. 68, 64). Their case is different from that of a third audience member, who made comments that were openly hostile to my anti-racist reading of the Roma's situation. If she had called the Roma "Jews," which she did not, her doing so could be seen as motivated by conscious reasons that involved deprecating the Roma by means of anti-Semitism. In contrast, the first two speakers' lack of hostility toward my paper makes it unlikely that conscious antagonism toward the Roma motivated their substitution of "Jew" for "Gypsy."

Both speakers who called the Roma "Jews" were fluent in English even though English was not their native tongue, thus confusion about the meaning of each English word does not satisfactorily explain the substitution of "Jew" for "Gypsy." This is not to claim that the fact that the two native Czech-speakers were using English was irrelevant, but that its relevance seemed to take the form of merely providing an opportunity for the unconscious to express itself. As Freud approvingly quotes Ferenczi, " '[i]t is by no means rare for someone who is not speaking his mother tongue to exploit his clumsiness for the purpose of making highly significant slips of the tongue in the language that is foreign to him' " (PEL, p. 87 n. 2). The term "exploit" here need not and, indeed, should not be understood as a conscious operation. It is the exploitation of verbal clumsiness carried out by the unconscious that makes the substitution of "Jew" for "Gypsy" a slip of the tongue rather than something else such as an attempt at a (poor) joke, which it clearly was not.[4]

Likewise, while there is a phonetic similarity between the beginnings of "Jew" and "Gypsy," the similarity seems to be more a convenient vehicle used by the unconscious for the expression of a hidden idea than a causal mechanism for the substitution (PEL, p. 81). As Freud says, phonetic laws "do not seem . . . to be sufficiently effective to disturb the process of correct speaking" (PEL, p. 81). They cannot explain, for example, why "Jew" in particular was uttered instead of some other phonetically similar word, such as "gentry." To understand *why* (and not merely *that*) "Jew" replaced "Gypsy," one must uncover the buried association of the two groups in the minds of Europeans, which concerns the scapegoat role that Jews and Roma have been assigned in Europe for hundreds of years. The most extreme example of this role can be found in the Nazi's attempted extermination of the Roma and Jews during World War II. A more complicated and equally sinister instance of it has emerged the last decade, in which guilt about the treatment of the Jews coexists with acceptance of rising violence and discrimina-tion directed toward the Roma in Central and Eastern Europe in particular.[5]

This analysis of a slip of a tongue begins to develop what I wish to explore further in this chapter: how Freud's work might contribute to critical race theory by developing an understanding of the psychic reality of racism and racial identity. Unlike race theory of the seventeenth through the mid-twentieth century, critical race theory theorizes race for the purpose of elimi-nating racism.[6] Perhaps because of psychoanalysis's reputation for being apolitical, few critical race theorists have turned to psychoanalysis for help in addressing the status of the concept of race or devising theoretical tools needed to fight racism.[7] This may be, at least in part, because Freud rarely explicitly discussed race in his published work. Critical race theory nonethe-less needs psychoanalysis because to be effective it must address the opera-tions of racism at unconscious levels. Racism today often involves unconscious mechanisms such as projection and repression for which psychoanalysis is needed to understand. Freud's work can be seen as rightly discouraging us from thinking, as some critical race theorists have assumed, that racism is merely a product of ignorance: a set of conscious, false beliefs that can be eliminated with proper instruction.[8] Appropriating Freud in this way admit-tedly will stretch his concepts beyond the areas to which he applied them, but such a stretch will be fruitful even if it does not always uphold the Oedipal shibboleth of psychoanalysis.[9] The result of a Freudian approach to race will be a greater understanding of the operations of racism than accounts that neglect the unconscious can provide.

Before exploring further the resources Freud's ideas offer critical race theory, however, the role implicitly played by race and racism in Freud's writings must be explicitly acknowledged if his work is to be an aide, rather than an obstacle to anti-racist projects. As Jean Walton has suggested, we cannot "elaborate a psychoanalysis of race without first exploring what we might call the 'race of psychoanalysis.' "[10] Freud's anxieties about race—which primarily revolve around the complicated relationship between Jews, non-Europeans, castration, and circumcision—must be reckoned with if a psycho-analytic approach to race based on his work is to minimize the chances of replicating them. I thus will return to Freud to use his concept of the super-ego to explore the formation of white identity through white privilege and white supremacy after examining some of the limitations of his work for critical race theory.

One last point before I do so, which concerns my use of the term "ethnicity" instead of "race." In the twentieth century, the concept of race has been scientifically discredited. There are no biological essences, genes, or physical features that necessitate dividing the human population into differ-ent races. For this reason, some have argued that race does not exist and thus that one should speak of cultural groups—ethnicities—rather than races.[11]

One need not, however, appeal to biological essentialism to insist on the reality of race. In today's world, race continues to thrive as a socially and psychically constituted reality that, among other things, privileges white people over nonwhite people.[12] In my view, this privilege is not adequately captured by the term "ethnicity." By implicitly positing Irish, German, Scottish, Italian, and other people who currently count as white as just another ethnic group among others, "ethnicity" tends to make white privilege invisible.[13] I thus use the term *race* not to endorse biological essentialism but to acknowledge the reality of white privilege so that it might be more effectively fought.[14]

CIRCUMCISION AND ANTI-SEMITISM

Although Freud rarely explicitly discussed race, his writings on castration and circumcision implicitly combine with his comments about Jews and Egyptians to deprecate non-Europeans and, moreover, to establish which inhabitants of Europe count as "real" Europeans. To see these connections, we must begin with the central role in Freud's psychoanalysis of the relationship between the Oedipus and castration complexes. For Freud, the Oedipus complex is "the nuclear complex of the neuroses" and, indeed, of all human psychic life, whether neurotic or not.[15] The Oedipus complex is composed of a child's sexual desire for the parent of the opposite sex and the related rivalry with and desired death of the parent of the same sex. For the male and female child, the Oedipus complex not only entails different desires for and hostilities toward his or her mother and father; it also involves a different relationship to castration. According to Freud, all children believe that everyone originally has a penis (although Freud suggests that male children come to this realization before female children do). The male child knows, in the sense of finding it self-evident, "that a genital like his own is to be attributed to everyone he knows, and he cannot make its absence tally with his picture of these other people" (TES, p. 195). Coming to understand that females do not have a penis inaugurates the castration complex, the collection of "severe internal struggles" with the fact of the absence of the penis that is attributed to females' having had their penises cut off (TES, p. 195). If girls have had their penises cut off, however, that means that it is possible for boys to suffer a similar loss as well—hence the fear of castration on the part of the little boy. In contrast, the little girl does not fear castration because she has always been castrated (which is not to deny her original possession of a penis since to be castrated, one must have had a penis at one time). Her participation in the castration complex takes the particular form of envying the boy's possession of a penis (TES, p. 195 n. 2). This envy eventually allows for a resolution of her Oedipus complex when she compensates for the lack of a penis with the desire to have her father's baby, whose symbolic fulfillment comes when she has a baby with her male partner (who himself is likely a symbolic replacement for her father).[16]

The boy's resolution of the Oedipus complex is much different, however. His desire for his mother will eventually be deflected on to other, more appropriate (and/or neurotic) object-choices because of the threat of castration that comes from his idealized rival–father. This threat is particularly formidable because it targets the most important component of a child's self-image, his penis. This is why Freud claims that the fear of castration is the "narcissistic precondition" of the male's Oedipus complex (TT, p. 161). The father, with his big penis and power over the little child, prohibits the male child's sexual access to his mother by means of a threat to the child's libidinal self-investment. He is awesome, in the most literal sense of the word. He is idealized as part of the child's identification with him at the same time that he is someone trembled before because he demands renunciation of instinctual desire.[17] The father, thus, is the linchpin holding together the Oedipus and castration complexes for the male child. In both, he plays "the part of a dreaded [and admired] enemy to the sexual interests of childhood" (TT, p. 161).

Castration is not, however, the only form of threat to the penis. Or, rather, while castration is the ultimate threat to the penis, it manifests itself in a variety of symbolic substitutions. According to Freud, some of these symbols are blindness, hair being cut, and teeth being knocked out.[18] The most significant for Freud among these manifestations is the one symbolic substitution that literally results in (part of) the penis's being cut off: circumcision. The removal of the foreskin of the penis "is the symbolic substitute for the castration which the primal father once inflicted upon his sons in the plentitude of his absolute power, and whoever accepted that symbol was showing by it that he was prepared to submit to the father's will, even if it imposed the most painful sacrifice on him" (MM, p. 122; see also MM, p. 91). The circumcised child is symbolically castrated; his power has been removed by his submission to his father. Because the elimination of the child's power takes place through the literal removal of part of his penis, however, circumcision is not so much symbolic circumcision as it is an ambiguous form of castration, both symbolic and literal at the same time. Its hybrid status as symbolic–literal makes circumcision the most fearsome substitute for the complete loss of the penis that is castration.

The alleged fearsomeness of circumcision helps explain Freud's claim that circumcision evokes a great hatred of Jews. While discussing the case of Little Hans, whose fear of his father's threat of castration had manifested itself as a fear of horses, Freud attributes an "unconscious train of thought" to Hans that, as "typical," is a widespread feature of the psyche. In this train of thought, one can see that "[t]he castration complex is the deepest unconscious root of anti-semitism; for even in the nursery little boys hear that a Jew has something cut off his penis—a piece of his penis, they think—and this gives them a right to despise Jews."[19] In this remarkable passage, Freud traces a direct link from castration to circumcision to anti-Semitism that depicts anti-Semitism as virtually universal, unavoidable, and justifiable—at least, for all males. On Freud's account, as the narcissistic precondition of the Oedipus complex, the fear of castration necessarily is found in all boys and men. As its most literal symbolic substitution for the fear of castration, the fear of circumcision thus also necessarily occurs in them. Because castration threatens the deepest source of a male's self-image and self-esteem, it (allegedly) is understandable for men to despise those who lack (a part of) the penis or who cut off (a part of) the penises of their children.[20] Even as the simultaneous pacification of that threat through its symbolic function, circumcision provides justification for anti-Semitism. As the quintessence of submission to the father, the Jew is hated by the particular type of man who wishes to be exempt from all authority and who resents those who remind him of its demands. As both the threat of castration and the means of avoiding that threat, circumcision is implicated in the unconscious source of a "right" to a particular form of racism. As a formative structure of the unconscious, the castration complex is the root that grows into and provides nourishment for the despising of Jews. By depicting hatred of Jews as typical and reasonable, Freud's account of circumcision and the castration complex thus naturalizes, rather than problematizes anti-Semitism.[21]

The unconscious also is a source of misogyny, and in such a way that misogyny and anti-Semitism inextricably intertwine. This is because, on Freud's account, the symbols of Jewish racial difference and women's sexual difference are virtually identical.[22] Immediately after his comment about the unconscious roots of anti-Semitism, Freud remarks that "there is no stronger unconscious root [than the castration complex] for the sense of superiority over women." From the point of view of the infantile complexes, "what is common to Jews and women is their relation to the castration complex."[23] Both the Jew and the woman are lacking in terms of the penis. Their difference in this respect is only one of degree, not one of kind. This explains further why there is an alleged (sexist) right to despise the (male) Jew: he has become feminized through the absence of (part of) his penis. He serves as the anxiety-producing image of the loss of masculinity.[24] The "enduringly low opinion of the other sex" that males often have for females thus also characterizes the opinion that the noncircumcised Aryan has of Jews (TES, p. 195 n. 2).

RELOCATING ANTI-SEMITISM:
(FAILED) STRATEGIES OF PROJECTION

If Freud is right that anti-Semitism is "typical" because of its roots in the unconscious, then on the logic of his account, we must conclude that anti-Semitism afflicts Freud no less than it does other men. The universality for males of anti-Semitism puts Freud, a Jew, in a particularly difficult position, however, since his internalized distaste for Jews is equivalent to an internalized distaste for himself. In response to this, he can be seen as seeking to free himself from his self-loathing in two ways. First, by speaking in his texts as a neutral (= raceless) man of science discussing the role of sexuality and gender in the unconscious, Freud brackets his Jewishness and thus is able to identify with the dominant, gentile race.[25] This is not to claim that Freud renounces his Jewishness, which he never did. It is to argue instead that the position of an (allegedly) neutral observer is a situated perspective that reflects the particular interests of a dominant group—in Freud's day as today, that of white, male, middle-to-upper class Christians—and that to occupy this position requires that women, Jews, and other marginalized groups set aside their distinctive perspectives and interests.[26] In reaction to his day's cultural image of the Jew as an inferior masculine type, Freud can be seen as taking up the perspective of this dominant group. He formulates the problem of the castrated/circumcised penis as a problem occasioned by women only, projecting all anxiety-producing traits of male Jews (including himself) onto women.[27] The triad of uncircumcised Aryan, castrated female, and circumcised Jewish male is collapsed into a dyad of the Aryan male and lacking female, the former with which the Jewish male aligns himself.[28] Sex and gender thus become primary in Freud's discussion of sexuality precisely by means of the erasure of race.

In addition to confining the allegedly disgusting aspects of Jewishness to women, Freud also can be seen as attempting to redeem the Jewish people through a combination of projection and identification that foists the origin of circumcision onto Egyptians. In his psychoanalytic account of the Jewish religion in which the Jewish people are alleged to have killed the "father" of their faith, *Moses and Monotheism*, Freud argues that Moses was Egyptian rather than Jewish. The truth or falsity of this claim and Freud's bizarrely fragile arguments for it are not my interest here. I want instead to examine why Freud insisted on making the claim when even he realized how weak his support for it was, when he knew it would offend other Jews, and when it interfered with the central theme of the book's examination of parricide by making only Moses a figurative father of Judaism.[29] The title of the first draft of *Moses and Monotheism* was *The Man Moses, a Historical Novel* (MM, p. 3). This fact has led some to suggest that Freud persisted in arguing that Moses was Egyptian because the format of the novel kept Freud from seeing how historically shaky his argument was.[30] But this suggestion does not explain why Freud pursued the idea of Moses' being an Egyptian in the first place. More helpful is the proposal that, in line with the anthropology of Freud's day, Freud conflated race and language: the etymology of Moses' name might have been Egyptian, which means that Moses likely was an Egyptian (MM, pp. 8–9).[31] Freud's account of what Moses gave the Jewish people, however, strongly suggests another explanation for making Moses into an Egyptian:

not that Freud inadvertently confused race and language, but that he was attempting to eliminate a key weapon used against the Jews by anti-Semites.

Freud emphasizes two practices that Moses brought to the Jewish people: monotheism and, most important for my purposes here, circumcision (MM, p. 26). If Moses was an Egyptian, then circumcision is not original to the Jewish people. It comes from Egypt instead. Freud is unequivocal on this point: "[t]he fact remains that there is only one answer to the question of where the Jews derived the custom of circumcision from—namely, from Egypt" (MM, pp. 26–27). By making Moses into an Egyptian, Freud thus can disassociate Jews from a key component of the unconscious root of anti-Semitism. Writing *Moses and Monotheism* from 1934 to 1938 during which time he was forced by the Nazis to immigrate to England, Freud's argument about Moses enables him to say to the increasingly anti-Semitic world around him that the activity that literally symbolically provokes the greatest threat to and makes significant demands on (masculine) gentile identity and thus that supplies a right to oppress those who practice that activity, is not inherently Jewish at all. Jews are not the source of the emasculation of the penis as is often mistakenly thought, and thus there is no reason to hate and fear them.

Moses and Monotheism was and is often read as an expression of hatred toward Jews because of its perceived attack on the Jewish religion.[32] While not denying that Freud's claim that the Jews killed Moses can function as an attack on Judaism, I see *Moses and Monotheism* as an expression of Freud's loyalty to fellow Jews by means of an attempt to dispel anti-Semitism. Freud hints that the only reason that Jews have embraced circumcision is that they do not want to admit to themselves that their religion has a non-Jewish source. He states, "[i]f it were to be admitted that circumcision was an Egyptian custom introduced by Moses, that would be almost as much as to recognize that the religion delivered to them by Moses was an Egyptian one too. There were good reasons for denying that fact, so the truth about circumcision must also be contradicted" (MM, p. 30). The portrayal of Jews here is of a people that are torn: they would be happy enough to disassociate themselves from circumcision but they do not want to acknowledge the Egyptian roots of Judaism, which such a disassociation demands. Freud is the Jew who is willing to make this difficult acknowledgment, not because his primary goal in this work is to destroy the Jewish religion (though this is his aim elsewhere[33]), but because the abolition of the link between Jews and circumcision is worth the destruction of Judaism.

This explains in part how what distressed Freud about the book as he was writing it both was and was not the claim that Moses was an Egyptian. Or, rather, the claim itself was not so much what disturbed Freud. What troubled him instead was one of the possible ways that his claim might be received. The danger of his book's main thesis is that Moses' lack of Jewish identity would be mistaken as a declaration of the illegitimacy of the Jewish people and that the Jews' murder of their founding father would be understood as justification for years of hatred and persecution of them. This reading would only intensify anti-Semitism, and indeed it is how the book usually is read today.[34] In the face of this danger, however, Freud insisted again and again that the "truth" about Moses must be made clear. In this sense, the claim about Moses' true identity did not distress Freud at all. It was the truth that would set the Jewish people free, as Freud cryptically suggests in the opening lines of the book: "we cannot allow any such reflection [concerning the difficulty of depriving Jews of Moses] to induce us to put the truth aside in favour of what are supposed to be national interests; and, moreover, the clarification of a set of facts may be expected to bring us a gain in knowledge" (MM, p. 7). What is often supposed to be a "national," that is, Jewish interest is the preservation of Moses' identity as a Jew. The real national interest, however, is the one that brings "a gain in knowledge"—not knowledge in the abstract, which has no connection to concrete, national interests, but the particular knowledge of the true origins of circumcision, which will help eliminate persecution of the Jews.

While not necessarily Freud's conscious intent, the effect of his argument that Moses was an Egyptian is not only to disassociate circumcision from the Jews. It also is to link circumcision to Egypt and to transform the type of racism supported by the unconscious from anti-Semitism to anti-non-European racism. Freud presents—again, not necessarily consciously—the Egyptians, not the Jews, as those who should evoke hostility because of the castration complex. Deflecting anti-Semitism away from the Jews, Freud does not dig up and destroy the unconscious roots of (at least one form of) racism, but instead relocates their "proper" target. This movement allows Jews to join the ranks of white Europeans by designating Egyptians, not Jews, as the truly savage, dark, exotic "Other" that evokes anxiety and fear because of its threat to the penis/phallus.

The fact that the skin color of Egyptians may not "objectively" differ much from that of Jews does not necessarily interfere with this transformation because racial classifications affect whether one's biological features are perceived as white or not. That is, race operates such that perceived biological differences are not so much causal determinations of racial classification as they are the result of those classifications themselves. Visual differences such as those of skin color serve to naturalize preexisting racial categories rather than to produce them. For example, when the Irish first immigrated to the United States, they did not count as white and were perceived as having dark skin.[35] Now that the Irish are considered to be white in the United States, their skin color is perceived as light. Similarly, if a group such as the Jews can establish itself as dominant rather than subordinate, then the skin color of its members will tend to be perceived as light because they are classified as white. And regardless of its "objective" tint, the skin color of those such as the Egyptians who are relegated to the category of the Other will tend to be perceived as dark because they are classified as nonwhite.

One clear example of Freud's identification with white Europeans in contrast with exotic Egyptians occurs during Freud's analysis of a woman's dream involving a rattlesnake's connection to Cleopatra, and thus Egypt, even though rattlesnakes are found only in North America. In that context, Freud offhandedly remarks, "[w]e will not blame her for her equal lack of hesitation in transferring the rattlesnake to Egypt, for it is usual for *us* to lump together everything which is non-European and exotic" (PEL, p. 66, emphasis added). The "us" that associates everything non-European with the exotic is not a generic, neutral population as Freud implies, but instead the population of white Europeans. This is a population of which Freud considers himself a member; he is part of the "us" to which he refers. Freud thus can be seen as sharing his patient's anxiety, which forms the "essential content" of her dream: that a family member "might make a socially unsuitable marriage, a *mésalliance* with a non-*Aryan*" (PEL, p. 67, italics in original).

Yet the situation is not quite this simple (if self-hatred can ever be said to be simple). Freud's identification with white Europeans through the projection of otherness onto Egyptians and other non-Europeans is not unequivocal. As alienation, projection serves to distance a person from something about herself that she does not want to recognize by foisting it onto another person. It can be seen as involving identification through a disavowal of identification: because you are like me, I can project my distastefulness on you, which means that you are not really like me because you are distasteful and I am not. Freud's projection of the otherness of Jews onto Egyptians means a partial identification of the two groups for Freud. Only because Jews share something (allegedly) disgusting with non-Europeans is Freud able to create a distinction between them via projection. This means that Jews occupy a liminal position between white Europeans and non-European Others. They both are and are not European and non-European, white and black, masculine and feminized. In Daniel Boyarin's words, for Freud "Jews are not white/not quite . . . at once the other and the metropolitan, the 'Semite' among 'Aryans' and the Jew desperately constructing his whiteness by othering colonized blacks."[36]

Freud's ambiguous identification of Jews and non-European Others means that his infamous writings on "modern savages" and "primitive races" not only can be seen as targeting historical and contemporary native and black peoples. They also implicitly, if ambivalently and anxiously, can be interpreted as concerning Jews. When Freud writes about the lack of inhibition on the part of "primitive men" and notes similarities between "savages" and children, Jews implicitly are included in the group of people who are not fully civilized (TT, pp. 200, 157). Moreover, Freud's brief observation that circumcision is frequent in "primitive races" explicitly strengthens the connection between "savages" and Jews (TT, p. 189 n. 61). His strategy of protecting Jews from anti-Semitism by projecting the perceived disgusting practice of circumcision onto another people thus ultimately fails. It fails not only because *Moses and Monotheism* was and is read solely as an attack on the Jewish faith, but also because the strategy of projection subtly aligns Jews with the very people from whom Freud tried to distinguish them. The unintended upshot of Freud's efforts is the message that Jews, like Egyptians and other non-Europeans, are "modern savages" whose lack of civilization poses a threat to civilized Europe and thus who are rightfully despised.

ON RACIAL IDENTITY: THE ROLE OF THE SUPEREGO IN GROUP FORMATION

Freud's approach in *Moses and Monotheism* can be seen as failing for another reason, one that is somewhat ironic. To the extent that the work makes deliberate arguments against consciously held beliefs about the Jews, it neglects the unconscious roots of anti-Semitism. Apart from additional unconscious strategies, therefore, it is unlikely to convince people that Jews are not the source of circumcision. Setting this irony aside, however, even if Freud's analysis of circumcision had not aligned Jews with Egyptians, it should be seen as a failure because it merely relocates, rather than attempts to eradicate racism based on circumcision. Although it might have been well intended, Freud's experiment with projection as a strategy against anti-Semitism does not directly contribute to a *critical* race theory. It does, however, demonstrate that Freudian concepts can be meaningfully applied to the topic of race, and it raises the question of whether approaches other than the one pursued by Freud might be more valuable. To explore this issue, I turn to Freud's analysis of the role that the superego plays in the formation of groups.[37] Understood in the context of critical race theory, the superego involves a type of identification that helps explain white privilege and white supremacy.

According to Freud, groups exist by means of libidinal ties that bind individuals together (GP, pp. 35, 60). Without the emotional "energy" of the erotic drives, a collection of individuals would be just that: an arbitrary assortment of unrelated individuals rather than a group whose members have significant connections with one another. As libidinal, groups are fueled, so to speak, by sexual drives, but this is not to say that group members necessarily pursue sexual unions. In many groups, sexual drives are diverted from this goal and express themselves in a less obviously sexual manner, such as that found in warm feelings toward group members, a desire to be near other group members, and a willingness to do things for group members, even to the point of sacrificing oneself in the process (GP, pp. 29–30, 92).

The libidinal tie among group members does not by itself explain a group, however. Or, rather, the libidinal tie does not come into being among group members alone; merely collecting some individuals together does not guarantee the formation of a group. The libidinal tie among group members depends on their emotional ties to a leader (GP, p. 50). The leader is the "object" external to the individual with which the individual identifies.

Identification provides a complex emotional relationship between the leader and each individual that binds the individuals together into a group and gives them an emotional connection with one another.

In many cases of identification, the external object takes the place of the individual's ego (GP, pp. 46–49), but in the case of group formation the external object takes the place of each individual's superego (GP, p. 61). The superego is "heir to the original narcissism," which is not a neurotic perversion but rather the emotional, loving attachment to one's ego that is fundamental to the instinct of self-preservation (GP, p. 52).[38] As the child matures, demands external to the ego are made upon it that it cannot satisfy. The superego, which embodies those demands, thus splits off from the ego and establishes an ambivalent relationship with it. Because it is an outgrowth of the ego even as it is functionally distinct from it, the superego can be a source of great satisfaction to the ego when the two coincide (GP, p. 81). Due to its origins in the inadequacy of the ego, however, the superego often conflicts with the ego. The superego's functions are those of "self-observation, the moral conscience, the censorship of dreams, and the chief influence in repression," and thus the superego is like a parent whose role is to establish high standards for the ego, demand that it live up to them, and punish it when it does not do so (GP, p. 52).

When an external object, such as the group leader, replaces the superego, the criticism and moral conscience provided by the superego are suspended. The externalized object that has now been internalized can do no wrong, and nothing done for the sake of the object produces any qualms of conscience (GP, p. 57). The replacement of the superego by an external object thus explains why Freud claims that there is a mental change forced by a group onto the individual and, more specifically, that this change is one in which the individual loses freedom, intellectual ability, restraint, independence, and originality (GP, pp. 7, 35, 78). Individuality is surrendered in the group, and the group comes to rule the individual (GP, pp. 22, 63). The loss of the superego means, in particular, that group members no longer have in place an agency to repress their unconscious drives. Since the unconscious is that portion of the psyche "in which all that is evil in the human mind is contained as a predisposition," individuals' cruel and brutal drives are freed by group membership to find direct satisfaction, and group members will do things that they would not usually do as individuals (GP, pp. 9, 15, 23).

WHITE SUPREMACY AND WHITE PRIVILEGE AS LEADING IDEAS

Freud is clear that a leader is essential to a group, properly considered, but he allows that an idea can substitute for the leader (GP, pp. 65, 40). An abstract "leading idea" thus can do all that a flesh-and-blood leader can do, namely, provide the libidinal ties that hold a group together by replacing the superegos of group members. Moreover, like leaders, leading ideas can just as easily be negative as they can be positive. "[H]atred against a particular person or institution might operate in just the same unifying way, and might call up the same kind of emotional ties" as positive ideas, like love, do (GP, p. 41). It is here that Freud's account of group formation is instructive on white racist identity. White supremacy can be seen as functioning as a leading idea that replaces the superegos of some white people. This binds a mere assortment of people into a consciously raced group of white people who share a consciously held, deprecating belief about nonwhite people. The belief in question here could be characterized as either a positive or negative one since the positive and negative forms of it are the inverse of each other: either the positive form of loving white people since they are (allegedly) superior to nonwhite people, or the negative form of hating nonwhite people since they are (allegedly) inferior to white people. In both cases, the belief about white supremacy serves as the object to which the group members have an emotional tie, and their emotional connection with this leading idea provides the emotional bonds between themselves.

Because the leading idea of white supremacy replaces group members' superegos, white supremacists lose the ability to criticize both their devotion to the ideal and the activities done in the service of it. The predisposition to evil—in this case, racist evil—that Freud argues lurks within the unconscious is no longer fettered by the moral conscience that says racism is wrong. The hostility felt by white toward nonwhite people, on which white individuals normally would not act, easily converts into cruel acts against nonwhite people for white supremacist groups.

Because white supremacy is a consciously held leading idea that forms extremist groups, this account of the formation of white groups may not seem particularly relevant to the lives of most white people today. Freud's comments about the unconscious suggest, however, that an account of the operations of racism must be broadened to include more than "fringe" groups of white supremacists. The evil that lurks as a predisposition in the unconscious lurks in the unconscious of *all* people. According to Freud, there is no eradicating these evil tendencies, only controlling the circumstances that either keep them contained, such as peace, or lay them bear, such as war.[39] Virtually all emotional relationships between people include an element of hostility, though it may not always be openly expressed or consciously acknowledged. This means that racial hatred is far more widespread than most people would like to think. Even racial groups that are close related, as are the English and the Scotch, despise one another, and such repugnance only grows as the differences between racial groups does (GP, pp. 41–42). Freud claims that once we understand that hostility toward others is at the core of the human psyche, "we are no longer astonished that greater differences should lead to an almost insuperable repugnance, such as the Gallic people feel for the German, the Aryan for the Semite, and the white races for the coloured" (GP, p. 42).

Freud tells us what most nonwhite people are consciously aware of, but that many white people are not: racism is not confined to the extremist fringe. In a world where racial differences exist, perceived racial differences often translate into the disdain of one racial group for another.[40] This disdain can and, Freud would add, should be repressed. In fact, for Freud, one sign of civilization is that no open hostility and aggression amongst different races exist.[41] Lack of open aggression does not mean that hostility toward other races has been eradicated from the unconscious, however. It instead means that civilized people have discovered ways of resolving hostile conflicts other than war and direct aggression.

The so-called advances of civilization over the last century have produced the transformation of white supremacy into white privilege for many white people. As a result, the social, political, economic, psychological, and other benefits that continue to accrue to white people because they are white often are not seen by white people today. Or, put another way, they are not seen as privileges. They are seen instead as part of the "natural," normal order of the world, as a way of living that includes no advantages that all other people do not have. In other words, if others do not have these "advantages," then it is because they have done something to forfeit them—it is their fault that they are disadvantaged. For example, as a white person, I do not usually worry about being tailed by store security guards who see me as a potential shoplifter; I generally enter stores psychologically comfortable and undisturbed. My comfort might seem normal and natural, that is, as a psychological state enjoyed by everyone or, at least, available to everyone and lacking only if one intends to shoplift. The fact that many black people are assumed to be potential criminals and often are followed in or not admitted to stores, however, reveals my comfort to be an instance of white privilege.[42] It is a psychological state *not* automatically available to everyone, but rather disproportionately available to white people because of their race and not because black people are responsible for (guilty of) forfeiting their right to psychological comfort.[43]

That white privilege operates unconsciously means that, while Freud does not make it in the context of group formation, a distinction can be made between conscious and unconscious leading ideas.[44] White supremacy is a leading idea that is consciously endorsed. The idea comes to replace the superego by means of a deliberate choice of which a person is consciously aware. This is not to claim that the unconscious is totally uninvolved in white supremacy but instead that consciousness plays a larger role in white supremacy than it does in white privilege. In contrast to white supremacy, white privilege is an idea to which white people are emotionally tied in ways of which they usually are not consciously aware. White privilege has come to replace the superego, but the replacement is not consciously noticed.

Whether a person is consciously aware of her leading ideals has implications for her awareness of groups to which she belongs that are important for my analysis of white racism. Because the white supremacist consciously affirms white supremacy as her leading idea, she is consciously aware of her membership in a group of white supremacists. In contrast, it might sound strange to describe a person as unaware of what groups she belongs to, and Freud does not discuss this as a possibility. Nonetheless, people who are not consciously aware of their leading ideas often are not aware that they belong to a particular group and that the group's attitudes affect the way that they view and interact with the world. This certainly is true of many white people with regard to their membership in whiteness. The seeming naturalness of white privilege often prevents it from being recognized as a leading idea. Unaware that white privilege is one of their leading ideas, white people often do not recognize that they belong to a group of whites who are tied together by the privileges and ideals that they share as white. This lack of awareness of group membership is apparent in those white people who do not see whiteness as a race or think that race is a topic that is relevant to black and other nonwhite people only. It is also manifest in the attitude of the white, well-intentioned liberal who declares that she does not see people's races and sees only raceless individuals instead. These are examples of white privilege because it is a privilege of those who are not racially oppressed to see or treat race as optional. People who are discriminated against because of their race do not have a choice of whether to view race as relevant. It is relevant because it often is forced on them by a racist world.[45]

But does it make sense to describe white people as unaware that they are members of a group when group membership is characterized primarily by emotional ties to the group's leading idea and to fellow group members? That is, can one have emotional ties to people and ideas without being consciously aware of them? On Freud's account, the answer is a qualified "yes." It might seem that emotions cannot be called unconscious since it is of the essence of emotion that it is something felt and thus something that enters consciousness. Strictly speaking, Freud tells us, this is true. It is not inaccurate to call emotions unconscious, however, because they can be misconstrued in the feeling or perceiving of them. Felt emotions are represented by ideas, according to Freud. The proper presentation of an emotion can be repressed, which forces the emotion to connect itself to another idea that is then interpreted by consciousness as the expression of the emotion. If and when the original presentation of the emotion is restored, the original emotion is appropriately called "unconscious" even though it was the presentation of the emotion and not the emotion itself that was repressed and unavailable to consciousness.[46]

In the group membership of whites, the emotional attachments felt toward the leading idea of white privilege may be unconscious in that the true representation of the emotion is repressed because it is currently not considered morally appropriate to feel. Another representation thus takes its place. The emotion in the case of white privilege—or, rather, the ideational presentation of it—might be something like distaste for or hatred of non-white people combined with affection for white people. Such an emotion is difficult to consciously acknowledge without causing considerable pain to the ego, so it is repressed or misconstrued as a different emotion, such as respect for all people regardless of race. A white person's felt comfort around white people can then be (mis)understood as merely an instance of the comfort felt around people in general, in other words, as *not* being part of an emotional tie toward white people in particular. White people thus could have a particular emotional connection with other white people as part of their membership in the same group without being consciously aware of it.

In contrast—and perhaps surprisingly—white supremacists can be seen as repressing affection for nonwhites. White privilegists (to coin a term) repress their leading idea of the inferiority of nonwhites and their emotions of hatred for nonwhites; they find it more painful to consciously claim the inferiority of nonwhites than to consciously endorse the opposite, their equality. White supremacists, on the other hand, find it pleasurable to feel hatred toward nonwhites and to consciously assert nonwhite people's inferiority, which suggests that what they find too painful to consciously acknowledge is again the opposite—their affection, in the sense of sexual attraction, for nonwhites. In both cases, the conscious beliefs and assertions of white people can be understood as reaction formations to their unconscious beliefs about nonwhite people. Whether the leading idea of the inferiority of nonwhite people is conscious (white supremacy) or unconscious (white privilege) hinges on whether hatred of nonwhites and a belief in their inferiority is accompanied by sexual attraction for them.

In the categories proposed by Elizabeth Young-Bruehl, white supremacists thus can be seen as hysterical racists, who need the racial other to exist as the site for all the racist's "dark," forbidden desires.[47] In contrast, white privilegists can be seen as obsessional racists, who fear the "contamination" of nonwhite people and thus often coldly and methodically work for their extermination. While I do not wish to claim that some forms of racism are "better" than others, from this perspective white privilege ironically appears more horrific than white supremacy. This is not to minimize the atrocities committed by extremist groups such as the Ku Klux Klan, but to suggest that rather than being a relatively "benign" form of white racism, white privilege might be even more destructive than white supremacy, even if (or perhaps precisely because) it is not as spectacular.

Returning to white privilege in particular, we should examine how the original emotion of hatred for nonwhites can be repressed if the superego has been replaced by the leading idea of white privilege. As the agency of censorship and the office of the moral conscience, the superego is the primary influence in repression, and thus its replacement might seem to mean that censorship could not occur. Yet it does. For this reason, more accurate than saying, as Freud does, that "the functions allotted to the ego ideal [superego] entirely cease to operate" when the superego is replaced by an external object (GP, p. 57), is to say that when the external object replaces the superego, the object takes over the functions of the superego. On this point, Freud gives the example of someone who is in love and the loved object replaces her superego. When this happens, Freud tells us that "in the blindness of love remorselessness is carried to the pitch of crime" (GP, p. 57); thus, criticism carried out by the superego, which primarily embodies the demands of parents (especially the father), ceases to function. But in the blind love that is willing to commit crimes for the loved one, criticism per se has not ceased to function. While Freud may be right that criticism of the loved object disappears, the loved object certainly can and might criticize the lover for not doing what he asks, for seeming to put her interests above his, and so on. Ultimately, however, whether we say that the critical agency of the superego has been eliminated or that it continues but with an allegiance to the loved one rather than to parents is a moot point. In both cases, criticism in the service of the external object continues when the object replaces the superego.

The situation is similar in the case of white privilege. On a Freudian analysis, when white privilege replaces the superego, the superego no longer functions to criticize the ego based on the internalized demands of one's parents. Criticism continues, however, in the service of white privilege. White privilege maintains itself largely by seeming normal, natural, and unobjectionable. It functions best by remaining invisible, that is, unconscious. White privilege thus can be seen as functioning as a censor of all emotions or ideas that expose it to conscious examination. Any emotion that threatens white privilege must be transformed into a different emotion that does not conflict with it.

CAN UNCONSCIOUS RACISM BE CHANGED?

I wish to close by examining the likelihood of eliminating white privilege given that it tends to operate unconsciously. Racism would be much easier to combat, after all, if it were merely preconscious, that is, not currently the object of conscious awareness. While it is descriptively unconscious, the preconscious is not repressed and thus is not dynamically unconscious.[48] If racism were solely preconscious, "all" that would be required to eliminate racist beliefs would be to want to and then to choose to change them.[49] As my Roma example demonstrates and countless other examples could confirm, however, a person can hold racist beliefs that she is incapable of recognizing and thus of changing, at least not on her own. As unconscious rather than preconscious, a great number of racist beliefs cannot be eradicated by simply turning one's conscious attention toward them. Given the unconscious life of race, we thus must ask: is there a way for the unconscious aspects of racism to become the object of conscious awareness? Can white people gain knowledge of their unconscious racist beliefs? If the answers to both of these questions are "no," then there would appear to be little hope for the eradication of racism.

To begin to address them, it is important to note that these questions ask two different, though related things, both of which get at the heart of psychoanalysis. Freud often charges his opponents with thinking that the unconscious is merely preconscious. What they do not realize is that the unconscious cannot be known; it is only supplied by means of compelling inferences.[50] Freud makes clear that "the core of our being, consisting of unconscious wishful impulses, remains inaccessible to the understanding and inhibition of the preconscious," and thus also to consciousness.[51] The answer to the first question above therefore clearly is "no": white people cannot become consciously aware of their unconscious racist beliefs.

Or, rather, not *directly* consciously aware of them. At the same time that Freud insists that the unconscious is not preconscious, he also proclaims that the goal of psychoanalysis is to make conscious what was unconscious.[52] Freud's method for the interpretation of dreams, which is the foundation of his version of psychoanalysis, is nothing less than *"the royal road to a knowledge of the unconscious activities of the mind."*[53] This goal only seems to conflict with Freud's insistence that the unconscious cannot be known because Freud makes a distinction between direct and indirect knowledge of the unconscious. We can gain knowledge of our unconscious beliefs—indeed, the practice of psychoanalysis would be pointless if we could not—but not direct knowledge, which is why it is important to maintain the distinction between the dynamic unconscious and the preconscious. The answer to the second question above therefore is "yes." On Freud's terms, white people can gain knowledge of their unconscious racist beliefs, but only indirectly by means of the process of translating the unconscious into preconscious and conscious processes.

Although the details of translation will vary from situation to situation, a few general things can be said about the process. First, it often requires the assistance of other people. For all its emphasis on hostility between people, Freud's psychoanalytic theory also makes room for cooperation and reciprocity by landing a devastating blow on the assumption of self-transparency that afflicts many theories of the self. Because the self is not a unity, it can keep secrets from itself.[54] Although no one has direct access to the unconscious, a person is just as (if not more) likely to be aware of another person's unconscious wishes, motivations, and beliefs than she is of her own. Human beings may be like prickly porcupines that cannot bear to be too close to one another, but at the same time they need each other to gain knowledge about themselves (GI, p. 41, n. 1). The asymmetrical relationship between a person's ability to recognize her own unconscious and to recognize that of another is apparent, for example, in the Roma situation in which Gypsies were referred to as Jews. While the speakers' slips of the tongue were virtually impossible for their audience to miss, they themselves could not hear them. It took the interruptions of the audience to enable the speakers to realize that they had replaced one term with the other.

Realizing that they had made a slip of the tongue did not, however, prevent the speakers from making future slips. While conscious recognition of one's unconscious racist beliefs is crucial to the possibility of eliminating racism, becoming consciously aware of their slips did not apparently result in a change in the two speakers' unconscious beliefs about the Roma. This might lead us to suspect that even in the case of white people who are sympathetic to anti-racist efforts, conscious knowledge of their unconscious racism will not change anything—except perhaps to produce wallowing in their guilt[55]—and thus that the charges that psychoanalysis is not useful for social and political work are accurate after all. But these conclusions would be premature. Translating the unconscious into consciousness inevitably will be difficult and laborious, which leads to the second general feature of this process. That the unconscious can indeed be altered through conscious awareness of it does not mean that such alternation will be a quick, easy, one-step fix (nor, again, that all people wish to eliminate their racist beliefs once they become aware of them). To assume so is to naively underestimate the magnitude and power of the unconscious. As Freud claims, "[i]t is doubtful how far the processes of this system [the preconscious or consciousness] can exert a direct influence on the Ucs [unconscious]; examination of pathological cases often reveals an almost incredible independence and lack of susceptibility to influence on the part of the Ucs."[56] Changing the unconscious by means of conscious influence on it takes a great deal of time and effort, and there is no guarantee of success.

Finally, bringing consciousness to bear on the unconscious is not the only way to change it, according to Freud. While gaining conscious knowledge of the unconscious is an important strategy in the fight against racism, Freud tells us that change can occur without the influence of consciousness at all. The unconscious of one person can influence the unconscious of another without either person's consciousness serving as mediator.[57] This type of change obviously is one that people have little control over; it cannot be deliberately willed. But by becoming consciously aware of one's unconscious racism, a person can consciously choose to place herself in situations in which her racist beliefs are likely to be unconsciously troubled rather than unconsciously supported. Pragmatist-feminist Jane Addams' experience at Hull House, in which she lived and worked with immigrants in Chicago for forty years, offers a prominent historical example of such a situation.[58] Joining an organization that works against racism also is a way that a white person might participate in a community whose members' unconscious beliefs are likely to affect her unconscious in anti-racist ways. Of course, belonging to such a group likely will result in greater conscious awareness of one's unconscious racism as well, but this is not the only way that unconscious change might take place. Ongoing physical and emotional proximity to other people can create conditions under which direct unconscious-to-unconscious interaction can occur.[59]

White privilege is all the more difficult to combat because it is unconscious. This is not to claim that the conscious affirmation of racism found in white supremacy is preferable to white privilege, but rather to note that different strategies for fighting racism will be effective in the twenty-first century, when a great deal of racism is unconscious, than were effective 100 or even fifty years ago, when a larger portion of racism was conscious. As Charles Mills has remarked, the racial contract that has held and continues to hold Western society together has transformed itself over the years from being an explicit to an implicit agreement among whites.[60] As implicit, the contract is not often the focus of white people's conscious attention. Challenging the contract today means that critical race theorists cannot concentrate solely or perhaps even primarily on consciousness. As difficult as the task will be, they—we—must attempt to undo the unconscious operations of racism.[61]

NOTES

1. Shannon Sullivan, "Racialized Habits: Dewey on Race and the Roma," presented at the First Central European Pragmatist Forum, Sterna Lesna, Slovakia, May 28–June 2, 2000; in *Pragmatism and Values*, eds. John Ryder and Emil Visnovsky (Amsterdam/New York: Rodopi Press, 2002).

2. Freud would tell us that laughter in this sort of situation is not uncommon: "Many of my neurotic patients who are under psycho-analytic treatment are regularly in the habit of confirming the fact by a laugh when I have succeeded in giving a faithful picture of their hidden unconscious to their conscious perception; and they laugh even when the content of what is unveiled would by no means justify this" (Freud, *Jokes and Their Relation to the Unconscious*, ed. and trans. James Strachey [New York: W.W. Norton, 1960] 211 n. 5). According to Freud, laughter occurs because the energy used to repress the previously unconscious belief has been freed up and is available for discharge (*Jokes*, 182).

3. Sigmund Freud, *The Psychopathology of Everyday Life*, ed. and trans. James Strachey (New York: W. W. Norton, 1960), 90. Hereafter cited in the text as PEL.

4. For Freud, the difference between a slip of the tongue and a joke "is simply a question of whether [a person] spoke the words with a conscious or unconscious intention" (PEL, 77).

5. On rising discrimination against the Roma, see Steven Erlanger, "Across a New Europe, a People Deemed Unfit for Tolerance: No Room for Gypsies," *The New York Times on the Web*, April 2, 2000, www.nytimes.com; Isabel Fonseca, *Bury Me Standing: The Gypsies and Their Journey* (New York: Alfred A. Knopf, 1995); and Helskini Watch Report, *Struggling for Ethnic Identity: Czechoslovakia's Endangered Gypsies* (New York: Human Rights Watch, 1992).

6. As Charles Mills explains, "contemporary 'critical race theory' . . . adds the adjective ["critical"] specifically to differentiate itself from essentialist [and racist] views of the past" (Mills, *The Racial Contract* [Ithaca: Cornell University Press, 1997], 126).

7. Exceptions to this claim include Elizabeth Abel, "Race, Class, and Psychoanalysis? Opening Questions," in *Conflicts in Feminism*, ed. Marianne Hirsch and Evelyn Fox Keller (New York: Routledge, 1990), 184–204; Michael Vannoy Adams, *The Multicultural Imagination: 'Race,' Color, and the Unconscious* (New York: Routledge, 1996); Tina Chanter, "Abjection and Ambiguity: Simone de Beauvoir's Legacy," *The Journal of Speculative Philosophy* 14, no. 2 (2000): 139–156; Christopher Lane, ed., *The Psychoanalysis of Race* (New York: Columbia University Press, 1998); and Kalpana Seshadri-Crooks, *Desiring Whiteness: A Lacanian Analysis of Race* (New York: Routledge, 2000).

8. An example of such an assumption can be found in Jason D. Hill's *Becoming a Cosmopolitan: What It Means To Be a Human Being in the New Millennium* (Lanham, MD: Rowman and Littlefield, 2000).

9. "The importance of the Oedipus complex has became [sic] more and more clearly evident; its recognition has become the shibboleth that distinguishes the adherents of psycho-analysis from its opponents" (Freud, "Three Essays on Sexuality," in volume 7 of *The Standard Edition of the Complete Psychological Works of Sigmund Freud*, 24 vols., ed. and trans. James Strachey [New York: W.W. Norton, 1960], 226n; hereafter cited in the text as TES).

10. Jean Walton, "'Nightmare of the Uncoordinated White-folk': Race, Psychoanalysis and H.D.'s *Borderline*," in *The Psychoanalysis of Race*, ed. Christopher Lane (New York: Columbia University Press, 1998), 395.

11. Two philosophers well known for holding this view are Kwame Anthony Appiah and Naomi Zack. See Appiah, "The Conservation of 'Race,'" *Black American Literature Forum* 23, no. 1 (1989): 37–60, and Zack, *Race and Mixed Race* (Philadelphia: Temple University Press, 1993).

12. I say "among other things" here since I do not think that the concept of race necessarily has a racist meaning only. Race can be a source of positive as well as negative value in people's lives.

13. I say "currently" because the ethnic groups that count as white have changed over the years. On this point, see, for example, Noel Ignatiev, *How the Irish Became White* (New York: Routledge, 1995).

14. It also seems important to preserve the term *race* to be able to account for the race-based discrimination that sometimes exists within the same ethnic group, as it has between Western (assimilated) and Eastern (immigrant) Jews. See Jerry Victor Diller, *Freud's Jewish Identity: A Case Study in the Impact of Ethnicity* (London: Associated University Presses, 1991), 39.

15. Sigmund Freud, *Totem and Taboo: Some Points of Agreement between the Mental Lives of Savages and Neurotics*, ed. and trans. James Strachey (New York: W.W. Norton, 1961), 160. Hereafter cited in the text as TT.

16. Freud, "The Dissolution of the Oedipus Complex," in volume 19 of *The Standard Edition of the Complete Psychological Works of Sigmund Freud*, 24 vols., ed. and trans. James Strachey (New York: W.W. Norton, 1961), 178–179.

17. Freud, *Moses and Monotheism: Three Essays*, in volume 23 of *The Standard Edition of the Complete Psychological Works of Sigmund Freud*, ed. and trans. James Strachey (London: The Hogarth Press, 1964) 122. Hereafter cited in the text as MM.

18. On cutting hair and losing teeth, see TT, 189 n. 61; on blindness, see TT, 161, and *An Outline of Psychoanalysis*, in volume 23 of *The Standard Edition of the Complete Psychological Works of Sigmund Freud*, ed. and trans. James Strachey (London: The Hogarth Press, 1964), 190 n1.

19. Freud, *Analysis of a Phobia in a Five-year-old Boy*, in volume 10 of *The Standard Edition of the Complete Psychological Works of Sigmund Freud*, ed. and trans. James Strachey (London: The Hogarth Press, 1955), 36 n. 1; see also MM, 91.

20. The example of the United States challenges Freud's claims about the universality of fear of circumcision and hatred for the Jews because of circumcision. Until recently, circumcision has been a routine medical practice in the United States for male gentiles and Jews alike, and most gentile men would consider a circumcised penis to be normal, not reprehensible. Let me be clear then that my description of Freud's account of circumcision is just that: my point is not to defend Freud against this challenge, but to describe how Freud (misleadingly) depicts the fear of circumcision as universal to males rather than as historically and culturally specific. While I do not have time to explore the idea and Freud himself never discusses it, the reasoning of Freud's account suggests it might present North American men as relatively effeminate and as experiencing the castration complex as women do—as penis envy—because of their lack of fear of and distaste for circumcision.

21. Daniel Boyarin, "What Does a Jew Want?; or, The Political Meaning of the Phallus," in Lane, *The Psychoanalysis of Race*, 216. It is not clear on Freud's account why or how females in particular can be anti-Semitic. One explanation, which I do not have time to pursue, might be that for Freud, female anti-Semitism is a form of self-hatred since, as I will discuss later, circumcised Jews are like females in that they both lack in terms of the penis.

22. Boyarin, "What Does a Jew Want?," 216.

23. Freud, *Analysis of a Phobia*, 36 n. 1.

24. Sander L. Gilman, *Freud, Race, and Gender* (Princeton: Princeton University Press, 1993), 9.

25. Gilman, *Freud, Race, and Gender*, 46; Boyarin, "What Does a Jew Want?", 215.

26. For more on this argument, see Sandra Harding, *Whose Science? Whose Knowledge? Thinking from Women's Lives* (Ithaca, NY: Cornell University Press, 1991).

27. Gilman, *Freud, Race, and Gender*, 46.

28. Gilman, *Freud, Race, and Gender*, 84; see also Boyarin, "What Does a Jew Want?", 229.

29. Marthe Robert, *From Oedipus to Moses: Freud's Jewish Identity*, trans. Ralph Manheim (Garden City, NY: Anchor Press/ Doubleday, 1976), 152–153.

30. Robert, *From Oedipus to Moses*, 153–154.

31. See also Robert, *From Oedipus to Moses*, 156.

32. Robert, *From Oedipus to Moses*, 158; Diller, *Freud's Jewish Identity*, 17.

33. See *The Future of an Illusion*, in volume 21 of *The Standard Edition of the Complete Psychological Works of Sigmund Freud*, ed. and trans. James Strachey (London: The Hogarth Press, 1961).

34. Robert, *From Oedipus to Moses*, 151.

35. See Ignatiev, *How the Irish Became White*.

36. Boyarin, "What Does a Jew Want?," 219.

37. In what follows, I will use the term *superego*, rather than ego ideal, even though Freud uses the latter in *Group Psychology and the Analysis of the Ego* (ed. and trans. James Strachey [New York: W.W. Norton, 1959], hereafter cited in the text as GP). I do this because, based on Freud's mature distinction between the two terms, "superego" better captures his meaning. As Freud explains in his *New Introductory Lectures on Psycho-Analysis* (in volume 22 of *The Standard Edition of the Complete*

Psychological Works of Sigmund Freud, ed. and trans. James Strachey [London: The Hogarth Press, 1964] 64–65), the ego ideal is a function of the superego by which the ego measures itself. Thus, the superego and ego ideal are not interchangeable, as *Group Psychology* implies, but rather the ego ideal is subsumed within the superego as one portion of it.

38. See also Sigmund Freud, "On Narcissim: An Introduction," in volume four of *Collected Papers*, trans. Joan Riviere (London: Hogarth Press, 1950), 31.

39. Freud, "Thoughts for the Times on War and Death," in volume four of *Collected Papers*, 295, 316.

40. Freud actually would make a much stronger claim than I wish to: that racial differences inevitably will translate into disdain. This means that on his account, the distinction between racialism (making distinctions among races) and racism (asserting superiority of one race over another) made by some critical race theorists does not hold (see Lucius Outlaw, *On Race and Philosophy* [New York: Routledge, 1996], 8, and Lewis R. Gordon, *Bad Faith and Anti-Black Racism* [Atlantic Highlands, NJ: Humanities Press, 1995], 92).

41. Freud, "Thoughts for the Times," 289–290.

42. Patricia J. Williams provides a striking example of such a situation in *The Alchemy of Race and Rights: Diary of a Law Professor* (Cambridge: Harvard University Press, 1991), 44–45.

43. The situation actually is much more complicated than I can do justice to here because of the ways that class and economic status intersect with race. For example, the "simple" question of who counts as white in the first place is already a question about class, economics, and, often, suburban identity. See France Winddance Twine, "Brown-Skinned White Girls: Class, Culture, and the Construction of White Identity in Suburban Communities," in Ruth Frankenberg, ed., *Displacing Whiteness: Essays in Social and Cultural Criticism* (Durham, NC: Duke University Press, 1997), 214–243.

44. Freud does not discuss conscious versus unconscious leading ideas in *Group Psychology*, but in "The Unconscious" he does make clear that there are conscious and unconscious ideas, which presumably could include leading ideas. See Freud, "The Unconscious," in volume four of *Collected Papers*, 109.

45. This is not to say that this is the only way race can be or is relevant to them. It can be something positive to endorse, but not on a Freudian account. See notes 12 and 40.

46. Freud, "The Unconscious," 109–111.

47. Elisabeth Young-Bruehl, *The Anatomies of Prejudice* (Cambridge, MA: Harvard University Press, 1996).

48. Freud, *The Ego and the Id*, ed. and trans. James Strachey (New York: W.W. Norton, 1960), 5–6.

49. I place "all" in quotations marks to indicate that I realize the difficulty of this task and thus that my statement is somewhat ironic. Far from insignificant, it would be remarkable for most people to want to eliminate racism. Even so, my larger point holds that preconscious racism generally is relatively easier—though certainly not easy—to combat than unconscious racism.

50. Freud, *Jokes*, 201.

51. Freud, *The Interpretation of Dreams*, ed. and trans. James Strachey (New York: Avon Books, 1965), 642. See also Freud, *The Interpretation of Dreams*, 651, and TT, 39.

52. Freud, *Beyond the Pleasure Principle*, ed. and trans. James Strachey (New York: W.W. Norton, 1961), 18.

53. Freud, *The Interpretation of Dreams*, 647, emphasis in original. See also *Jokes*, 211, 217; "The Unconscious," 98; and TT, 109.

54. Freud, "The Question of Lay Analysis," in volume 20 of *The Standard Edition of the Complete Psychological Works of Sigmund Freud*, ed. and trans. James Strachey (London: The Hogarth Press, 1959), 188.

55. My point here is not to deny that guilt can be a powerful and important motivation for social and political change, but rather to note that in the particular case of white racism, white people often—and to the frustration of nonwhite people—consider their guilt and self-absorption to be a sufficient contribution on their part to the fight against racism. White guilt thus sometimes can operate problematically as a substitute, rather than as motivation for social and political transformation.

56. Freud, "The Unconscious," 126.

57. Freud, "The Unconscious," 126.

58. See Jane Addams, *Democracy and Social Ethics* (New York: Macmillan Co., 1902) and *Forty Years at Hull-House: Being "Twenty Years at Hull-House" and "The Second Twenty Years at Hull-House"* (New York: Macmillan Co., 1935).

59. I have focused on the ways in which positive change might take place by means of this method, but the other side of the story should also be told. There are no guarantees that positive, desired change is the only kind that might occur. Unconscious-to-unconscious interaction in groups can also, for example, fortify one's unconscious racism. Because of the lack of conscious guidance in it, this method of attempting to change the unconscious strikes me as the most dangerous and least appealing way to transform the unconscious described by Freud. This is a criticism of the method rather than of Freud, however, for his brief remarks about this approach are purely descriptive, not prescriptive.

60. Mills, *The Racial Contract*, 72–77.

61. I am very grateful to Sherry Brennan for reading and discussing Freud with me. My thanks also go to John Christman, Vincent Colapietro, Jon Mills, and Emily Zakin for helpful comments on earlier drafts of this chapter.

ABOUT THE CONTRIBUTORS

JON MILLS is a psychologist and philosopher in private practice in Ajax, Ontario. He received his Ph.D. in philosophy from Vanderbilt University, his Psy.D. in clinical psychology from the Illinois School of Professional Psychology, Chicago, and was a Fulbright scholar of philosophy at the University of Toronto and York University. He is currently Chairperson of the Section on Psychoanalysis of the Canadian Psychological Association and on Senior Faculty at the Adler School of Professional Psychology in Toronto. He is also Editor of Contemporary Psychoanalytic Studies, Editor of the Value Inquiry Book Series in Philosophy and Psychology, and on the Editorial Board of the journal *Psychoanalytic Psychology*. He is the author and/or editor of six books including most recently *The Unconscious Abyss: Hegel's Anticipation of Psychoanalysis*, and *When God Wept*, an existential novel.

TOM ROCKMORE is Professor of Philosophy at Duquesne University. He received his A.B. in philosophy from Carleton College, his Ph.D. from Vanderbilt University, and his Habilitation à diriger des recherches at the Université de Poitiers. Among his multiple fellowships, teaching and research positions, and awards for excellence in scholarship, Professor Rockmore is a Consulting Editor for *Studies in Phenomenology and Existential Philosophy* and *Studies in Continental Thought*. Having published over twenty-five books, his most recent contributions are *Cognition: An Introduction to Hegel's Phenomenology of Spirit*, *Heidegger and French Philosophy*, and *Irrationalism: Lukács and the Marxist View of Reason*.

STEPHEN DAVID ROSS is Professor of Philosophy and Comparative Literature at Binghamton University, State University of New York, where he founded and continues as Director of the Program in Philosophy, Interpretation, and Culture. He is the author of many books on metaphysics, aesthetics, value theory, and ethics including, *The Ring of Representation*, *Injustice and Restitution: The Ordinance of Time*, and *Plenishment in the Earth: An Ethic of Inclusion*. He has now embarked on a multivolume project on giving and the good published with State University of New York Press.

JOHN RUSSON is Associate Professor of Philosophy at the University of Guelph. He has had academic appointments at Harvard, the University of Toronto, Acadia University, and the Pennsylvania State University. He has published extensively in ancient philosophy, German idealism, and continental philosophy and is the author of *The Self and its Body in Hegel's Phenomenology of Spirit*, and *Human Experience: Philosophy, Neurosis, and the Elements of Everyday Life*.

JOHN SALLIS is Edwin Erle Sparks Professor of Philosophy at Penn State University. He earned his Ph.D. in philosophy from Tulane University and pursued postdoctoral training at the Universität Freiburg and the Université de Paris. Considered one of the leading American continental philosophers of our day, Professor Sallis has held endowed professorships at Loyola University and Vanderbilt, and is Editor of *Research in Phenomenology*. His most recent books include *Force of Imagination, Chorology, Shades—Of Painting at the Limit, Double Truth, Stone, Delimitations, and Being and Logos*.

SHANNON SULLIVAN is Associate Professor of Philosophy and Women's Studies at Penn State University and is the Review Editor for the *Journal of Speculative Philosophy*. She has published numerous articles in continental philosophy, American pragmatism, and feminist theory and is the author of *Living Across and Through Skins: Transactional Bodies, Pragmatism, and Feminism*. She is currently completing a book manuscript titled *The Seductive Habits of White Privilege: Pragmatist-Feminist Reflections on Race and the Unconscious*.

MARIA TALERO is Assistant Professor of Philosophy at Rhodes College in Memphis, Tennessee. She studied philosophy and political Science at the University of Toronto before taking her Ph.D. in philosophy at Penn State University. She specializes in nineteenth- and twentieth-century European philosophy and has a special interests in cognitive psychology, twentieth-century literature, and the visual arts.

WILFRIED VER EECKE is Professor of Philosophy at Georgetown University. He received his Ph.D. in philosophy at the University of Leuven, Belgium, his M.A. in economics at Georgetown University, and pursued training in philosophy, linguistics, and psychoanalysis at Paris, Freiburg, and Harvard. Among his numerous publications include *Negativity and Subjectivity* and *Saying 'No.'*

BRUCE WILSHIRE is Senior Professor of Philosophy at Rutgers University. He is considered one of the leading figures in connecting American and European phenomenologies, and in 2001 received The Herbert Schneider Award from the Society for the Advancement of American Philosophy for lifetime achievement in American philosophy. Among his many publications include, *William James and Phenomenology*, *Role Playing and Identity*, *The Moral Collapse of the University*, *Wild Hunger*, *The Primal Roots of American Philosophy*, and *Fashionable Nihilism*.

EMILY ZAKIN is an Associate Professor of Philosophy at Miami University. She has published articles in feminist theory, contemporary continental philosophy, and psychoanalysis, and is currently finishing a book manuscript entitled *Fantasies of Origin: Sexual Difference and the Birth of Democracy*.

INDEX